COME ON, PEOPLE

COME ON, PEOPLE

On the Path
from Victims to Victors

BILL COSBY & ALVIN F. POUSSAINT, MD

THOMAS NELSON
Since 1798

NASHVILLE   DALLAS   MEXICO CITY   RIO DE JANEIRO   BEIJING

Published in Nashville, Tennessee, by Thomas Nelson. Thomas Nelson is a trademark of Thomas Nelson, Inc.

Thomas Nelson, Inc., titles may be purchased in bulk for educational, business, fund-raising, or sales promotional use. For information, please e-mail SpecialMarkets@thomasnelson.com.

"I Am a Black Woman," published by Wm. Morrow & Co., 1970, by permission of the author.

"Mother to Son," copyright © 1994 by The Estate of Langston Hughes, from *The Collected Poems of Langston Hughes by Langston Hughes*, edited by Arnold Rampersad with David Roessel, Associate Editor. Used by permission of Alfred A. Knopf, a division of Random House, Inc.

Managing Editor: Alice Sullivan

Library of Congress Cataloging-in-Publication data on file with the Library of Congress.

ISBN 978-1-59555-092-7

Printed in the United States of America

07 08 09 10 11 QW 6 5 4 3

To those who have worked for justice
so that we can all walk the path
to become victors.

Contents

CONTENTS

CONTENTS

Sing a song full of the faith that the dark past has taught us,
Sing a song full of the hope that the present has brought us;
Facing the rising sun of our new day begun,
Let us march on till victory is won.

From "Lift Every Voice and Sing"
JAMES WELDON JOHNSON, 1899

INTRODUCTION

A guy called in to a radio show: "For forty years, Bill Cosby has never really shown that he is black or said that he was black. So now that he is wealthy and nobody can hurt him, now he's going to stand up and be black."

Let's try to break that down. After forty years, I decided that I would hop on a streetcar, head downtown, and join the "black club." Here is how I imagine that encounter went.

"May I have my card, please?"

"And where were you forty years ago?"

"I apparently wasn't black then—or black enough in any case."

"So okay, but you want your card now?"

"Yes."

"Okay, I suppose we will give you a card now."

"Thanks."

"And what is it you want to say?"

"I want to tell the truth, and the truth often hurts."

"No, you can't tell the truth now."

"Why?"

"Because we are told that you've only been black for a year or so."

"Yes, but the numbers that I have are very true, and even if some people think I am not black enough for them, the numbers speak for themselves."

"What kind of numbers?"

"Like 70 percent of our babies are born to single women, or even when we do get married, we have a divorce rate of 60 percent."

"Why should I believe you?"

"Don't. Listen to Malcolm X. I don't know if he was black long enough to qualify either, but forty-five years ago he was saying many of the same things, telling people to get off of welfare because welfare made black people lazy."

"Was Malcolm black enough? He did have red hair after all."

"Dr. King didn't. Du Bois didn't. All the best writers turned the mirror around to say, 'While you are thinking about the enemy, don't forget about the enemy within.' That is all I have been saying."

"But what will the white people think?"

"Forget about the white people."

"Forget about them?"

"They're covered. How many speakers speak out every day about racism, whether it's systemic or whatever? Even if there is truth to what they say, they sedate themselves with it."

"That's heresy. What would Farrakhan say?"

"Even Farrakhan has said quit being concerned about white people; build your own strength first. That's from a man who is the minister of a group called 'black.' But apparently I'm not black."

"Only for a year or so, and even then you didn't have your card."

"Well, in that last year or so, just look at the numbers of shootings, the stabbings, the overdoses, the school dropouts, the meaningless acts of violence toward each other in our community. Can I talk about those or should I just shake them off like a bad cold?"

"A year is not a lot of perspective."

"Maybe so, but many of us come from a time when you really didn't see much of these kinds of things. So we have a basis for comparison."

"But you weren't black back then."

"You may not think so. But the white people did. And even if I wasn't black in your eyes, I was in theirs, and the people of my generation suffered the kind of indignities that people of yours can barely even imagine. So please allow us our perspective."

"Well, all right."

"And I have seen enough to know that, no matter what people tell you, this mayhem is *not* a part of our culture the way our music is. This violence is *not* a part of our culture the way our literature is. And this vulgarity has never been a part of our culture before. I'm asking you to be a voice against that kind of thinking, a voice that will no longer be shut out or shouted down."

"You're asking a lot."

"I know that."

We know that. For the last three and a half years, I have been holding community call-outs in cities around the country. My longtime collaborator, Dr. Alvin F. Poussaint, has been following these discussions along with me. The responses of the people have helped us understand some of the issues I've been addressing. Throughout this book, you will hear the voices of real people in different cities who participated in the call-out town meetings.

The voices at the call-outs—and in this book—will tell you how they moved, how they recovered, how they picked themselves up, how they went forward. We cheer them and we *amen* them. Yet how many of you are facing the same thing? How many of you are looking at perfectly healthy friends and family who have done nothing since they dropped out of high school other than a little hustling and a little welfare? How much is that person worth to the community or to the state or to himself or herself?

We ask these questions of everyone who cares about the future of young black people in America—parents especially, grandparents, foster parents, godparents, teachers, social service workers, and good citizens of every color. You are the "you" with whom we have the honor of conversing.

This book will cover selected topics that mirror the concerns of the different people—rich and poor, young and old, educated and uneducated, married and single—who attended the call-outs. The trials of black people are at the core of *Come On, People* But the problems they face are similar to those of all poor and alienated groups, regardless of race. We can all learn from each other and be allies in changing the behaviors and institutions that limit our young people's chances for success.

In this book, we look at the issues with an eye on what we need to do to help our youth and reenergize our neighborhoods to move in positive directions. African Americans must never give up the struggle to eliminate the racism and classism in our society that continue to present obstacles to success for the poor. People in the village work best to change their communities when they are educated, healthy, and mentally strong. We can change things we have control over if we accept personal responsibility and embrace self-help.

Listening to the people is key to mobilizing for change, to creating better communities for our children. If we are to gauge where we are today and where we have to go tomorrow, we have to look at the past as well as the present. Once we find our bearings, we can move forward, as we have always done, on the path from victims to victors.

Come on, people. We can do it!

Bill Cosby

1

WHAT'S GOING ON
WITH BLACK MEN?

For the last generation or two, as our communities dissolved and our parenting skills broke down, no one has suffered more than our young black men.

Your authors have been around long enough, and traveled widely enough, to think we understand something about the problem. And we're hopeful enough—or desperate enough—to think that with all of us working together we might find our way to a solution.

Let's start with one very basic fact. Back in 1950, before *Brown v. Board of Education,* before the Civil Rights Act and the Voting Rights Act, when Rosa Parks was still sitting in the back of her Montgomery bus, when the NBA was just about all white, back in those troubled times, black boys were born into a different world than they are today.

Obviously, many civil rights leaders had hoped that with the demise in the 1960s of officially sanctioned forms of segregation and discrimination, black males would have greater access to the mainstream of American society. They had fully expected that these young men would be in a better position in every way—financially, psychologically, legally—to sustain viable marriages and families. Instead, the overall situation has continued to go downhill among the poor who are mostly shut out from the mainstream of success.

How is that possible?

There is one statistic that captures the bleakness. In 1950, five out of every six black children were born into a two-parent home. Today, that number is less than two out of six. In poor communities, that number is lower still. There are whole blocks with scarcely a married couple, whole blocks without responsible males to watch out for wayward boys, whole neighborhoods in which little girls and boys come of age without seeing up close a committed partnership and perhaps never having attended a wedding.

BUILD ON OUR LEGACY

In 1950, we still feared our parents and respected them. We know that for a fact because we were both in our early teens that year and were both testing our limits.

We and the others in our generation weren't saints. We'll be the first to admit that. We were filled with piss and vinegar like many teenage boys—white, black, and otherwise. If we saw something we wanted and didn't have any money—and trust us, few of us ever had money—we thought about taking it, sure. But something called "parenting," something that had wormed its way into our heads from the time we were still in the womb, said to us, *If you get caught stealing it, you're going to embarrass your mother.*

The voice didn't say, *You're going to get your butt kicked.* We knew that and expected that from experience. No, that inner voice said, *You're going to embarrass your mother. You're going to embarrass your family.*

As we became older and grew more interested in girls, our hormones raged just as boys' hormones rage today. The Internet may be new. Cell phones may be new. But sex, we don't need to tell you, has been around since Adam and Eve. So has shame. We knew that if one of us got a girl pregnant, not only would she have to go visit that famous "aunt in South Carolina," but young Romeo would have to go too, not to South

Carolina maybe, but somewhere. It would be too embarrassing for Romeo's family for him to just sit around in the neighborhood with a fat Cheshire cat smile on his face.

And there was something else we understood: that girl likely had a daddy in the home. And he'd be prepared to wipe that grin off Romeo's face permanently. This was what parenting was about. It wasn't always pretty, but it could be pretty effective.

<u>Parenting works best when both a mother and a father participate.</u> Some mothers can do it on their own, but they need help. A house without a father is a challenge. A neighborhood without fathers is a catastrophe, and that's just about what we have today.

Can we fix this? Can we change it? We don't have a choice. We have to take our neighborhoods back. We have to go in there and do it ourselves. We saw what happened in New Orleans when people waited for the government to help. "Governments" are things. Governments don't care. People care, and no people care like parents do—well, except maybe grandparents and other caregivers, and thank God for them.

CALL-OUTS

Richard Rowe, in Baltimore, reported on one path to change: *Twenty years ago in this city we started the "Rites of Passage." Nobody else was doing it on the East Coast. We started looking at how the African-American male was going downhill. Twenty years from now, I hope we will not be having this same type of conversation. The purpose of our program is to nurture young men who can maintain, protect, and provide for a family and a community.*

The problems start early for black boys, and we can all see it. Call it ADHD or learning differences or whatever you like, but our young black males can act up a Level 5 storm in class. The fact is that little boys are diagnosed with ADHD approximately three times more than girls. Also, black boys are diagnosed with higher rates of mental disabilities and emotional problems than black girls, white girls, and white boys.

To be sure, little boys in general are more aggressive than little girls. In some cases, too, teachers are wary of black boys and too quick to dump them into special education classes. This kind of racial profiling and discrimination against active, aggressive black boys by school personnel accounts for some of the discrepancy in the numbers, but the bottom line is still bad.

Why is the problem so grave? A mother can usually teach a daughter how to be a woman. But as much as mothers love their sons, they have difficulty showing a son how to be a man. A successful man can channel his natural aggression. Without that discipline, these sons often get into trouble at school because many teachers find it difficult to manage their "acting out" behavior. If you think we're exaggerating, talk to a teacher.

CALL-OUTS

Some words of wisdom from Dr. Bernard Franklin in Kansas City: *In our culture too often boys are reared and taught by women who want boys' behavior to be like girls'. But boys were never, ever created to sit still. Boys are active, always have been, always will be.*

And so sometimes mothers have to pass them on to uncles or other men. We also have to figure out how to get more males in the classroom so that these boys can have active participation with another man in their lives.

There is another thing that little boys don't do any more: go to church. When we were kids, once a week we had to get dressed to the nines in clothes we'd rather not wear and spend an hour sitting and kneeling quietly in a place we'd rather not be. But this was a useful and necessary discipline. We learned how to sit still. We learned how to sit quietly. We learned self-control, and we knew the consequences if we didn't. We could always go out and play ball when church was over, a little wiser for the experience.

Today, many boys don't go to church and couldn't even put their clothes on straight if they did. Many of these kids have never tied a tie or buckled a top button or shined their shoes. Sadly, the first real suit many of them get to wear is colored orange. And what's really unfortunate is that the beltless, droopy-drawered look you see on the streets is a fashion straight out of prison. Boys like the defiance of the look, and some make it part of their permanent identity, but that look doesn't get anyone a job.

ACKNOWLEDGE THE PROBLEM

As these boys move through school, their behavior goes from bad to worse. The schools don't help much because they are often of terrible quality. Even the good schools are designed to favor girls, whose language skills tend to develop earlier than boys.

The boys are much more likely to end up in special education programs than girls, or white boys for that matter. Special education at its best is helpful for kids who need it, but too many kids are warehoused in these classes and never make it back to the mainstream. And if the drugs or the warehousing doesn't work, the schools finally just suspend the kids or expel them. Troubled black boys in schools are more than twice as likely to be suspended as white boys or Hispanics, and this does no one any good except the neighborhood drug dealers.

> **CALL-OUTS**
>
> Gregory Payton, in Cincinnati, talked about his journey: *Going into the service, flying around the country, fixing battleships—that's a good life. But what I couldn't figure out was, if it was so good, why did I put my whole life in a tube? I'm talking about a crack pipe. I put everything I ever had in that tube, and nothing came out the end but smoke.*
>
> *After coming out of the shipyard, I quit. When I say I quit, I quit everything. I gave up. I gave up on me. I was homeless.*

But when I started listening to people, I started changing. And when I started changing, some things happened to me. And one of the things I did was I went back to work. But you know, in Cincinnati, they don't have ships. So I had to go back to college.

You have to have a vision. You have to have people who believe in you too. You have to have people who support you. You feel support. You feel love. They seem like small things, but yet, they're so big, and they're so great. One of the things I do know is that we all make mistakes. But where I work now, they have a little sign on the door, and it says: a smooth ocean never helped build a sailor's skills.

What I found out is that it starts with me and it ends with me. I can't blame anybody for anything. I just gotta keep my head down and keep moving. The thing I do now is I just don't quit anything.

When the boys get suspended or expelled—admit it, parents—there is usually a good reason. The problem is that not all of us will admit it. Our boy gets sent home, and what do we do? We get angry at the teacher or the principal or the school board. We call a parasite lawyer like those we see on TV. "No, Mrs. Jones, it's not their fault! How dare they punish little Jovon! Let's sue." By the first grade, we're encouraging the kids to use "the other dude did it" defense, and some of them never forget it. They'll keep repeating "The other dude did it" like a mantra right up to the day they die, all too often courtesy of the state of California or Texas or Florida, (at this time the leading states in applying the death penalty).

To be sure, the justice system disfavors black males, and some are in the system who should not be. But tragically, too many of our sons deserve to be right where they are.

Those black boys who do make it to high school drop out more often than they graduate. Without a working dad in the home, or in their lives, most of them fail to learn the kind of basic hands-on skills that would help them find an entry-level job.

Working fathers can teach their sons about the necessity of hard work and about the need to show up on time and stick to a job. A working parent can also introduce them to a rather simple device that all of us hate but that most of us have learned to live with—an alarm clock. Getting up when you're tired and going to school or work is not something that comes naturally to anyone. It's something that kids have to learn at home.

One advantage that African-American kids have over most people in the world is the ability to speak English. It's the international language of business. To be a success anywhere on the globe, you have to speak it. But we're letting this advantage slip away too.

Many of our kids don't want to speak English. In our day, we used to talk a certain way on the corner, but when we got into the house, we switched to English. Everybody knows it's important to speak English except for some young people you see hanging around on the corners.

You can't land a plane in Rome saying, "Whassup?" to the control tower. You can't be a doctor telling your nurse, "Dat tumor be nasty." There is no Bible in the world that has that kind of language. We used to blame the kids for talking this way until we heard some of their parents. Some black parents couldn't care less. Too many teachers, of all ethnicities, couldn't care less too.

Most black employers we know want to see the entire community prosper. But even they don't want to hire boys who can't dress properly, and who speak as if English were a second language. When we see these boys walking around the neighborhood, we imagine them thirty or forty years down the road wandering around just as aimlessly, and we want to cry. The problem is they don't see themselves down that road.

These boys don't really know what the word *future* means. Neither did some of their parents. And that's why they're just hanging out at the bottom for five or six generations, trapped in housing projects that were built to stabilize people just long enough to get a job, move out, and move on. Even if there were more affordable housing out there, many of these guys would not be able to find their way to it!

Face the Facts

Black males are failing at alarming rates in the schools. Their rates of suspension and expulsion from school far exceed that of other groups. Given the high drop-out rate, the number of black men entering and graduating from college is far below the number of black women. Currently, in college and professional schools, black women outnumber black men two to one. And if you don't think that causes a problem for female students, you haven't talked to one.

Is it something about being an African-American male? Aren't we smart enough? Black Americans fought to open doors of opportunity— and now black immigrants are walking through these doors while too many of us are hanging out on the street corners. There is certainly institutional racism—particularly against black men—but racism doesn't explain everything. Black men are, in fact, lagging. If it weren't for the relative success of recent black immigrants in schools and college, the statistics would be even worse.

Enough young black males behave badly at an early age that they set the norm for other black boys. The stereotype of the angry and potentially violent black male can lead to racial profiling by teachers in the early grades. This makes it doubly difficult for those boys who are trying to behave and trying to get ahead to succeed. Soon the kids begin to stereotype themselves. These images lead to low expectations for achievement, which then become a self-fulfilling prophecy. Check the numbers:

- Homicide is the number one cause of death for black men between fifteen and twenty-nine years of age and has been for decades.

- Of the roughly sixteen thousand homicides in this country each year, more than half are committed by black men. A black man is seven times more likely to commit a murder (excluding military actions) than a white man, and six times more likely to be murdered. (Black mothers live with these numbers. We don't know how they sleep at night.)

- Ninety-four percent of all black people who are murdered are murdered by other black people.

- The life expectancy at birth of black men is sixty-nine years, compared to seventy-five years for white men, eighty for white women, and seventy-six for black women.

- In the past several decades, the suicide rate among young black men has increased more than 100 percent.

- In some cities, black males have high school drop-out rates of more than 50 percent.

- Young black men are twice as likely to be unemployed as white, Hispanic, and Asian men.

- Although black people make up just 12 percent of the general population, they make up nearly 44 percent of the prison population.

- At any given time, as many as one in four of all young black men are in the criminal justice system—in prison or jail, on probation, or on parole.

- By the time they reach their midthirties, six out of ten black high school dropouts have spent time in prison.

- About one-third of the homeless are black men.

This is madness! Back in 1950, there were twice as many white people in prison as black. Today, there are more black people than white in prison. We're not saying there is no discrimination or racial profiling today, but there is less than there was in 1950. These are not "political" criminals. These are people selling drugs, stealing, or shooting their buddies over trivia.

And when these kids get out, they are no longer kids. Many are hardened cons, and they are then recycled back into the community with the same antisocial, violent skills that got them sent away in the first place.

Keep Your Cool, but Not Too Cool

We'll be the first to remind you it's not easy being a black man in America; it never has been. If we seem hard on our brothers, it is only because we know how hard they will have to work to regain control of their destinies.

Over time, we admit, we have had to adapt in unique ways to survive, to maintain our sanity, and to excel in areas that were open to us. One important way that black men have tried to maintain their dignity and to keep control of their anger is by being "cool." Even successful black athletes have had to work at being cool in provocative situations as a way of saving their jobs—or even their lives.

For better or worse, we invented "cool." Being cool, incidentally, is a male thing. For black men, being cool has been a way of projecting strength and manhood in a society that stereotyped us as trouble. It has never really caught on with women, many of whom don't quite understand its roots or its value. Men tend to. That's why it has intrigued males all over the world.

Coolness is very attractive as a cultural force. Let's never forget that black men have made major contributions to American culture as a whole—in music, in fashion, in literature, in oratory, in science and medicine, in sports, in dance, and yes, even in comedy. In fact, no group of people has had the impact on the culture of the whole world that African Americans have had, and much of that impact has been for the good.

Still, for all its superficial appeal, coolness can shut down other emotional reactions and shield us from our true inner feelings. Being cool is protective, but that protection comes at a price. Playing it cool is not entirely harmless and can interfere with our emotional health.

To be cool is to be emotionally detached, at least on the surface. For some, showing emotions is uncool, unmanly. Expressing the kind of emotions that any good father should express—like warmth, love, caring, and grief—is almost impossible for someone who has spent his whole life stuck on being cool. Many who feel abandoned by a parent protect themselves from being hurt by putting on a cool detachment. Better to put on those bad shades and shut off the world.

But when that cool mask comes off, watch out! We have some powerful macho emotions beneath the surface, and when men and boys who have never really learned to deal with their emotions "lose their cool," there can be hell to pay.

These guys can explode in the kind of rage and violence that make no sense to anyone, not even themselves. How many times have you heard a dude say, "Dunno" when asked why he shot a buddy or beat his girlfriend or hurt his baby? And he may not know. This is the "hot" side of "cool." If these young men are hurting, they want to put the hurt on someone else—with painful results for themselves and others.

One of the challenges we face as a community is how to channel the anger in young black men. This anger has a lot to do with what their so-called friends and family have done and continue to do to them.

Many young men have channeled a lot of their aggression into a competitiveness that helps them achieve in education, the arts, and other professions.

LIFE LESSONS

It helped to have an involved father who was a music teacher, but what distinguished Wynton Marsalis from the beginning was his willingness to study and work hard. Recognizing his seriousness, the New Orleans Philharmonic invited Marsalis to perform with them when he was fourteen.

Tanglewood's Berkshire Music Center admitted Marsalis at seventeen, their youngest student ever. From there, he was off to New

York. Along the way, he also managed to earn the Eagle Scout award, the highest honor in scouting.

Still in his forties, Marsalis has emerged as the premier jazz musician of his generation and is an inspired composer. He has won nine Grammys and the Pulitzer Prize for Music, the first time ever for a jazz recording. The trumpeter has also proven to be a caring human being. In the wake of Hurricane Katrina, he organized a benefit for his hometown called Higher Ground and did everything within his power to resurrect the flooded city.

Such drive is usually all for the better. Success in sports or academics or entertainment or business makes us all feel like we've got something going on, and it diminishes our own inner sense that we are not good enough. Black men feel less angry when they get recognition from others for their accomplishments.

Still, many men adopt the "cool" stance in social settings even when they don't have to, even though it accomplishes nothing, even where it is inappropriate, even if it leaves a mate or a child feeling out in the cold—and that's a frightening place to be.

TURN OFF THE HEAT

If cool is a problem, at least we've had generations to deal with it, to integrate it into our lives. Now "hot" may be a bigger problem still. Rappers, particularly gangsta rappers, have ushered in a hip, bold, profane, aggressive style that has few pretensions of being "cool." Rap builds strongly on traditions from slavery that encourage an in-your-face style of confrontation and a verbal "ranking" on each other. Some male rappers have pushed this style to an art form of sorts, and many have pushed it beyond art of any sort.

Hot leads to trouble too. Hotheads offend easily and let no offense pass without revenge. They are like those dudes you see in a Musketeer movie who insist on a duel to the death in response to the slightest "dissing." The very idea of a "war" between multimillionaire rap stars is absurd. But rap stars have parents too. And those parents mourn the needless deaths of their sons. There is nothing cool about cold-blooded murder—nothing at all.

Black boys, much more than girls, feel the need to carry on these traditions as part of their identity of being hot and/or cool. When boys hang on to so-called Black English in the classroom and verbal confrontations in the street, they may be hanging tough with their homies, but they are handicapping themselves in the game of life. They can "trash-talk" or "play the dozens" better than anyone on the planet, and that still isn't going to get them a job or into college.

GET SMART ABOUT SEX

Gangsta rap makes our young people tough, but not so tough that they can walk through prison walls. It can jazz them about sex, but it can't begin to make them good fathers. No matter how often or how publicly they grab their crotches, crotch-grabbing isn't even going to get them a bus ride downtown.

Here's the sad and stupid part. The more socially impotent the black man is feeling, the more he will rely on sexual conquests to prove his manliness. There's a lot of bragging that goes on among black men when sex and paternity are their main claims to fame. Some will see getting a girl pregnant and having a child as proof of their virility. But what it really proves is their insecurity.

Many young women are equally insecure. When a young man whispers to a girl, "If you really loved me, you'd have my baby," she finds this kind of "sweet" manipulation difficult to resist. Even though many teenage girls are demanding that their beaus use condoms, others keep quiet out of fear of losing their lovers.

Real men act responsibly, and they sure as hell don't walk away from the mothers of their babies. Real men make a commitment to these young mothers. If they do not marry them, at least they should take care of their children.

Unfortunately, not all boys become real men. In our poorer neighborhoods, in fact, few do. We deceive ourselves if we deny that there is a crisis among black families. Roughly 70 percent of black babies are born each year to single mothers. The mothers are not all teenagers either. The rate of teen pregnancies has come down. These single mothers are often women old enough and educated enough to make good choices.

The fact is, though, that many of the black females who used to get married when they became pregnant are no longer doing so. There is less shame and less embarrassment. But more than that, some black women simply don't want to marry the fathers of their babies because these men appear to have little else to offer beyond the sperm. Many of these men are unemployed and unemployable.

Recent studies by scholars at several major universities and as reported in leading newspapers show that a critical mass of young black men is becoming "ever more disconnected from the mainstream society" than they used to be, much more so than white or even Hispanic men.

In poor communities, more than half of all black men do not finish high school. What happens to these guys is not at all happy. Despite a strong economy for the last two decades, most have not hooked into the job market in any meaningful way.

These studies show that the percentage of unemployed young black males continued to climb even as the stock market did. By the year 2000, after eight straight years of economic growth, 65 percent of black male high school dropouts in their twenties did not have regular employment. These were just about the only people in America who didn't. They couldn't find work, they weren't looking, or the warden wouldn't let them out to look. By 2004, that percentage had increased to a preposterous 72 percent, almost four times more than among Hispanic dropouts. Even including high school graduates, half of black men in their twenties were jobless in 2004.

Because so many black men are unemployed, underemployed, and incarcerated, they are not proposing marriage, and if they did, their proposals might not be taken seriously. A father takes care of his children. These men have trouble taking care of themselves. The relationship between them and the mothers of their babies is often strained, or worse. Society keeps laying the problem on the "unwed mother." You never hear anything about the "unwed father." We have to talk more about these men and to these men if we are ever to see them assume their responsibilities as men.

What aggravates the problem is the absolute shortage of black men. Due to their naturally shorter life span, the high rate of death from homicide and accidents, the imprisonment factor, and other problems that take men off the street, there are many more available black women than men at every age level. The odds favor the men and often spoil them.

Not too long ago a television show featured a thirteen-year-old mother who had somehow managed to have two of her suitors appear on the show for a paternity test. One of the boys was black, the other Puerto Rican. They were fifteen- and sixteen-year-old best friends, who both had had sex with this young girl during the general time she had conceived.

The word *shameless* comes to mind. Why these people would wash linen this dirty not just in public but on national TV is still another sign that all is not well in the world. Why someone would encourage them and reward them is even more troubling.

In any case, the Puerto Rican boy said he was planning on joining the army. The black boy said he was going to college. Both said the baby would mess up their lives and wanted no part of him. When the results were read, the Puerto Rican kid whooped in relief, the black kid groaned in despair, and the girl cried.

"I'm still going to school," said the reluctant dad smugly. The fact that a sixteen-year-old can say this on TV without worrying about sounding like a heartless jerk gives you some idea of where his training came from. Neither he nor his own mother wanted anything to do with that baby. And no one called him an "unwed father."

TONE DOWN THE CULTURE

The Ku Klux Klan could not have devised a media culture as destructive as the one our media moguls, black and white, have created for black America. Too often on TV news programs, black males are shown as abusive, irresponsible, absentee exploiters. This image may reflect a certain reality, but the media should also provide positive models, and not emphasize the negative.

In 1995, the Million Man March in Washington DC brought together hundreds of thousands of black men who publicly affirmed their responsibilities to their families and children. But even that was not enough to counter the flood of negative imagery.

What do record producers think when they churn out that gangsta rap with antisocial, women-hating messages? Do they think that black male youth won't act out what they have heard repeated since they were old enough to listen?

Oh yes, then there's *nigga* a thousand times a day, every day. Martin and Malcolm and Medgar Evers must be turning over in their graves. They put their lives on the line. Why? So our young people can pick up where white people left off and debase themselves instead of being debased? Talk about lowering self-esteem.

WALK BACK IN

When people say, "I never liked the Huxtables," we know why. People who don't like Dr. Heathcliff Huxtable don't like—or don't know—their own fathers.

We can't speak honestly of black culture in America unless and until we honestly address the issue of the estrangement of fathers and their children.

The situation is by no means hopeless. We just have to get these fathers to realize that the children they sired are their children and always will be their children. By walking away, they have punished their children. They leave these children feeling abandoned. Once they come and claim their children, and feel the joy and the beauty of a hug, they will at least begin to understand what fatherhood is all about. But let's not kid ourselves either. This is much easier said than done.

For no good reason we can understand, society seems to be telling young black men that fatherhood is no big thing. Society tells young people in general to look after number one and to worry about everyone else later, if at all. Like the sixteen-year-old on the TV show—if you don't like the outcome, walk away. Even if you get married and you're not happy, walk away. With all the temptations to walk away, the black divorce and separation rate today is 50 percent higher than the white rate. And black women who divorce are considerably less likely to remarry than white divorcees, partly because of the shortage of black males.

Without being told and told often, young men simply do not know or understand what a father's responsibilities are. Many of them have never seen a real father in action. Many do not appreciate that fathers are important to a child's healthy development or that unemployed, separated, and unwed fathers can still interact with their children and contribute significantly to their well-being.

CALL-OUTS

A wise voice from Compton, California, John Hill: *The environment is not you. You can rise above those things that have happened to you. Those of you who are raising your children—turn off the television, take some time, sit down and read with them.*

Talk to them, motivate them, help them to become something that they want to be. That's what you have to do. The teacher does not raise your children. Teachers teach. Your job is to raise your own children. You can't give over that responsibility to somebody else. And please, whatever you do, don't let the gangs raise your children.

Gangs don't raise your children. And to all of them here, we have got to become fathers in our neighborhoods, fathers to our children,

and fathers to every child in that neighborhood. We have to understand
that we have to be there; the children are only getting 50 percent
because only the mother is there.

SISTERS, HANG IN THERE

Black women, bless their hearts, are more loyal to black men than we
deserve. Still, they are not afraid to write about the strains in the relationships between us.

Many black men have heard this outcry and heeded it. They have
decided to organize, to raise not only their own consciousness but that of
other young black males as well. Today, just as black men as a group are
more aware of their chauvinism, black women are more aware of the
unique struggles of black men. Yet, despite our common history of victim-
ization, we are still victimizing each other—with black males inflicting the
most damage.

The reasons for this are not hard to figure. As gender barriers began to
crumble in the late 1960s along with racial barriers, women entered the
workforce in droves; more recently, there has been an enormous influx of
immigrants. These factors led to the displacement of many black male
workers. At the same time, the shift to new technology and service jobs left
many black men without the education and skills to compete for any except
the lowest paying jobs. The job market became more competitive for poor
black men with few job skills and inadequate educational preparation.

CALL-OUTS

Some thoughts from Darryl Green: *Young girls need to have a rela-*
tionship with their fathers as well. If that father is not present in the

young girl's life, nine times out of ten she is going to have something wrong with her in the dating process when it comes to knowing what a man is. When I look at my seven-year-old daughter now, I realize that I'm the first man she is ever going to know in her life. And if I screw that up, she is going to be screwed up. So I'm saying to men as Dr. Cosby has said, "We need you all to come back home, fellas." Enough is enough. We need you at the crib. Drop the kids off at school in the morning. Pick them up in the afternoon. We need you to have an active role in their lives.

Black men and women have begun to harbor racial stereotypes about each other. Black males who already feel insecure around white people resent feeling a similar kind of insecurity around "strong" black women. But no one can take a man's physical power away, certainly not women. That's why sometimes—too often—black men overcompensate with rage.

They direct their destructive rage against black women in any number of unfortunate ways—verbal abuse, battery, even rape. Meanwhile, gangsta rap musicians cheer them on.

Unable to fight back, women can unknowingly transfer their rage toward their sons—just because they are male. Black boys in female-headed households feel the hurt most when the mother is angry with a black male. If they hear their mom say, "Black men ain't worth s—," the boys wonder whether that includes them. When their moms yell, "You're no good, just like your father!" all the doubt goes away.

Black males and females must take the time to talk about their relationships with each other and with the children. Open discussion, with guidance from counselors, about the sexual and parental tension in black communities is something we all should encourage.

Some black men have already decided to acknowledge that pain and to make their brothers aware of it too. Black men have rallied and formed such organizations as 100 Black Men and Concerned Black Men to help vulnerable young black males and to serve as role models and mentors. Civil rights organizations have developed various "black male responsibility" projects, and some school districts have considered the merits of organizing all black male schools to address their needs.

Low expectations coming from a teacher can cause a child to fail. Coming from a parent, low expectations can crush the soul.

STRIVE TO SUCCEED

As history has shown, we are a resilient people. We overcome. In the face of all of the obstacles that even the most challenged of our children face, we continually come across stories that give us cause to smile and to hope.

What these stories have in common are two things: kids with the will to survive and succeed and adults who have taken the time to help these kids along. In the story that follows, we add a third element: the power of friendship.

One night, while a freshman at Putnam Vocational Technical High School in Springfield, Massachusetts, Loren Wilder went roller-skating. When he returned home, he found his whole world turned upside down.

The police had raided the apartment and arrested his mother for drug dealing. She would spend the next several years in prison. Wilder finished the ninth grade at his uncle's house and started the tenth at his sister's. When she left for Puerto Rico, he was on his own.

Wilder's buddy, Jimmy Hester, wasn't faring much better. After years of moving from place to place with his desperately unsettled mother, Hester broke off their tumultuous relationship and left home. He was fifteen years old and determined to drop out of school altogether.

A phone call from Wilder convinced him to come back to Putnam, where they both played football. "If it wasn't for Loren, I wouldn't be where I am today," said Hester.

At Putnam, their coaches kept a close eye on the boys, who would soon rent an apartment together. The school's guidance counselor also kept an eye on them. The parents of their friend Wesley White watched over them as well.

The *Springfield Republican* ran an article on the three boys, then seniors, about how they clipped coupons and hunted for bargains to help save money for college. As of this writing, with a little help from adults who read the article, the young men are doing just fine. All three of them are juniors in college in good standing. When possible, they come back to Putnam to help mentor those in situations like their own.

GIVE FATHERHOOD A SECOND CHANCE

Many black men, including the poor, have been struggling with the challenges of a new model of fatherhood, one in which they play a greater role in the child-rearing experience. Black men benefit from feeling the pleasures and satisfactions of being involved with their little ones. Many complain, however, that the mothers shut them out.

How do we change that? If the father has been cruel or indifferent to the mother or to the child, how can we ask the mother to give the man a second chance? It's never easy for anyone involved. Still, if a mother has a difficult—but not violent—relationship with the baby's father, it is important to get counseling to help them work through their issues for the sake of the child. Parents should not use the children to manipulate each other. There are counselors in churches, health centers, and community agencies who can help parents learn to work together.

If the father is physically abusive and refuses to change, the mother has no choice but to shut him out. And the father should honor any legal restraining orders until he gets his act together and convinces the authorities that he has. In the meantime, for her children's sake, the mother should try to find "substitute" fathers among relatives, mentors, and community organizations.

The fact that a black father is unemployed or underemployed should not disqualify him as a parent in the mother's eyes. These men can play an important role in the household. If fathers take on more child-care and household responsibilities, it lessens the burden on the mother. By participating in the life of the family, men can help relieve the stress that is frequently found in low-income households, as well as strengthen their children's development.

Children who spend time with their fathers will develop closer family connections and will benefit from the individual attention as they share in day-to-day activities. There are committed fathers out there. We all know the story of the Williams sisters, Venus and Serena, who are both world-class tennis players. Twenty years ago, their father, Richard Williams, told his little girls they were going to be tennis champions. With the strong support of both their parents, they started on a tennis court in Compton, California, and went on to play on international courts. Mr. Williams believed his daughters would win, and win they did. Dream dreams for your children. They don't need to become international superstars, but they do need you to lift them up so they can succeed in life.

CALL-OUTS

Dr. Willie Barber, of Baltimore, shared his thoughts: *I talk to fathers who want to see their children, but the mom will not allow it, or the in-laws will say, "No, he's not coming around here." So there are a lot of barriers.*

Sometimes it is tough to forgive people for what they have done. We have to help women deal with that. We have to educate them about the important role that fathers can and should play in their children's lives.

In recent decades, there have been many programs developed to meet the special needs of black men and their roles as fathers. Fatherhood training programs now exist in many communities around the country. If you do not have one in your community, contact a social service agency, church, or health clinic to urge them to set up such a program. Fatherhood programs are also a way of encouraging young black men to bond with each other for mutual support.

Finding ways to enable black fathers to connect with their kids is crucial to the kids' well-being. As should be obvious by now, black men often have to overcome some very real hurdles to connect with their children. These include child-support difficulties, incarceration, lack of education, and unemployment. In some of the harder cases, the men avoid their children for no other reason than that they see themselves as bad role models. What they need to understand, though, is that from the moment they commit themselves to that child, and as long as they honor that commitment, they can still be a good role model. Our kids, thank God, don't ask for a résumé or for references. They don't need to see our bank accounts. They just want us in their lives.

Constructive programs, especially for ex-inmates, are sprouting up in some communities, and we need many more of them. It is in these areas that we need policy changes and a criminal justice system that will support such programs. This is where black people's historic role as activists comes in.

The Dellums Commission in Washington DC on which Dr. Poussaint served as honorary vice chair, issued a 2006 report that recommended, among other initiatives, the repeal of mandatory sentencing, an increase in the minimum wage, and a restriction of zero-tolerance policies in schools.

We must listen to these voices of wisdom and fight for state and local governments to help us salvage as many black men—and women—as possible. This includes financial support for programs providing counseling, education, and job-training skills. Men need a good steady job that gives them a chance in life; otherwise, they end up back in jail or on the streets. Such men can become permanently alienated from the world, which can be hell on the community and heartbreaking for the children.

When all is said and done, the black child is our future. It's time for us men to think of the future, to straighten out our acts, to say to ourselves, *I am more interested in raising my child than any issue I had before. I'm going to behave or get help, but it's about the child.*

No matter how useless or hopeless a father may think he is, his role is simply to *be* there. If he makes that commitment, he is a much better man than he thought he was.

ROLE MODELS, PLEASE APPLY

For many black males, chances for success seem slim in many fields because they lack role models. They don't have a clue as to what's out there. How many kids in even the smartest Crips set in South Central have parents who have decent jobs? How many of them have available dads at all? How many have moms who are doing something more than just getting by?

Without working parents in the home, or in their lives, how do these boys learn about work skills? From the get-go, respectable careers in the trades are all shut off to them. Unlike their grandparents, they don't have to worry about segregated unions. But they do have to worry about developing their own skills, and that's a greater worry still.

CALL-OUTS

Some thoughts from Dr. Curtis Adams Jr. in Baltimore: *In order to be a full-grown man, you must see one in action. It's not just what that man says but what he does. The little things done day in and day out demonstrate what makes a man. And when a boy does not see this, he is deprived, and he feels it. Having said that, girls need to see a good man as well. A woman will not know how to pick a good man if she has not seen one.*

Despite the obvious gains that people of color have made in most jobs and occupations, many poor young black males still believe that important upper-level occupations exclude them because they are black. You can tell them this is a new day all you want, but they are still stuck on yesterday. It's much more comfortable to have someone to blame other than ourselves. That's just human nature.

We must reach out to black youth, particularly black boys, to show them all of the opportunities that are available. But more than show them, we've got to lead them, and that takes mentoring and tutoring and coaching.

These kids see all the bad role models you can imagine—drug dealers, pimps, you name it. But positive role models do exist. We're talking about ordinary black men doing an honest day's work as cab drivers, counselors, bus drivers, doctors, lawyers, and businessmen, and coming home at night to the mother or caregiver of their children.

LIFE LESSONS

When Benjamin O. Davis Jr. entered West Point in 1932, there were many of his fellow classmates who rather wished he weren't there. To discourage Davis from staying, his fellow cadets would not eat with him or room with him and barely spoke to him except when they had to.

Benjamin O. Davis Jr., though, had something going for him that his classmates did not count on. That would be Benjamin O. Davis Sr. The senior Davis had enlisted in the U.S. Army as a private and served with the legendary Buffalo soldiers. By the time his son entered West Point, Davis had worked his way up to colonel and understood full well the opportunity that West Point presented. When the son talked of quitting, the father steeled his son's resolve. The son persevered and in the process taught his fellow cadets a life lesson, as memorialized in the 1936 yearbook entry on Davis:

> The courage, tenacity, and intelligence with which he conquered a problem incomparably more difficult than plebe year won for him the sincere admiration of his classmates, and his single-minded determination to continue in his

---

chosen career cannot fail to inspire respect wherever for-
tune may lead him.

It was not good luck or white guilt that led Davis to command
the famed Tuskegee Airmen in Word War II or to become the first
African-American general in the United States Air Force. It was a
combination of personal grit and paternal steel.

DON'T COUNT OUT THE EX-OFFENDERS

Our young men see the bad guys making all that jack and wooing all those
women, but what they don't see is the twenty-thirty-forty years the bad
guys spend rotting away in prison. And many do end up there if they don't
end up dead. In California, seven times as many men are in prison now as
there were just twenty-five years ago, and way too many of them are black.

We have met with men who have paid their debt to society for the
crimes they committed, clear-thinking men, a combination of Black
Muslims and black Christians working to heal the inner spirit that has
been so badly damaged. It is marvelous to look at the faces of the young
inmates as they heed the words of these full-grown men, who speak to
them without profanity about the great wisdom that they have inherited
but so far mismanaged. And these young men are listening.

This is not the scary ranting we saw in the film *Scared Straight*. These
men know the Spirit. They are talking brother to brother and father to
son. The Christian men are talking about how God paid them a visit and
how those visits changed their lives.

These men are not afraid to go up to the junior gangsters they see in
the street and have conversations with them. This is what we mean by
putting a body on these boys. These men provide a counterforce to the
recruitment efforts of the Crips and the Bloods and other gangs.

As a society we could do more. We could envision a system in which those who come out of prison wanting help are sent to a local community college. There, at the least, they could finish their GEDs and get reacquainted with the job market.

Those with the interest could complete a two-year program and become what we might call "psychological behavior technicians." Armed with a two-year degree and some serious life experiences, they could have an important positive impact on youngsters coming up. If these ex-felons wanted to go on, they would not have to stop at two years. They might want to get a four-year degree, or their master's, or maybe even their doctorate. There is no reason we cannot save most of them.

The media can help. They can show black male role models across a spectrum of occupations. Right now, sports and entertainment figures predominate. Not surprisingly, many black youth aspire to careers as athletes and entertainers. Who can blame them? But for every guy who makes the NBA, there are a thousand who just dream about it. Dunking over your head is of much less use in the real world than designing a bridge or reading an X-ray.

CLAIM YOUR CHILDREN

We are calling on men, all men, the successful and the unsuccessful, the affluent and the poor, the married and the unmarried, to come and claim their children. You can run the biggest drug cartel in America or win the Super Bowl, but if you haven't claimed your children, you are not a man.

You can make all the excuses you want, but no one can stop you from claiming your children. It's not about you. It's about them. If you have not come to claim your children, you have stolen their hope. You have stolen any kind of feeling that they are worth something. They will likely have no sense of the past, little pride, and even less faith in the future. They will see fathers at the mall or on TV and they will wonder how stupid or ugly they must be to have driven their fathers away.

In going around the country, we have talked to people who create their own solutions, who don't wait for the government or anybody else to provide funding, who start their own schools and community centers and mentoring programs. Many such programs have already been created by civil rights organizations, settlement houses, churches and mosques, and black fraternal groups. We have to focus on healing these emotionally wounded children.

CALL-OUTS

A word from Mr. David Miller: *In the city of Baltimore, with 70 percent of our males dropping out of school, it is very clear we are looking at a community-based tragedy. So let's talk about a community-based solution—I and some others started our own Saturday schools for black boys. We didn't wait for the government or anybody to provide funding. We stepped out on faith and decided to raise the money.*

This experience is based on the life of Paul Robeson. So we have a very vigorous academic component. We have a vigorous lifestyle component. And parental involvement is magnificent. You can no longer wait for school districts to do for our children what we know God intended us to do.

So what I would like to see you do is to start a program in your community. We have to instill fundamental life skills—how to dress, how to act, how to talk, what to do when stopped by the police. We need to do things that will keep our boys close. We also need to teach our boys that they can be entrepreneurs, that they can create their own economic destiny.

As Mr. Miller shows, you don't stop an epidemic by cursing the world as unfair. You don't stop an epidemic by condemning yourself as a loser. You stop an epidemic by becoming an activist and stepping up and being a man. Every male, if he wants to, can be one.

CALL-OUTS

In Baltimore, Richard Rowe and Earl El-Amin led the audience in the African-American fathers' prayer: *First, I will work to be the best father I can be. I will openly display love and caring for my children. I will teach by example; I will be there for my children at all times. I will encourage them in family values; I will never say negative and discouraging things to my children; I will teach my children to be responsible, disciplined, fair, and honest. As a father, I will attempt to provide my family with love and security. From this day forward, I will hold sacred my role as a father and stop making excuses.*

There are great responsibilities parents assume in raising a child. And for a black child, those responsibilities often weigh heavily. Raising a child, in fact, may not be for everybody. But once any adult brings a child into this world, the child's well-being must come first. And that's the way it has to be.

2

IT TAKES A COMMUNITY

For the record, your authors were born three years and one hundred miles apart in Philadelphia and Harlem, respectively. Not to give too much away, but we each finished high school before *Brown v. Board of Education* and had successfully launched our careers before the Civil Rights Act of 1964. We know a little bit about black communities and have seen a good deal of change over time—some of it good, some not so good.

Since the 1954 *Brown v. Board of Education* decision to end school segregation, black people have made tremendous strides in a relatively short period of time. There have been extraordinary accomplishments on all fronts that seemed unthinkable fifty years ago. Yes, problems remain, but no one can deny that African Americans have helped make America great. We are far from invisible.

As we face the future, black people must remember that our success in American society is shown in black achievement throughout all of our nation's institutions. Despite the fact that racial discrimination has not been eliminated, black strength lies in our resolve to keep on keeping on, never quitting, never giving up, never yielding to the role of cooperative victim.

The background we provide here on slavery and its legacy is not designed to provide excuses for anyone. It is rather a way of helping black people and others understand how iron shackles can evolve into psychological ones. Our goal isn't to wallow in the misery such shackles can cause but to break free of them all. Come on, people; if anyone understands freedom, we do!

GO TELL PHARAOH

As old as your authors are, we weren't born into slavery, and neither were our parents. We can't begin to imagine what it must have felt like to have been a slave yearning for freedom but not knowing when the day of glory would come. Those of us who think we have it hard today don't know what "hard" means. Our ancestors did. They suffered in physical and psychological ways, humiliation being part of the package.

One way slaves survived such brutal conditions was to turn the Christianity they had learned into a liberation theology. The stories of the Hebrew slaves became their own. Even as slave owners used the Bible to justify slavery, black people used the Bible as God intended—to give people hope for a time when there would be true justice.

The story of Moses leading God's people to freedom resonated in the Underground Railroad, the name for the clandestine organization that smuggled people out of slavery.

LIFE LESSONS

Among the most successful of the railroad's conductors was Harriet Tubman. Born into slavery in Maryland, Tubman fled north when she learned that she was to be sold into the deep South. She continually risked her newly found freedom by leading nineteen successful excursions back into Maryland to free her family, friends, and others she did not even know—as many as three hundred people in all. "I never lost a passenger," she said. During the Civil War, she helped plan and lead the raid at Combahee Ferry that freed more than 750 slaves. Tubman lived for fifty years after the Emancipation Proclamation and was an activist for equal rights. In

---

honor of her brave efforts to free the enslaved, she will be forever known as the "Moses of Her People."

One well-known black spiritual captures the story of Moses and makes it come to life: "Go down, Moses, way down in Egypt's land, tell old pharaoh to let my people go!" Another old spiritual speaks mournfully of our burden: "Nobody knows the trouble I've seen. Nobody knows but Jesus." Christianity offered hope, if not in this life, then in the next. One widely popular black spiritual, "Swing Low, Sweet Chariot," says it best:

> *Swing low, sweet chariot,*
> *Coming for to carry me home . . .*
> *I looked over Jordan, and what did I see?*
> *Coming for to carry me home,*
> *A band of angels coming after me,*
> *Coming for to carry me home.*

Religion and the spirituals gave black people the strength to bear up even though freedom would not come for centuries.

BREAK THE SHACKLES

Slaves were happy on the plantation—slave masters told each other—having a grand old time. Oh yes, you can just imagine that! This "cheerful darky" image was meant to blunt criticism and even gain support for the institution of slavery. The stereotype of the happy-go-lucky slave endures even today. It continues to affect the way people think and behave, often to the detriment of black people.

Many slave owners argued that black people were really like children, that they preferred the subordinate role. This was perpetuated by the custom of referring to black men and women as "boys" and "girls." As slaves, black people didn't have to "suffer" from behaving like adults—making decisions, earning an income, accepting responsiblity for their own lives. According to slavery's defenders, slavery protected these dumb and docile creatures from themselves. If set free, they would likely go broke or insane.

We're serious! That's what people really thought or, at least, what they told each other they thought.

That slavery itself could drive a sane man mad, and even to suicide, was a fact that went right over the heads of most slave owners. One Louisiana slave master was upset that his slaves were fleeing his plantation in droves and heading north to freedom. He was quite frustrated about losing his property and profits. The slave master called on Dr. Samuel A. Cartwright for help. After studying the situation, Dr. Cartwright concluded that slaves who ran away to freedom were suffering from a mental illness, which he called "drapetomania," or runaway mania. The reality is that black people suffered deep mental trauma from slavery, which contributed to "drapetomania." This was not because of their "childish needs" but because they sought freedom. Escape is the natural response of the healthy individual to captivity. Just imagine how many slaves were suffering from post-traumatic stress disorder as it is defined today. The trauma that the slaves experienced was so profound that its legacy is sometimes described as post-traumatic slavery syndrome.

Under slavery, a black life did not count as much as a white life. Slaves had little protection beyond the good will of their "masters." Imagine being a slave and waking up in the morning wondering about the day ahead: *Let's see—I got about twelve hours of cotton picking wrapped around some episodes of random abuse. Hot damn!* Happy? Be serious. Historians have spoken of "good" slave masters, but—like the circles of hell—there were only shades of bad. An evil institution can produce no pure good.

There were, however, some slave masters who set their slaves free, and there were sympathetic white people, especially in the North, who helped slaves escape through the Underground Railroad. The abolitionists fought hard to end slavery in America, and many died trying. Still, despite some bright spots here and there, white supremacists had real clout in this nation for very nearly all of our first two hundred years. For black people to hold their heads high even today means getting rid of internal feelings of inferiority. This can be difficult given the very definition of a "black" person in America. Historically, slave masters defined a person with any known black ancestry as black—which makes African ancestry a taint on white purity. The way race is defined in the United States makes no biological or genetic sense. It exists primarily as a tool for political and psychological oppression. It is time to make the escape from psychological slavery.

THINK FREEDOM

The Emancipation Proclamation, written in 1863 during the Civil War (1861–1865), finally freed slaves in the South from bondage. It was a great day for America, and a glorious day for African Americans. After slavery, there was a short-lived period in the South called Reconstruction, when black men started businesses, bought property, voted, and even served in Congress.

But old habits die hard, especially racist ones. When Northerners wearied of Reconstruction, the old South reared its head and imposed "Jim Crow" segregation. Later endorsed by the Supreme Court, Jim Crow laws were reinforced with violence and lynchings by, among others, the notorious Ku Klux Klan, a hate group that was often openly embraced by Southern states. De jure segregation reigned for nearly one hundred years and was not to be eliminated until the great struggle of the civil rights movement beginning in the mid-1950s.

During that century, segregationists enlisted "science" to maintain a status quo that warred with the United States Constitution. If science could prove black inferiority "objectively," segregationists could insist that black brains were smaller and less developed and justify a paternalistic caste system for white people and for black people. Science has long been a powerful weapon of the privileged. Even today, some academics continue to compare biased IQ scores of black and white people to justify differential treatment, without weighing the impact of centuries of slavery and racial degradation on black performance.

Although few acknowledge it—who would?—the doctrine of white supremacy has sunk deeply into the minds of too many Americans, black people included. It has slithered its way into the psyches of poor black youth with low self-esteem, who equate academic success with "acting white." No offense, but we flatter white people unduly to equate success with whiteness. And if success is "white," then are we saying that to "act black" is to fail?

Again, we wonder how these stereotypes affect black people today. Are we too dependent? Do we rely too much on white people or "the system" to rescue us? Do we lack faith in our own ability to run things? Has the legacy of slavery affected even our current mental state?

Too many white people, and some black people, believe that many poor black youth are uneducable, particularly black males. This position harkens back to the notion of poor genes determining poor performance rather than poor environment or poor schools or a self-degrading music scene. We need to avoid putting down an entire culture. We must separate the good from the bad while treating black communities with respect.

Remember the Triumphs

A word of appreciation: African Americans are a remarkable people. By any measure, we are a strong people. We are a resilient people whose hopes and dreams could not easily be squelched. Defying the odds, iconic black men and women have risen up to fashion America's history: Nat Turner, Frederick Douglass, Harriet Tubman, Booker T. Washington, W.E.B. Du Bois, Mary McLeod Bethune, Thurgood Marshall, Rosa Parks, Dr. Martin Luther King Jr., and Dorothy Height, to name only a few giants out of a cast of thousands who have had a deep influence on events here and abroad. Black history is interwoven into the fabric of American history. From oppressed, down-but-not-out victims, black people became warriors. In the process, we have forced America to live up to its promise of freedom and justice for all. This is one epic story: how we broke the chains of bondage to achieve victory and freedom.

To be sure, the problem of race in America runs deep and complicates interactions among us all. Yet there are more friendships across ethnic and racial lines in America than ever before. To their credit, white workers marched side by side with black people during the civil rights movement in the 1960s, and many were beaten—or worse—in the process. No one should question the deep commitment of such workers when they put their lives on the line. They gave much to local communities, helping their neighbors with education, health, and the acquisition of job skills. We salute the sacrifices made by such workers in the battle for black liberation. Many non-black people work in programs located in black communities across America. Black people welcome such help and commitment. It has made a difference. We wish there were more dedicated people like them serving in our schools and in our governing bodies. If we had more allies in the non-black communities, the racial divide in America could be quickly bridged.

For all the woes of segregation, there were some good things to come out of it. One was that it forced us to take care of ourselves. When restaurants, laundries, hotels, theaters, groceries, and clothing stores were segregated, black people opened and ran their own. Black life insurance companies and banks thrived, as well as black funeral homes. African Americans also owned and prospered on family farms. Such successes provided jobs and strength to black economic well-being. They also gave black people that gratifying sense of an interdependent community with people working to help each other.

In the era before welfare checks and food stamps and subsidized housing and Medicaid, families were strong too. They had to be. And if the nuclear family faltered, as sometimes happened, the extended family— grandparents, aunts, uncles—reached in and lent a helping hand, because if they didn't no one else would. This was the world your authors were born into. It was far from free and even further from perfect, but it worked. As we all know, however, something happened, and it wasn't necessarily good.

CALL-OUTS

Lauren Lake, speaking at a Birmingham call-out, talked about our responsibility to make things right: *We just have to do a few things. We need to have a vision. We need to have a vision of a better life. We need to see things differently—the way that our ancestors did—and know that it is possible. We need to be accountable not only to ourselves but for ourselves and others. We need . . . to be accountable for the ways that we contribute to what is going on in our communities today.*

The first thing we need to do is restore the black family. . . . There used to be a mother and a father. There used to be a sister. There used to be play cousins. There used to be a fake Auntie. There used to be Mr. Tyrone who lived around the corner. All of whom could give you a whupping if they saw you doing something wrong. I want the black family returned.

We need to rebuild our communities. Ladies and gentlemen, we need to go back into our entrepreneurship-style thinking as people of color. There was a time when we couldn't go into the neighborhood restaurant, so we opened our own, filled with good food. And not only did we open it, we supported it. Ladies and gentlemen, we have to invest in ourselves, in our communities.

We have to get out and vote. We have to get out and vote because we are powerful, so powerful that people of color have the power in each and every election to choose the candidate they want to win. It is the people of color who, if they banded together and voted in one accord, could choose the candidate they want to win. And not just choose them based upon what we usually do, but choose them based upon what we require them to do for us.

REJECT VICTIMHOOD

Black families have to come to grips with the legacies of slavery and seg-regation, which continue to burden them. This is particularly true for families who suffer the double whammy of being *black* and *poor* in a society not thrilled with either. These twin handicaps make it more dif-ficult to leap over the hurdles on the track to success.

The high rate of poverty among black people owes something to the aftershocks of slavery and segregation. When slaves were emancipated, they were virtually all poor. They never received their promised forty acres and a mule. Most were left destitute, far behind even their poor white countrymen in a ravaged postwar countryside.

Poverty really stresses people out. This will come as no surprise to those of you who see the effects all around you. It is a risk factor for all kinds of social and emotional problems. Given such major hurdles, past and pres-ent, it is amazing how much many of us have managed to accomplish. This is an affirmation of our ability to move from victims to victors.

Our ancestors, to their credit, did not accept victimhood. They fought back as individuals and as a people. Most refused to become pas-sive victims of the system. This tenacious drive to be victorious is a qual-ity that will help us meet the current challenges in our communities. By strengthening black families, whatever their structure, and nurturing black children, we can save black youth from alienation, defeat, failure, and hopelessness.

Despite the naysayers, black people—with the help of supportive social policies—can shoulder the remaining challenges and eliminate the barriers to black success. The driving force for change has been the activism of African Americans and others who take up our cause. The key word is *activism,* yesterday, today, and tomorrow. Getting active and fighting back promotes good mental health for all of us, especially the poor. Passivity takes us nowhere. Activism is what gets us where we want to go.

Sometimes people with a victim mentality feel hopeless and do self-destructive things that make their lives even worse. It is time to redirect that energy. It is time to think positively and act positively. Black communities and families must provide our youth with the love and guidance that keep them strong and on that positive path. This is easier said than done. The fight against the institutional dragons outside the gates and the self-destructive ones within will take a whole lot of Saint Georges.

African Americans have achieved in spite of the most malignant forms of racism and are succeeding today despite the legacies of those practices. Blaming white people can be a way for some black people to feel better about themselves, but it doesn't pay the electric bills. There are more doors of opportunity open for black people today than ever before in the history of America. Black people who thus far have not achieved must be made to realize that these doors are tall enough and wide enough for them to walk through with their heads held high.

DEFINE THE VILLAGE AND DEFEND IT

When politicians come courting the black vote, they like to say, "It takes a village." Black people routinely respond, "Well, yes, okay." But no one seems to ask the questions that should come first: What is a village? What makes a village? Who acts for the village? Who speaks for it? One person? Two people?

Properly understood, the village is everyone. We've got to see ourselves as part of the village. We can no longer just say, "I'll let the rest of you handle it," because if each individual lets someone else handle it, no one handles anything.

Ask yourself: If Rosa Parks had apologized, stood up, and sat in the back of the bus, would we have had a Montgomery Boycott? Would we have had Selma? Would we have had the Civil Rights Act of 1964 and the Voting Rights Act of 1965? Are we waiting for one person to make the move instead of moving together?

Although they have made their own share of mistakes like everyone else, the Black Muslims have never been the kind of folks to sit in the back of anyone's bus. What is more, they have always believed in their community. Neither of your authors is a member of the Nation of Islam, but we know what we see.

Okay, we see that they sometimes frighten people. They wear suits and dark glasses and bow ties. They sell bean pies. But they're not afraid to walk up to the local drug dealer and say, "Brother, you can't do that here. Brother, this is my family. Brother, you're in the wrong neighborhood. You're going to have to take that out of here. And by the way, if you want to clean yourself up, brother, we have something for you to read."

That's what the Muslims do. And the Muslims get out and about. They're in the communities. Bean pie, fish, and cookies may not sound all that appetizing, but they sound a lot better to our ears than crystal meth, angel dust, and crack.

CALL-OUTS

Nation of Islam minister Tony Muhammad, of Compton, California, thinks so too: *Brothers and sisters, let me tell you. What we need is in our community. What we have got to stop doing is looking outside of our community and look within our community, and we don't care what the title is—get away from labels. If it's the Nation, if it's Christian, if it's Buddhist, if it's Oobooboo, all I want to know is, do you have a program that's saving our children?*

I went to Koreatown today and I met with the Korean merchants. I love them. You know why? They got a place called what? Koreatown. When I left them I went to Chinatown. They got a place called what? Chinatown.

Where is your town?

We're going to go street by street, block by block, and I'm getting with every pastor because the religious men and women, it's our fault that the streets have gone wild. You hear what I said? It's our fault.

We can take Compton. But we are going to need your help. We are going to need your support. So I want to get together with all the top educators, and I guarantee you if you allow us to help you, we can turn Compton around.

WALK THE WALK

Throughout history, we have come to think of a sanctuary as a protected place, a place where the anxieties and animosities of the bigger world just kind of melt away. Today America's black communities are anything but sanctuaries. We believe that they can be and should be and, one day, will be. But we have to make it happen. We all have to remember that this— right here—*this* is the village, the only village, the place we go when we go back home. We are the village, each individual—the village is us. We are the beautiful people. If we want to make a change, it is the God in us that gives us our strength. Now, we can look up and say, "Thank you, Jesus." That is good and just, but still, remember, the Lord helps those who help themselves.

Are we making sense? The next time Jesse Jackson comes your way, you have to give him more help than: "Jesse is coming and Jesse's going to solve it." You have got to do more than just walk with Jesse, because Jesse's going to get back on the plane. Then you all go back and eat potato salad or coleslaw, catfish, or whatever. And it's over. You wait for the next big name to come to your village, the village now known as "We Don't Do Nothing 'Til Somebody Comes Village."

If there's no movement from you, nothing happens. Nothing *good* happens anyhow. Jesse Jackson comes and goes. The politicians come and go. And everything else remains the same. Remember, you are the village— individually and together. And we need you to speak, to stand up. We need all of you to get up, to stand up. It's not difficult. And when people tell you, "You can't get up, you're a victim," that's when you know that it is the devil you're hearing, no one else.

Help Carry the Cross

Historically, even churches were segregated, and that forced us to create our own vibrant spiritual centers that served as the bedrocks of our community and, in many communities, still do.

In black communities, even today, most of us are Christians. We know Jesus very well. We know that Jesus walked the walk, talked to the people. We know that he carried the cross for us. But unfortunately, we have not helped him carry it. Today, we are letting Jesus drag that cross, and we are standing here just watching him. And many of us are saying, "Oh, isn't this terrible. Somebody ought to do something!"

Others are bothering Jesus with their own trivial requests—"Dear Lord, sorry about that cross you're dragging, but can you help me win the lottery?" "Sweet Jesus, please let my car start this morning"—while remaining quiet about the devil's work going on right under their own noses, sometimes by their own children. We have to stop sedating ourselves. We have to get moving because the devil works 24/7.

Jesus and his apostles spent just about every waking minute outside, walking the neighborhoods. They moved around, and they talked to the people who needed help and then helped them. Too many Christians today wait until Sunday to do their talking and then insist that the people come to them. They need to be out there in the community on the other six days—helping people, including the young people, live by Christian principles such as, "Do unto others as you would have others do unto you." It would save us all a lot of pain.

The black church has always been a force for black people throughout the worst times in our history. The church is a key player in the black extended family. We would not have much of a village if we didn't have the church and other faith-based organizations. Reports show that people who are involved in church fare much better than those who are not. The church needs to reach out more, particularly to our poor youth. We want "Amen" to be more than a word. It's time for active Christians to talk to young men about their responsibility for acknowledging the children that they have helped to bring into this world. Irresponsibility is not some kind of "culture thing." Don't let it be.

When that youngster tells you, "I'm bad. I'm a man. I'm this. I'm that," you say, "No, you're not! You're hurting somebody. When you abandon a child, that child is likely to grow up wanting to hurt someone else."

If these children are not helped, they're going to pay somebody back for what happened to them. And folks, it's important to remember that they all live in our village. They don't go away until they are sent away, and then it is too late. We will talk more about this later.

Let us add a modern-day wrinkle to the Rosa Parks legacy. Back then, we were singing, "We shall overcome *some day.*" Some day? That made sense fifty years ago. But today, it can't be some future "some day" we sing about. We moved past "some day" a long time ago. "Some day" was your day. "Some day" was our day. At the latest, that "some day" has to be now. It has to be today, folks.

Martin Luther King Jr.'s "one day" has to be now too. In his "I Have a Dream" speech, his dream was that his four little children "will one day live in a nation where they will not be judged by the color of their skin but by the content of their character." He was talking about children advancing to become strong, beautiful people—not abandoned by their parents, not drug addicted, not irresponsible. What we see around us today in our poor neighborhoods is a nightmare, not a dream. This is not the picture that King and other leaders took those whuppings for. This is not the image that those poor people had while being dragged from their homes by the Ku Klux Klan. This is not the future for which their ancestors escaped slavery or resisted it. No, none of our forbearers sacrificed their lives so that their children's children could call each other "nigger." Not one of them.

Some Christian ministers have misunderstood—not all, but some—and have let their people linger in sedation and apathy. In Genesis, a contract was set up between the two people whom God created and God. The nature of it was that they would look after the garden, namely the earth. Some of their descendants have done a wonderful job, and others have caused a huge mess. Today, no matter where we happen to be, we should still be looking after our part of the garden.

The poor often do not feel that responsibility because they do not believe they own anything. But we must help them understand that even if they do not own the building, they pay for the space they are living in. They pay for the entryway, the steps, the hallway. Why not make those areas pleasant to the eye, pleasant to all of the senses? The philosophy that "I don't own this, therefore I will let it fall apart" is incredibly stupid and self-defeating. We are all given part of God's garden to maintain, and why would we not rather smell the roses than smell the stench?

CALL-OUTS

Deborah Johnson, in Washington DC, offered a response to our criticism of the church: *There are Christians and there is a church. And there are some churches that are doing just what you said is not being done by some people. We have a thing called the Warding Learning Community, and we have a faith-based church called the Temple of Praise. And the Temple of Praise is a church that is going out into the community and really compelling the people to come and do better with their lives through education, through programs that deal with drug addiction and other kinds of things.*

I can tell a story about how the Christian movement has been so important to me. Some years ago, I was brought from the West Coast to a place called Cincinnati, Ohio, as a baby. Today, I do not even know who my mother is. But it was the saints. It was the members of the Church of God and Christ. When I came, one of the bishops taught me how to live, how to be a lady, how to protect my virginity, oh yes, and how to be educated . . . They reached down and they helped me.

Whatever the Christians are not doing, whatever the people who are in other denominations are not doing, let this be a lesson to all of us today that we need to find a mechanism by which we can also tell our stories about how we're impacting people's lives.

REPLACE VICTIMHOOD WITH NEIGHBORHOOD

Too often the word *victim* shows up in our discussions. We have all driven through lower economic neighborhoods where there are three and four families living in a one-family house, and the music is loud enough to wake the dead. It seems as if the folks living there are trying to drown out their own feelings. This culture is sedating. It encourages people to see themselves as victims, as being incapable of helping themselves, of feeling anything but totally defeated.

It is typically the overwhelmed single mothers, absent fathers, and black youth who are most inclined to sedate themselves. They sedate themselves with music or waiting for Jesus to come help them or the government or the lottery or a lover or some crack or, if nothing else, a bag of burgers. But there are no solutions here, just a wallowing in sedated victimhood. It's always someone else's fault.

The self-sedated don't pay attention to what older people say. As a matter of fact, they will probably run in the opposite direction. The 1950s was a time when older people talked and young people listened. The old folks were prepared to set the young straight if need be, and the young took the medicine. Today more than ever, we need our seniors to say to the wannabe victim, "Here's how you begin to help yourself. You have to fight back."

We know that there are forces that make the effort to escape poverty difficult. We know the pathologies that depress those in poor neighborhoods—the overburdened single parent families, the absurdly high dropout rate in schools, the consequent joblessness, the violent street gangs, the drug dealing, the crime, the incarceration, the deaths at an early age from a gun blast fired by an angry fellow black man. These forces are decimating our communities. Many people in these communities, who are trying to make it, find themselves struggling against their fellow African Americans who are so lost in self-destructive behaviors that they bring down other people as well as themselves.

But for all the talk of systemic racism and governmental screw-ups, we must look at ourselves and understand our own responsibility. This sense of empowerment is expressed in the inspiring words of poet Mari Evans:

> *Speak the truth to the people.*
> *Talk sense to the people.*
> *Free them with reason.*
> *Free them with honesty.*
> *Free the people with Love and Courage and Care for their being.*
> *Spare them the fantasy.*
> *Fantasy enslaves.*
> *A slave is enslaved;*
> *Can be enslaved by unwisdom*
> *Can be re-enslaved while in flight from the enemy*
> *Can be enslaved by his brother whom he loves,*
> *His brother whom he trusts,*
> *His brother with the loud voice*
> *And the unwisdom.* *

We need to steel ourselves with the will to get better, the will to win, the will to move, the will to act. Then we will succeed. We cannot accept the current state of affairs. For all the external hassles we face, we are not helpless. We can overcome the odds and succeed in spite of the obstacles. But first we have to try.

We heard a prizefight manager say to his fighter, who was losing badly: "David, listen to me. It's not what he's doing to you. It's what you're not doing."

That principle can be applied to many of the social ills that plague black communities. A people armed with the will to get better, armed with the will to win, and armed with knowledge that we must move forward and take action will succeed and will reclaim our dignity. Fighting back in itself is therapeutic. Striving for success is like love: it's better to have tried and failed than never to have tried at all.

---

*"I Am a Black Woman," published by Wm. Morrow & Co., 1970, by permission of the author.

Dr. Hillary Wynn, of Panama City, Florida, reinforced our point: *There are so many ways that we can act out our responsibility to our communities. Foster care is one of the largest, biggest, most profound ways . . . But it could also be something as big as adoption and making a commitment to a child. People who do mentoring are contributing to their community. If you would just start volunteering two to three hours a week anywhere, you would have contributed to your community.*

We can't wait for everybody else to do it. The social service agencies, child protective services, they are overwhelmed. They don't pay them worth a doggone and they have so many cases. And sometimes they may do inappropriate things. Or because of a lack of experience, they can't do everything. We have to take more responsibility and stop being afraid.

Speak Up, Speak Out

If we don't speak up, who will? If we don't take time out to believe that there is a tomorrow, who will? If we don't take time out to make sure that our friends who never voted, vote, who will? If we don't vote out people who are taking us for granted, who will?

And let's make sure our voting makes sense. Let's study those people running for office. Let's see if we should be voting for them just because we share a skin color. Let's not vote for somebody just because they stood in our church and said, "Today, I feel as black as any person sitting in the pulpit." No. We want action. And if we demand it and vote for it, we're going to get it.

There are many times, though, that we have to take action ourselves. If the Ku Klux Klan were coming again, what would we do? We'd grab our children, throw them under the table, put them under the bed, put bodies on them, get the guns, and be ready.

But how do we respond to a crack cocaine dealer? How do we respond to a dysfunctional school system? How do we respond to the criminals in our midst? How do we respond to those people who are unraveling the moral fiber of our village?

Our community has accepted things for too long—just flat out accepted things.

What things? In our mind's eye, we see a boarded up house with weeds about six feet tall. The city is supposed to cut the weeds on the empty lot. We ask the woman who lives in an apartment next to the house, "Mamma, when was the last time the city came to cut down these weeds?" She answers, "Never."

This woman and others sound disgusted, but we haven't heard anybody say they've gone down to city hall to complain about it. People keep saying the Lord will find a way, but does anyone really believe that Jesus has nothing better to do than come along and cut these weeds? Better that a minister organize some men, and they cut down the weeds. Then they should take all the weeds that were cut, put them in a truck, drive down to whatever division is supposed to cut the weeds, and dump it on their steps. Oh yes, and be prepared to go to jail! King did. Mandela did. You can too. You'd be in good company. But the message will be clear to the city and to the community: No, we are not going to do the city's job, but see how nice it looks when we do. This is where we live, and we want it to look better.

The media may say we're preaching to the choir. Well, we love the choir. We love the choir because they show up every time, they know the songs, they sing with their hearts, and lots of other people hear them and get inspired.

TALK TO THE POLICE

Because we are encouraging people to speak out, to begin to put pressure on the police to chase the drug dealers out of the neighborhood, we thought we would provide a model of how that conversation might go. It should be very calm and respectful, with neither one challenging the other or trying to show the other up.

Officer: Mr. Cosby, when you ask the people to march on the police station, to march on the police, I think it's important for you to know that we are underfunded and undermanned and even underwomaned, or however you say it in English.

Cosby: Let me ask you a question if I may, and please don't get angry with me.

Officer: Okay.

Cosby: I just want to ask some questions if you don't mind.

Officer: Okay.

Cosby: Do you have a house?

Officer: Yes.

Cosby: Wife?

Officer: Yes.

Cosby: Children?

Officer: Yes.

Cosby: Across the street from your house, people are dealing drugs. You got me?

Officer: Yes.

Cosby: What are you going to do about it?

Officer: What am I going to do about it?

Cosby: Yes, what are you going to do about the drug dealers dealing across the street from your house?

Officer: Well, because of the difficulty of the situation from past experiences, not in my neighborhood mind you, but knowing what I know, I would probably set up a sting operation.

Cosby: You would set up a sting operation?

Officer: Yes, I would.

Cosby: My next question is about your superior officer.

Officer: Yes.

Cosby: Wherever he lives, he has a house, wife, and family?

Officer: Yes, he does.

Cosby: A hundred yards away from where he lives is a drug dealer or dealers. Would he probably do the same thing?

Officer: Probably, for sure.

Cosby: Then my next question is obvious, isn't it?

There is a smile across the officer's face.

Cosby: My question, sir, is what is the difference between your children, your wife, your home, and the children, wives, and homes of the people who are complaining to you about drug dealing in their neighborhood? Does a sting cost less in a policeman's neighborhood?

If lower economic people would begin to behave the way middle and upper economic people behave when things are going on in their neighborhood, on their turf, the "annoyance" factor would begin to at least move the ball in the right direction. The laws should not be enforced differently for certain people or certain neighborhoods. The law should be the law wherever you live and be enforced accordingly.

TAKE BACK THE COMMUNITY

We have to begin by taking back our neighborhoods. We have to be involved. The people who need help are right here, right now, standing on that corner. We need a revolution in our minds and in our neighborhoods. We have lost many of the kinship bonds that historically held us together as a community. The spirit of caring and self-help that sustained us for centuries is now largely a cultural memory. We had high moral standards as a community, and even if we didn't always meet them, we were moving forward and succeeding.

But today many social and political forces have changed our standards. What was considered unacceptable decades ago is now acceptable.

No longer is a woman stigmatized because she is pregnant without a husband. No longer is a boy embarrassed if he tries to run away from being the father of his child.

We are not suggesting that a nuclear family or marriage is the only model. What we care most about is children being raised properly to succeed. In general, two people in partnership and their extended families provide the best home with the least emotional strain and financial hardship. But whether yours is a two-person family or a single-parent one, it needs to be a strong, loving family.

In many neighborhoods, parenting is not going on. Children are not being raised with a respect for learning and education. Parents do less caring and directing, often abandoning their kids to the destructive influences of the media. We need to improve our parenting. New approaches must be considered. But, most of all, the basic love and nurturing of a child must be there.

Even under difficult circumstances, it is possible to be an effective parent, to raise successful and productive children who did not go to jail, join gangs, or become drug dealers or junkies. How did they do it? It's important to know so we can transmit and teach these critical lessons to all parents in the community. It is certain that such parents did not adopt a passive, defeatist victim mentality. They wanted to be victors for their children and for themselves.

CALL-OUTS

William Pollard, in Washington DC, exhorted us to start where we are: *There was a captain lost at sea and he needed water. So he signaled another ship that he wanted fresh water. And the captain of the other ship yelled over, "Cast down your buckets where you are!"*

And the first captain yelled back, "I'm at sea, I'll get salt water. I don't want to do that. So I'm not going to cast my bucket down." He repeated that he needed water to drink.

And the second captain yelled over again, "Cast down your buckets where you are." And the first captain wouldn't do it. So the ships got closer. And the second captain said, "Look, brother, you're at the mouth of a river. Cast down your buckets where you are and you can get fresh water."

Our challenge is to cast our buckets down where we are. We have to look to our families. We have to look to our neighbors. We have to look to our community, to our churches, to our organizations. We have to cast our buckets down where we are and pull them out and help each other up. This is what we want to do tonight. This is what this call-out is all about.

MAKE A DIFFERENCE

One person can make a difference. Reginald Wilson, in Washington DC, talked to Bill Cosby about his mentor.

Wilson: My mom died from AIDS when I was twelve. And my dad died when I was, like, fourteen. So, right after my dad died, Timothy came into my life. I know about the foster-parent thing because my brother and I were raised by someone that's not any kin to us, but Timothy promised my mom, before she passed, that if anything should happen to her, that he would take care of my brother and me.

He's been a blessing in my life. I'm an assistant teacher right now at an artistic school. But a lot of times, I just reflect back on when we used to talk and things like that and how I used to take a lot of things for granted.

And just like he said, my life is now my own. I know that now, and he's also helped me spiritually and getting involved in the church and getting involved with Christ. And I like to say my life is on a better path and I've been married for seven months.

Cosby: At fourteen you have got a lot of things coming at you, if you can remember. You have, at fourteen, a lot of decisions to make. Along comes this gentleman, who made a promise to your mother. Your father's gone. But this gentleman is on you, isn't he?

Wilson: On me like white on rice.

Cosby: Well, now, we don't have to get racist.

Wilson: Brown rice, brown rice.

Cosby: Brown rice, brown rice. But the thing that's important here, that all of us can relate to, every person in this audience, when we're growing up, old people like me. You look at the kid and you see more in that kid than the kid sees in himself or herself. Now, all this gangsta rap crap, this thing they call "culture," they've got our children saying things on TV, like, "I don't listen to old people because they don't know what they're talking about." But old people can see through you as if they had X-ray vision. And they come to you, or they came to you, and they told you about yourself. And even in your state, old people told you, didn't they?

Wilson: Yeah.

Cosby: And it's very important for us to understand this, ladies and gentlemen. Don't be set back by these voices that are saying, "You are too old to speak up." This young man, at age fourteen, a man made a promise to his mother, and he kept it. So he knows this man. He didn't have his father. But he has this man. And he's very fortunate.

STAND ON THEIR SHOULDERS

And when we move forward, we stand on the shoulders of those who fought in the struggle to bring greater opportunities to all. These elders are our legacy. Hear the inspirational remarks given by Dr. Dorothy Height, former president of the National Council of Negro Women, who spoke passionately at one of our call-outs in Birmingham, Alabama.

Dr. Dorothy Height spoke from her heart: *The first time I came to Birmingham, I was the woman in what they call the Big Six—with Martin Luther King Jr., Roy Wilkins, Whitney Young, James Farmer, and James Forman. And I came because of the bombing in this church that killed four little black girls in 1963.*

Dr. King called, and he said, "Can you bring some women down to talk to the mothers and to the women in the community?" Because they were disturbed. It was one week later that we decided to come. And on the Sunday morning that we were to come, I heard on a television that the Gaston Motel, where we were to stay, had been bombed. And so I called the fourteen women I had lined up to come.

One by one, they said, "Well, I'm going. They need us more now than ever before." And as we came, Wyatt Walker shepherded us through bayonets and yellow hats, and it was a fearful sight. We spent our time with Mrs. Gaston at her home because we could not go to the motel. But I'll never forget that day because among other things, one of the mothers spoke to the group these eloquent thoughts:

I asked my eight-year-old why she was marching. And she said to me that she was marching for my freedom. My freedom? I asked what she meant, and she told me that if I were free, I wouldn't have to take her to New York to buy her clothes. We could buy them here. And she could go to Tiny Tots Town here too. And that made an indelible impression on me.

And today I was led into town to find that the chief of police is a woman. And then to be presented this beautiful key to the city by an African-American mayor, and there was one before him, but I'm just so pleased. In other words, we've come a long way. But we're not there yet.

We must never forget what the struggle has been. Our young people today are going through open doors, and they don't know how they got opened. And so, they don't care about things that are important.

I'm ninety-four now, and the most important thing is we've got to carry the message. We have to carry the message that the people of all races have worked together to bring us to where we are today.

You know, we sing in the church, "God will take care of you." But I've also learned, God helps those who help themselves. And this is an occasion where we are helping ourselves. Everyone in this room can help us even further, by carrying the message.

We have to help our young people understand the importance, not only of their education and their schooling, but also of the way in which they learn how to deal with problems and issues. They have to be able to get away from just dealing with personal concerns and be concerned about others. Mary McLeod Bethune, who was a great mentor to me, always said, "I want to see my people rise as high as they go, but never forget to help one another as they go along."

And Harriet Tubman put it another way when she was leading people from slavery into freedom. She said to them, "Look backward, move forward, but keep going."

Keep going!

3

WE ALL START OUT
AS CHILDREN

If this isn't an extraordinary time to be born, we don't know what is.

Our kids are coming into a country that, while imperfect, is one of the freest, most prosperous, and most diverse in the history of the world. But with that freedom come temptations. We've got children being born, young people coming up, who ought to be given every opportunity to use those great brains of theirs, to exercise their wills, to share their hearts, to become the leaders of the world.

Yet, despite this opportunity, we see so many of our black youth squandering their freedom. Crime, drugs, alcohol, murder, teen pregnancies, and drop-out rates in city high schools of 50 percent or more are devastating not only to black children but also to black communities, and the entire nation for that matter.

Come on, people!

We feel that an important element in this crisis is the breakdown in good parenting. We're not telling you something you don't know. In too many black neighborhoods, adults are giving up their main responsibility to look after their children. In all corners of America, too many children are getting the short end of the stick as extended family networks collapse and community support programs fail to replace them in any significant way.

It doesn't have to be like this. In the pages that follow, we'll share with you some of what we have learned over time, much of it through reading and research, and some of it the old-fashioned way, through sheer hard knocks. Since we have a little experience in the parenting game ourselves, please bear with us while we offer some instructional hints.

Let's start with some of the problems young people face today, problems that are different from the ones we faced and are in many ways more dangerous.

Then we'll get to the solutions.

IT ALL STARTS WITH CHOICE

We address this conversation specifically to those who have some responsibility for the well-being of black kids—parents especially, grandparents, foster parents, godparents, teachers, social service workers. In some cases, you may be directly responsible for the child; in other cases, indirectly. But in all cases, even if you are just coaching a parent through parenthood, you, too, are a "caregiver." There is no more important job.

Let's start at the beginning of the parenting process. And no one we know speaks more powerfully to the issue of life's beginning than Dr. Xylina Bean, chief of Neonatology at King Drew Medical Center in Compton, California.

CALL-OUTS

Dr. Xylina Bean: *Each and every one of you has a responsibility to protect children—your child, my child, your next-door neighbor's child. You have a responsibility. Grandparents? Aunts? Uncles? Neighbors? Play aunts? God aunts? Every single one of you has a responsibility for children. Every single one of you.*

I may say some things that make you a little bit uncomfortable. I believe you have a choice as to whether to have children or not have children. You actually have that choice. Now I do believe that once the choice was made to have a child, that you pretty much gave up all the choices you had for the rest of your life or at least until that child had a life.

It's real simple. Now let's start with the idea of when do you start protecting children. You start protecting children when you decide to have one. And you decide to have one. It was not an accident. It didn't just happen. We all know you've got to do something in order to have one, okay? So it's not accidental. It's not incidental. And one of the things that I am really tired of is all of these incidental babies. They just "incidentally" happen. You can decide who gets to be your baby's daddy.

And there are people that you should just decide should not be. You have a right to decide that. And you should decide that. That's the first decision you ought to make. Because whoever that person is, is supposed to be there for that child. I didn't say for you. I said he is supposed to be there for that child for the rest of his life.

And by the way, I would think that some of you baby daddies might want to ask some questions about who's having your baby and make sure it's somebody that you want to have something to do with for the rest of that child's life.

That's the way it works. Both of you are supposed to have something to do with that child for the rest of its life. And you're not supposed to move from one to the other and have a new baby daddy every year because it just happens to be the one who's willing to pick up the tab today. So, you start protecting the child when you decide to have one. You decide on the person you're going to have it with and you make a commitment to it.

SOME GOOD WAYS TO SAY
WELCOME TO THE WORLD

Now that the child is on the way, what happens next? Good question, and now is the time to ask. Most everything we've learned about this issue, we've learned from the women in our lives. So we approach the subject with some humility.

Keep those adolescent bodies in shape.

If African Americans are going to turn from victims into victors, we all must start paying attention even before pregnancy and birth occur. Our young women should try to stay in good health before they get pregnant. Obesity and Type 2 diabetes, for example, can increase health problems for the infant.

Remind them they may have a baby on board.

Don't hesitate to tell the teens in your charge about the importance of good health. A young girl may be smoking and drinking and taking drugs not knowing she's pregnant. Grab that girl and say, "Honey, are you crazy?" Remind her that smoking and drug and alcohol use put that baby-to-be in real danger. Substance abuse and poor health can lead to premature birth and worse. And even if the babes come out kicking and screaming, they will face heightened health risks and developmental problems down the road.

Get that girl to the doctor.

As soon as a young woman in your care misses a period, remind her to check with a doctor to see if she is pregnant. If she doesn't have a regular doctor, she should go to the community health center or call the area hospital for help. Don't know where to turn? Well, as they say, let your fingers do the walking—in this case, the running. It's that important.

Prenatal care is the care a woman and her unborn child receive before the baby is born. The earlier prenatal care begins, the better for the baby.

Prenatal care is very important, but black women, particularly the poor, often do not get it. Many women wait until the second or sometimes third trimester of pregnancy to check in with a doctor. That is way too late! Early visits are important because complications during pregnancy can endanger the mom's health as well as the baby's. The infant mortality rate remains twice as high for black babies as for white babies. Keep that in mind!

Keep that sanctuary sacred.

A mother's womb is like a sanctuary for a baby. It should not be defiled. We can talk all we want about an imperfect health-care system, but that we can't control. What we can control is what is going on when the child is in the womb. Is the mother taking crack cocaine, heroin, alcohol, other drugs, or even marijuana? Is she being physically abused? Is she eating a healthy diet? Those of you who care should know. If the baby spends her first nine months in a cozy, clean environment, chances are she'll hit the world in good health and stay that way.

Track the baby's environment.

When a child is born, it enters a brave new world and has nothing to say about it except for the occasional squawk. Caregivers are sometimes handicapped by not knowing about the environment that baby had in the womb and how the mother maintained it. They usually know even less about the father and his habits. It's important to remember that drugs and alcohol abuse affect sperm just as they affect eggs—and, in most neighborhoods we know of, it still takes both to create a baby.

LET'S NOT FORGET THE MOTHER

A pregnant young teenage girl has what? She has a baby in her womb. Otherwise, she has no credentials, no clear picture of life ahead, and little idea of motherhood.

The pregnancy may be an accident or an attempt by the girl to punish herself, or even a trap to secure the boy who fathered the child. The new mother's emotions can vary wildly depending on her motivation for getting pregnant.

But please don't be angry with us for bringing up this subject. We do so because the message has to get out—loud and clear—to vulnerable young females. The truth is that we don't know who they are or what they are thinking. So many of these girls have not finished their education and are heading down the road without a map. They have a lot of rough-going ahead of them.

It's important for you—as a parent, a grandparent, a teacher, a friend—to remind any young girl of the value of an education and also the fallout of leaving school before she graduates. At thirteen or fourteen or fifteen, she cannot begin to anticipate the emotional turmoil ahead. When we were that age, we know we didn't have a clue.

If the girl is lucky, she will find her way to a good educational program. This can be a real shot in the arm because she will likely be more focused than when she was not yet pregnant. She better be. She may also get more attention, the kind of attention she really needed beforehand.

Even the most caring single parent at home cannot provide a model of a two-parent family for girls or boys. How can these children hope to know what a two-parent partnership means? How can they aspire to create a two-parent family of their own? They don't even see intact families on TV anymore. It seems to us that single parenthood will lead to more single parenthood unless marriage—or committed partnerships—are actively supported. So support them, people! Talk them up!

CALL-OUTS

Dr. Susan Wilson, in Kansas City: *It's the old adage of babies having babies. And I think that you have to ask the question, why do babies have babies? Have we ever asked that question? Well, studies show that girls who don't have goals—or even parents who talk to them about goals—think that the only thing that they can do to sustain their self-worth is have a child.*

A girl is not going to tell you, "Well, I'm gonna have a baby because I feel bad about myself." But with most of the young mothers that I talk to, if you look deep enough, that's the issue.

A lot of times these young girls haven't gotten male attention because their fathers are absent. We talk about boys needing their fathers. Girls need fathers too. I talk to nine-, ten-, eleven-year-old girls who didn't have fathers, and I make them aware that because they don't have a father, they have that special need in their hearts for male attention.

And if a girl doesn't understand that she needs that, she is going to get that attention from boys. A lot of our girls will tell us that they have sex because they think that's the only way to be popular, the only way to get attention.

The young guys have the same self-esteem reasons. Having a baby is like a notch on their belt.

So we have to go into this with our eyes open, mothers and fathers: this sweet young girl who's twelve, eleven, even younger, may be sexually active.

GOOD IDEAS ON MAKING THE BABY FEEL AT HOME

Now that the baby has arrived and is well and at home, it's not about the parent anymore. It's about the baby and how to take care of that precious little gift. If you're the mom, don't be afraid to ask for help. If you're the mom's mom, don't be afraid to give it. Unlike a cell phone, babies don't come with an instruction manual, and they are a whole lot harder to maintain.

Get the parents back to class.

Mothers who have regular prenatal care also have the chance to attend classes after delivery where they can ask questions and learn about the care and feeding of an infant. Most mothers *and fathers* want to know what is normal or abnormal, and how to handle emergencies. Encourage them. In this society, we do little to educate young people on how to parent—we have to take courses to get a driver's license but not to care for a child.

Share your wisdom.

Instructions about even routine tasks like changing diapers, burping, and giving a baby a bath can help parents have more confidence. Do not assume that the parents will know.

Feed the little tiger.

In prenatal classes and after delivery, health workers can instruct the mother in how to successfully breast-feed. Pediatricians strongly believe that the best nutrition for a baby is breast milk—it keeps the baby healthy and protected while his or her immune system develops. One more thing we've learned: if parents choose to use formula, they should make sure it contains Omega-3 fatty acids. Tell the new parents. They'll appreciate the tip.

Cuddle them to contentment.

Breast-feeding also requires cuddling, which encourages a strong bond to develop between mother and child. Fathers can bond with the baby by holding the baby when comforting is needed and assisting in bathing and diaper changing.

Protect the baby.

For babies, crying is a way of communicating, and parents will come to recognize the baby's different screams and squawks and whoops. Folklore warns us that you spoil babies if you pick them up too much when they cry. But we'll go with what the pediatricians tell us. They say that there is no such thing as "spoiling" a baby. If a baby is upset and gets no comfort, you can do harm. Babies need to feel safe and protected.

Real men change diapers.

Diaper changing? That's right, brother. It takes a real man to change a baby's diaper. And as we dads have learned, when that baby is ours, the whole process doesn't seem nasty at all—well, not too nasty anyway.

Two parents work better than one.

The connection to two parents is important to a child's development. Come on, people, of course it is! The fact that nearly 70 percent of black babies are born to single mothers and often don't have the benefit of a father in the home, or even in the babies' lives, is more than sad. In these situations, it's important for you mothers to connect with other family members and friends to get support for you and the baby.

Keep your appointments.

To support your babies, you parents should be absolutely sure you keep well-baby clinical appointments. Doctors and nurses can monitor whether a child is growing and developing normally. Dads, pay heed— it's important for both you and the mom to go to appointments, maybe even alternating. Taking care of a baby is hard, and sometimes scary, but we parents know that the hard work is always worth it.

KEY CONCEPTS IN BRINGING UP BABY

Okay, you've just celebrated the baby's first birthday. The grandparents are disappointed that he can't recite Dr. King's "I Have a Dream" speech or play "Take the A Train" on the eight-note piano they gave him, but you're glad they are there. New babies and new parents prosper when they are part of a caring community.

Give new parents all the support they need.

Their lives are busy and the demands are many. That's the reason it is important to stoke those traditional kinship bonds with extended family and friends. Please do as much as you can to assist them.

Sing to those little ones.

Don't be afraid. Smile at them, sing to them, play music for them. Babies like all kinds of music, but they must be protected from lyrics that glorify sex or violence or use the N-word. No gangsta rap, please!

Go easy on the TV.

You don't need to buy videos for babies. No research that we know of says they do any good for anyone. Bug-eyed fixation on a screen can make them into little automatons, who never learn how to play or relate to their parents and playmates. Let's face it: too much TV watching is a big problem in many black homes. It worries us that any parent would hook their young one on the TV.

Do your own babysitting.

Too many parents and caregivers use TV excessively as a babysitter, which is not good for a child's learning. Caregivers should do the babysitting, not the TV.

Blocks are still cool.

Playing with blocks and toys involves all the senses of a baby and young child—touch, smell, taste, vision, and hearing. Even adults like to play with blocks. Try it.

Books are even cooler.

Parents and caregivers who read picture books to children help wire those children's brains for language and images. Talking and smiling and explaining things to babies, even when you know they don't quite understand, helps stimulate brain development. "Here is a sheep. What does a sheep say? Baaa." We confess. We crusty old grandpa types enjoy this as much as the kids do.

Patience saves lives.

Crying babies can test the patience of even the best of parents and caregivers. When nothing quiets the little one, some people yell and carry on and even hit the baby. "I just lost it," the boyfriend says. Well, you better find it quick! That's no excuse. Shaking a baby can cause severe brain damage for life; it can even kill a child. Shaken Baby Syndrome causes hundreds of injuries and deaths each year.

If you feel angry enough to hit or shake a baby, get your body out of the room and calm down. This is the one time leaving the baby to cry alone is safer. Acting out violently with a child can lead to serious injuries for the child and serious repercussions for the parent or caregiver—like prison.

Screen sitters carefully.

All too often the mother yields the care of her child to someone who thinks of that child as a nuisance. The reality is that a "boyfriend" is much more likely to abuse a child in his care than is the father of that baby.

You can always find help with social service agencies, but if the danger is too great for the child, the baby or child may be taken from you and placed in foster care. If that happens, remember: your child's health or life is more important than your pride.

SEVERAL GOOD REASONS TO SPARE THE ROD

As the little ones become not so little, they will begin to test the adults who care for them. The challenge you face is how to respond.

Many black parents use physical punishment—not just spanking, but also hitting, slapping, and beating kids with objects. African Americans sometimes use the term *whupping* when punishing their kids. This may very well have a connection to the slave experience. That isn't like jumping over a broom at your wedding. It is definitely not a part of the slave experience you want to reenact.

Physical punishment often escalates.

In confirmed child-abuse cases, two-thirds of parents started out using physical punishment as "discipline," and it later got out of control. In other words, the parent or caregiver "lost it" and left bruises, cuts, or broken bones. When parents rely on physical punishment, there is inevitably a greater risk for child abuse. Again, find whatever you "lost," and find it quickly.

Beating does not make you a better parent.

Some of you parents and caregivers believe in "beating the devil" out of the children in your care to make them "good boys" or "good girls." You may think that if you don't beat your children—even in public—you are not being a good parent. You can take the word of Doctors Cosby and Poussaint on this one—many of the world's best parents never beat their children. Besides, the devil doesn't get beat all that easily.

You're the boss.

As a grown-up, with all your years of experience, you should be able to out-argue your child. Remember, you're the adult. If you tell a kid he has to clean his room and he snaps back, "My friend doesn't have to clean up his room," then you stare that kid down and say, "And where does your friend live? Not here." End of argument. You're the boss.

Children need to learn "why."

Meeting children's violence with violence doesn't help anyone but the bail bondsman. Young children need to learn what is off-limits. It is much better to restrain them and say something like: "No hitting or biting; it hurts," or "You wouldn't want someone to hit or bite you," or maybe "Mommy and Daddy don't hit or bite you." In this way, kids learn *why* they shouldn't hit or bite. Inflicting your own counterviolence may work in the short term, but in the long term the child doesn't really learn that it is wrong.

You don't want to send the wrong message.

Parents and caregivers should consider that when they beat their kids they are sending a message that it is okay to use violence to resolve conflicts—especially if one party is bigger and stronger than the other. Children may take this lesson into the street and use violence against others, and you know where that leads and how quickly. Actions do speak louder than words. The real message children get is that it's okay to use violence.

Children need to learn self-discipline.

Children are not as likely to learn self-discipline if the main reason for being good is to avoid getting hit. One thing we've found is that kids whose main form of domestic discipline was the rod often get wild in environments where the rod is spared, like the classroom. These kids often act out in unruly, disrespectful ways. Not only do they disobey their teachers, but they may also curse them or even attack them physically.

Spanking doesn't stop tantrums.

Wise parents know that hitting a child who is having a temper tantrum only ratchets up the tantrum. In our experience, ignoring the tantrum gets the best results. What's more, if children have too much fear of a parent, they may project that fear onto others or simply withdraw.

Parents are tempted to hit for the wrong reasons.

We have all seen parents and caregivers who beat their kids, not to discipline them, but to exorcise their own demons. They may be angry about a neighbor or upset about work or out of sorts with their partner, and they take that anger out on the child with minimal or imagined provocation. In other words, the child serves as a "whupping" object for peevish adults. These caregivers hide behind the word *discipline* to cover the true reasons for their anger and violence.

SOME SCARS NEVER HEAL

We ask all parents and caregivers to look inside themselves and review all of the reasons they beat the kids in their charge. Like anyone in authority with physical power over others, they should have their own rational "rules of engagement" and honor them.

Sometimes when talking to black audiences, we hear some of the adults testify that their parents beat them when they misbehaved and it was for their own good. What we do not know, however, is whether they grew up to be normal, law abiding citizens *because* of the beatings or *despite* them.

In fact, one recent study found that 94 percent of black mothers agreed that "a good hard spanking" is a useful disciplinary technique, compared to 65 percent of white women and 46 percent of Asian-American women.

We are not saying that parents who occasionally spank children will damage them. The adults who feel spankings helped them were more likely to be the ones who were occasionally spanked. Unfortunately, those who were spanked excessively or abused as children are less likely to show up in our audiences as responsible adults.

Despite the damage caused by violence in the home, many black parents have told us that physical punishment is part of black culture and thus plays an important role in disciplining children. In some cases, they suggest that beating kids into docility protects them from having confrontations with white people, which could lead to severe punishment and sometimes death.

That argument may have had some merit during slavery, or even in the era before civil rights, but it makes no sense as a cultural practice today. Some black parents use hitting in small doses, and others do it excessively. Something to think about: Some mothers and fathers beat their children regularly with an ironing cord or belt or worse for the slightest transgression. Some of these beatings leave scars. The parents may even believe that when the child sees the scars he'll remember to be good and obedient.

The scars within, however, never heal. These beatings often produce angry children who treat others as violently as they have been treated. They may seem compliant to the person who beats them but only because they have been scared into submission. Later they may become enraged and rebellious and more likely to hit back or run away.

Many of these kids engage in violence because, to them, discipline means getting hit. When they were beaten to be "good," they failed to learn how "good" could be accomplished without getting hit or even *why* it was important to be obedient, to have self-control, to be respectful to adults, to know the differences between right and wrong.

> ### LIFE LESSONS
>
> "The only thing my old man ever gave me was a beating," so remembered Sonny Liston, a former heavyweight champ whose life outside the ring was a testament to the lasting damage of child abuse. Liston had fled his father and his Arkansas home at fifteen and headed straight into a life of crime. The only place he ever did feel at home, in fact, was in prison. Despite his extraordinary boxing talent, Liston never could find his footing in the real world. Less than ten years after first winning the championship, he died alone in Las Vegas of a heroin overdose, the raised welts on his back a lasting reminder of his father's "discipline."

In addition to creating an angry and possibly violent child, beatings can cause symptoms of anxiety, depression, and even post-traumatic stress disorder (PTSD). Beaten children can develop learning problems in school that contribute to school failure and high drop-out rates.

Of course, not all kids who get hit develop such symptoms. Much depends on the amount, kind, frequency, and method of the "spankings." In a loving environment, an occasional swat may do no harm, but it is better not to hit. In a home where children feel unloved or unwanted, however, beatings may ratchet down a child's already shaky self-esteem.

In fact, not all children who suffer actual child abuse develop symptoms of PTSD or become violent. Kids can be pretty tough. They may have protective factors in their genes or in the environment that give them the resilience to survive various traumas. Still, children who are beaten are at a higher risk for stress, anxiety, and depression. You know it. We all know it.

Oh yes, we oppose paddling in schools as well and for the same reasons we oppose it in the home. Teachers can become as challenged as parents. They often paddle to release their anger at the kid, not to help him. There are other risks to school paddling. Many of the kids who act up have emotional problems such as <u>attention deficit hyperactivity disorder (ADHD)</u>, bipolar disorder, or other problems that require medical evaluations, counseling, and treatment. Paddling cures no psychological problem that we have ever heard of. It may even aggravate the problem. What amazes us is that it is still allowed in twenty-one states.

In fact, in school districts where they allow paddling—mostly in the South—black kids are paddled at two to three times the rate of other kids. Often the same kids are paddled over and over again. This is a clear sign that this strategy is not exactly working.

You can't beat a mental disorder out of a child. Yet studies show as many as one in ten children has a diagnosable mental disorder, and these are likely the kind of kids who are beaten. In our activist agenda to turn victims into victors, we have to fight for mental health services in our communities, especially those linked to school. Too many black kids with mental health problems are booted from school without getting the care they require.

When trying to create healthier neighborhoods and schools, all concerned parties should review the fallout from physical punishment. Some experts, who have researched violent offenders and murderers, say the most important thing people can do to cut down violence in America is to cut out the physical punishment of children.

We expect many of our battle-hardened friends to dismiss this discussion. After all, they survived! But we think black parents and community groups need to consider the high cost of physical punishment. Several countries, such as Sweden and Germany, have banned the spanking of children. Here, it is still the parent's right to spank or not. But "seize the rod and swat that child" is no longer the best medicine when so many other more effective parenting strategies are sitting on the shelf.

WHEN DOMESTIC VIOLENCE GETS OUT OF HAND

If you visit your local prison, you'll find that a disproportionately high percentage of those inside—men and women—have been victims of child abuse, including sexual abuse. Studies find a strong correlation between being abused and committing abuse. There is a real cycle of violence here.

With the high rates of violence, suicide, and homicide among black youth, those of you with children in your care should be extremely cautious about any kind of punishment—especially beatings—that produces anger and encourages violence in children. Homes should be a sanctuary for love and peace, not a hotbed of anger and violence.

Psychological Abuse

You should be aware that psychological abuse can be just as damaging as physical abuse. Although bruises to the soul are not as visible, they are just as painful. Words like "You're stupid," "You're an idiot," "I'm sorry you were born," or "You'll never amount to anything" can stick a dagger in a child's heart. Racial slurs twist that dagger. Imagine mothers and fathers hitting their children and saying, "Nigger, I'll kick your f—— black a——." It happens. It's awful. It's degrading. We've all heard it, and it only leads to more problems for the child.

You don't need a doctorate to understand that parents are more likely to abuse their kids when those parents have been abusing drugs or alcohol. Why, we ask, must that awful word *abuse* be so common a word in our vocabulary? If you are a substance abuser, think of the children and get help. There are programs locally to assist you. Being sober and in control of your life will greatly benefit the kids. Don't be afraid or ashamed to ask for help.

Sexual Abuse

Preventing the sexual abuse of our children has to be a high priority. Girls especially, but boys too, have suffered from the many varieties of this abuse, all of which can produce stress symptoms and long-term harm.

Wary of being thought gay, boys may be much more reluctant to tell people about the abuse, and more likely suffer in silence. Children who have been sexually abused—whether by relatives, friends, or strangers—feel violated and betrayed. The violation is even more extreme in cases of incest, where a family member commits the abuse. It may be difficult for them to trust others—ever—and it gets in the way of healthy social and sexual relationships when they grow up. A high percentage of girls who have been sexually abused become prostitutes or engage in other antisocial behaviors.

LIFE LESSONS

At age nine, after shuttling between her mother's home and her father's for several years, Oprah Winfrey settled in with her mother in Milwaukee. As bad as the poverty and insecurity were, what truly unsettled the young Oprah was her ongoing rape at the hands of a nineteen-year-old cousin.

The rape stripped Oprah of her innocence and deprived her of her sense of self. With each violation, Oprah descended deeper and deeper into self-hatred and eventually into self-destructive behavior. At fourteen, now fully out of control, Oprah was sent by her mother to live with her father in Nashville.

At Vernon Winfrey's home, Oprah found the love, care, and structure that she so desperately needed. With her roots reestablished, she was able to begin the long hard journey back to wholeness, and we are all the better for it.

As history has shown, we are a resilient people. We overcome. It is reassuring to see giants like Maya Angelou and Oprah Winfrey, who were sexually abused, rise to great heights. Their openness about their personal histories has encouraged parents to protect their children and support them in reporting sexual advances by adults.

We must protect our children. We have no higher priority. The simplest protection is to teach them—from a very young age—that their bodies are their own. No one—not even a relative—has a right to touch them in a way that makes them uncomfortable.

But sometimes some of us bring people into our homes who have no business being there. Let's say your daughter tells you that such a person is fondling her, but since the guy's paying the rent or giving you some money, you continue to pretend it's not really happening. Or maybe some visitor is fondling your son, and you sense it, but you just keep letting the guy come in, and you push the thought of what he might be doing out of your mind. You can put it out of your mind, but your children never will. They have been wounded.

CALL-OUTS

Cindy Dittus, of Greenwood, Mississippi, on the nature of abuse: *People with disabilities are at a four times greater risk of being abused than the general population. Studies show that in about 97 percent of abuse cases, the person with the disability knows the person who perpetrates the crime.*

It can be sexual abuse. It can be verbal abuse. It can be emotional abuse. Many times, a person who has been abused will become an abuser. A lot of times, too, our children cannot communicate what has actually happened to them. Parents don't realize what's happened to these kids until there's a behavior that comes out. They'll do something out of the ordinary or act in a strange way, and it's up to someone to find out what has happened, what caused the behavior.

Even for the best and most attentive of caregivers it can be difficult to help children who have been abused, especially in those cases where the abuse has become chronic.

CALL-OUTS

Dr. Lewis King, of Compton, California, spoke to this challenge: *One of the issues that confronts many of you is not the child who has a dream, but the child whose dream has been deferred as a function of abuse or molestation early in life. Where does all of that pain go? What can you do to help?*

The first thing you need to know is you have to be able to listen to that child. It may take two days. It may take a year. But you have to discover what happened to that child.

Spousal Abuse

The home should be a sanctuary. When kids watch their mother being beaten by her husband or boyfriend, it becomes something else altogether. It is not a sanctuary, either, if a woman attacks the man or if the house is noisy with cruel slurs, including racial ones. That kind of house is no kind of home.

Domestic violence wrecks homes and damages the children in them in ways uncountable. If you know a woman who is being abused, have her contact a women's shelter, an abuse hotline, or a social services agency. Pronto!

Hospital emergency rooms often have information about where to go for help. Women should report physical violence ASAP to the police to get protection and restraining orders because their lives are at risk. On the plus side, police are much more sensitive to family violence than they used to be.

Thousands of women have lost their lives in domestic disputes, and too many of us have stood by, not wanting to get involved. The effects of domestic violence are so devastating to children that social protection agencies now consider domestic violence itself as a form of child abuse. You help the kids by helping their moms find assistance and counseling.

Sibling Abuse

Social agencies and law enforcement often overlook still another devastating form of domestic strife: sibling violence. It's a growing problem. Today, so many more kids with different fathers or even different mothers live under the same roof and compete, often unequally, for whatever attention is going around that there is bound to be bad blood. And we're not talking pigtail in the inkwell here. We're talking cuttings and broken bones and worse. This may be more widespread than you think because parents are understandably reluctant to report it. To them, it may seem like a lose-lose proposition. But when sibling rivalry crosses into violence, it can destroy a family, and it happens all the time.

We must find ways to stop it. But not many kids want to report a sister or brother to the police for physical assault, nor do the parents or caregivers. But if you're the adult in charge, you have to take a leading role and keep these brothers and/or sisters from hurting each other.

You should encourage bonds of love and caring between sisters and brothers. This is especially necessary in blended families. You need to be careful not to pit children against each other, not even to say, "Why can't you be like your brother?" A nonviolent home is the best one in which to love and nurture children to their fullest.

RAISING VICTORIOUS CHILDREN

Victorious children are kids who live happy, healthy, loving, and cooperative lives, kids who enjoy learning and exploration, kids who embrace the future. They don't get that way by themselves. Each one of us who comes into their orbit has an opportunity to inspire them to victory.

Researchers have discovered that one of the most critical times for intervention is during the first five years of life. During those years, babies and children are still growing rapidly in body and mind. There is rapid growth of the brain—literal and figurative—as a child interacts with his environment. During these early years, we are laying the foundations for learning and healthy emotional growth.

Millions of black children have achieved at the highest levels in all occupations and professions, and millions of parents and caregivers have made their success possible.

LIFE LESSONS

Guion Bluford was born in Philadelphia in 1942 and had an early interest in model planes, which his parents encouraged. At Penn State, Guion moved from model planes to aerospace engineering, testing himself against the best. Not easily contented, he went on to get his PhD in aerospace engineering with a minor in laser physics.

An Eagle Scout as a boy, Guion really took off in the United States Air Force. He flew 144 combat missions, many of them over Vietnam, but he was still just testing his wings. In 1979 he joined NASA as an astronaut, and in 1983 he flew the first of his four missions into space. In 1997, Guion was elected to the International Space Hall of Fame. "Don't be afraid to learn," he tells young people, "and don't be afraid to explore."

People like Guion Bluford should not be the exception. All black parents can do right by their children, and all black children can succeed. There is no reason why not.

In the home every day, parents can help their children develop. Children have an innate desire to learn about their world and environment, and they need a coach, a guide.

Caring for infants and children can be taxing at times, but it is also full of many pleasures and emotional rewards. This is revealed frequently when you ask a mother or father how their young child is and they say, "He [or she] is such a joy!"

We hope more black parents can someday say the same. Those who do say those words understand that with enough hard work this "bundle of joy" will blossom into a treasure for life.

Kids need to be told that they have the potential for genius in one field or another; they just have to go out and find it. They have to stop believing that they "can't do it" and be reminded often that, yes, they can. Those of us who care, parents especially, have to take time to help our children develop this self-belief. These are our kids, and this is our future. There is no guarantee. But the chance for success is far better if we try than if we just let our kids get their education in the street.

Some Good Ways
to Discipline Children

Children require structure and predictable rules. Above all, they require attention. Back in the day, parents *bothered* their children when they came home from school. Some parents may not have known how to do long division. They may not have known how to write or how to construct a business letter. But they knew how to prod their children because they wanted them to be something.

Parents back then might have said, "Well, what did you do today in geometry?" They may have thought *isosceles* was a guy from the Bible and that a *hypotenuse* was a big ugly animal in Africa, but they knew their kids. They would make us go upstairs, get the book, bring it down, sit with them, and go over it. And even if they didn't understand, they'd pretend to. They pretended to because they knew kids needed an education. That need hasn't changed.

Share your experience.

A wise parent or caregiver shares her wisdom. She tells children about useful social skills as well as about the need to be responsible and orderly.

A child who is disciplined will be more obedient and also more organized as a student. He'll do better in school and in life. Of course he will!

Educate your children.

Good discipline is key to supporting the learning and education that our children need. Kids do better academically and are less likely to drop out if they take more responsibility for their school success. Self-disciplined people are more likely to succeed at whatever they do.

Distinguish discipline from punishment.

This is not just a word game. Discipline and punishment really are different things. Discipline may include punishment but aims for a much higher goal. Discipline includes other ways to shape a child's behavior for the long term, not just for the short term. The aim of good discipline is to teach children self-control and the difference between right and wrong, which becomes part of their inner character.

Behave the way you want your children to behave.

Children learn discipline in ways that parents need to be aware of. For instance, children will learn right and wrong by watching what their parents do. If parents lie, the kids will. If parents use racial slurs, so will the kids. If parents use violence at home, the kids will use it in the streets—the same with alcohol and drug abuse and cigarettes. This stuff starts early. We know a kid whose first words were "lousy bum," and he used them—echoing his old man—to address an Eagles wide receiver who dropped the ball in the end zone.

You parents and caregivers who don't want the kids to do these things, don't do them yourselves. That's the first step. If you have other bad habits, like being sloppy or late, don't expect the kids to be neat or on time. You can say, "Do what I say, not what I do" all you want, but when you turn your head, the kids will do what you do. *Actions speak louder than words.* Whatever behaviors and attitudes you want for the children, you'd better model them in your life.

Tone down your language.

As a parent or caregiver you should consider the language you use within the four walls of your home. Curb the yelling and the angry tone. For instance, imagine yourself at dinner. Listen to yourself say, "Pass the bread." Then ask yourself, *How am I saying it? Do I sound like a parent who cares? Or do I sound like a prison guard?* Your kids can tell the difference.

Listen to your children.

Think about sitting down with the children in your charge and asking them—with a smile and a relaxed expression—the very simple question, "What makes you happy?" They'll be glad to answer that. And ask, "What makes you sad?" Don't even get into anger. Just ask, "What makes you sad?" And then you can deal with it from there. Try that every day, just *talking* to the children.

Reward good behavior.

The best kind of reward is praise. If a child usually makes a mess at the table, praise her when she *doesn't* make a mess. And make sure she helps to clean up the mess she does make. In this way, you are helping to reinforce the behaviors in your child that you want to continue.

Make the punishment fit the crime.

Penalties help, but they should not be excessive and should be linked with the misbehavior that you are attempting to modify. For instance, if your kid is not getting enough sleep because she is staying up too late, the penalty could be an earlier bedtime. The reward could be a compliment when she wakes up refreshed in the morning and looking like a million bucks.

Set limits wisely.

Children need limits set by parents or caregivers, often to protect them. You can't let your kid run out into the street where he might get smacked by a car. You restrain him and say very firmly, "No, no—dangerous. You can get hit by a car!" There is no need to spank. You took the time to explain, and you were firm. With repetition, the child will get the message and learn not to run into the street.

Setting limits also involves setting rules that children are expected to follow. Tell them that dirty clothes go in the hamper, garbage goes in the trash, food goes nowhere near the bedroom, and adults are to be respected, not talked back to.

Let older children set their own rules.

To a point, of course, it's helpful to let older children help set the rules. This is particularly true for teenagers. Kids can even help determine what the penalty should be when they break a rule, such as curfew. You have the final say, but at the same time it helps children to participate in setting household rules.

Be consistent.

Children need to know what you expect from them by the limits you set. And you must be consistent. If there is no TV on school nights, there is no TV on school nights. Period. Stick to these rules no matter how loudly kids whine. If you let them change your mind by throwing a fit, they have won a victory that is not good for them or for you. In fact, you will have validated the outburst by giving in. Sometimes adults cave in because they feel the children won't love them if they don't. But, in the long term, children will love and respect adults more if they are consistent. And remember, consistency doesn't mean being rigid when you realize circumstances have changed.

State the rules positively.

Parents and caregivers should put a positive spin on rules. For instance, "Please put dirty clothes in the hamper" works better than "Don't throw your dirty clothes on the floor." "Treat family with respect" is more useful than "Don't smack your little sister." Too many "Thou Shall Nots" encourages some children to defy authority or express anger.

Even with the positive tone, you still have to be firm and consistent.

Give children choices.

You can also discipline children by giving them choices. Do they want to take a bath before or after dinner? When the kids choose the time, they have made a commitment to take a bath, which is what counts. Do they want to wear the black pants or the green pants to church? They get the choice, but you have just told them they are not wearing jeans.

Likewise, you can let them choose from a variety of foods as long as the choices are all good ones. Children who are given choices feel respected. They are also learning independence, which becomes especially important during adolescence. Children who are allowed to make small choices at young ages are better prepared to deal with the larger choices when not so young.

With proper discipline at home, kids behave well when they are away from home and out of sight of their parents or caregivers. Disciplined kids are less likely to disrupt the classroom or bully and intimidate other kids. Your self-disciplined child is someone you can count on to take responsibility for what he does and is less likely to do what others want him to. Disciplined children know the difference between right and wrong and are less likely to go wrong, and today there are a whole lot of ways to get there—illicit drug and alcohol abuse, premature sexuality, violence. You name it, someone is doing it. But it doesn't have to be your kid.

GETTING THE COMMUNITY INVOLVED

Here is a tough question for you: What do we have to do to get that extended family back again? We see its absence particularly in cities where so many black families feel isolated and alone in their own neighborhoods. Unfortunately, the places where African Americans have historically gathered, like church and school, don't pull people together the way they did in the past.

Still, churches, schools, settlement houses, and other agencies do exist and do have a lot to offer, but they have to be more proactive today in reaching out to parents, including fathers. Young parents have lost touch with these institutions and are often shy about reaching out on their own. They could benefit from programs in which they spend time with other parents. They would not feel so isolated, so alone, so alienated. We believe that knowing effective parenting skills is so important for our children's well-being that all students should have required courses in parenting and child development in middle and high schools.

New parents often look for information and advice from other parents. We have to think of new ways to form groups of parents helping parents. Groups like Effective Black Parenting and Parents Anonymous—for parents who need help in maintaining their self-control and improving their parenting skills—are helpful. Black mothers, fathers, grandparents, teachers, and other caregivers should search out such programs in their communities. The costs of isolation and alienation are much too high.

| LIFE LESSONS |

Stanley "Tookie" Williams looked back upon his early years in Louisiana as a kind of paradise lost. His grandmother was a sweet, kind, Christian lady who shared her love and warmth with all sixteen of her children. His grandfather was a strong, loving man who worked tirelessly on the railroad to support the children. Williams remembered the church they went to as being alive with music and spirit. His grandma's food was "heavenly" too, particularly the sweet potato pie and cornbread.

This natural community helped compensate for the lack of a father in Tookie's life. His father had abandoned the family before Tookie's first birthday. Looking for opportunity and a fresh start, his mom uprooted him when he was six and brought him to Los Angeles. There they had all the freedom they wanted, but none of the community. That was gone forever.

Without a community's roots to hold him, Tookie went as far wrong as a boy could. Needing family, Tookie found it in building the Crips, a violent gang that has spread throughout the United States and South Africa. After being convicted of murder, he was placed on death row. In prison, Tookie changed his perspective from that of a gangbanger to a voice against violence, including writing a book series for young people to prevent their gang involvement. On December 13, 2005, the state of California executed Stanley "Tookie" Williams. This tragedy did not have to happen.

Raising children is a tough job. It not only takes a village, but it also takes a village that actually cares. That means a lot of hands-on work from us all. We need to remind new parents that they are the ones who are going to build confidence in their child, that it is their job as a parent to build protection for their child. That's not to say that they should wrap the kid up in some kind of cocoon and screen out the world. No, we mean a protection that involves the parents being fully in their child's world.

Parents should know everything about their children. Kids express themselves with what's posted on their bedroom walls, with what's written on their clothing, with what's hidden under their beds, with what's on their minds or in their hearts. We all should pay attention. If parents and caregivers can't protect kids when they need it, the kids will likely never have confidence in their parents or caregivers or in themselves.

Young parents can learn from example, good and bad. We need to remind them to observe the things that they see their friends do with their children, the good things that work and the not-so-good things that don't. These observations will help them adjust what they are doing to protect their own children.

The need to support parents and children has to be high on all of our agendas. Black organizations, sororities, fraternities, and local programs—including Boys and Girls Clubs of America, and Big Brothers

Big Sisters—have provided greatly needed child mentoring programs in black neighborhoods.

Many of these mentors have made a world of difference in the lives of black children. This is also a way of linking successful adults with struggling young people. These kids need real, honest-to-goodness role models, not the thugs, pimps, and drug dealers they see on TV or even on their own streets.

Remember, good mentors do not have to have a college education. People who simply want to help children make good mentors. Mentoring is an important step in building broader kinship bonds in the community.

Ways to Build Strong Bodies and Minds

In the past, many parents believed infants just needed to eat, sleep, and be kept clean and they would develop well enough. This is not the case any longer and never really was. Children need to experience life and interact with others to grow into healthy human beings.

Many African-American parents have done the right things—intuitively perhaps—to raise successful and emotionally secure children. The following are some thoughts on giving your kids an even better start in life:

Get the little ones off the couch.

Today, too many children have the animated guys on their Playstation do all the physical activity for them. This does not help them stay healthy and slim. It doesn't do much for their minds either. Get the kids out for a walk or a bike ride. Play catch with them. Take them to the playground. Get them involved in organized sports—but not at the expense of school or family time.

Don't overfeed your children.

Three out of four children who are obese at thirteen will be obese all their lives. Overweight kids develop health risks—and serious self-esteem issues—so be careful not to overfeed a child, particularly with high-calorie, high-fat, high-sugar foods. When they ask for a Baby Ruth, hand them a baby carrot. We could write a book on this alone.

Serve good food.

As the children get older, introduce them to healthy meals with non-fried food, whole grains, lean meat, fish, chicken, and lots of fruits and vegetables. Too many of our kids have developed a junk food habit. We like pizza and macaroni and cheese as much as the next guy, but these should not become the main staple of your meals. Follow the advice about nutrition given by your doctor, nurse, or nutritionist.

Eat dinner as a family (and turn off the TV).

Eating together does a lot of good things at once. You get to catch up with what your kids are doing. You get to share your parental wisdom. You get to teach them some table manners, and you get to control what they eat.

Speak Standard English.

Use Standard English when you have your kids together, not Black English. They'll hear enough of that in the streets. Pediatricians insist that it is important to assist language development at every opportunity.

Work on your own language skills.

You should check out your own speech. This book is written in Standard English. If you don't understand what Standard English is, reading aloud to your children can help you learn. Or watch the news and pay attention to the difference between the way they speak and the way you speak.

Another thing we all can do is to encourage schools and community agencies to develop programs to help adults learn Standard English. Books are written in Standard English, and schools teach in Standard English.

Starting a child off right is important to his or her later success. Using a rich vocabulary at home will not only help your kids' speech development but their intellectual growth as well. We all have a keen interest in seeing black children develop a positive self-esteem in a society that doesn't always esteem them.

If you are a parent or caregiver who wants to understand the effect that language can have on someone's life, watch the movie *My Fair Lady*. All cultures discriminate against people who have not mastered the standard language, and when race is involved, it is much harder for a nonstandard speaker to feel competent or even at home in the culture.

Your kids are coming of age in a world that may be wary of them. They have to know how to navigate in that world. That's why Standard English is so important.

THOUGHTS ON RAISING
BLACK CHILDREN IN THE UNITED STATES

A positive self-concept is very closely linked with feelings of competence. It is well-known that children taught to cope with their surroundings have a better sense of self. Children who feel a sense of mastery or "fate control" in relation to the environment are less susceptible to feelings of inferiority. On the other hand, children who are overprotected and experience feelings of helplessness may not have a positive self-image.

Many black children have survived the hardships in poor environments because their parents helped to teach them independence and self-reliance. Because the public schools remain deficient and often poorly attuned to the needs of black children, black parents have a responsibility to educate their children throughout their development, and that responsibility begins with a long look in the mirror.

Reflect on your own self-image.

You must ask yourself, *Am I ashamed of being black, or am I proud?* You may feel inferior and believe most of the stereotypes about black people, and you may be passing these feelings along.

Examine your feelings about skin color.

You may have issues about your children's skin color and hair texture. We have seen it go both ways. Some parents favor a light-skinned child over a darker one. Some feel more protective of the dark-skinned child because "she will have a harder time in life." Avoid both courses if you can.

Review your beauty standards.

If you still refer to "good hair" and "bad hair" or "nappy hair," it's time to think about the origins of the message you're sending—and the potential impact.

Value the black experience.

Another matter to consider is how you share the black experience at home. Do you usually put black people down, or do you point out black success stories? Do you read your children books that include black characters? Do their picture books show black children? Are your children's books multicultural, or are they mostly just the traditional tales featuring white kids?

Help children feel at home in their skins.

What kind of dolls do your girls and boys have? Do they reflect a variety of ethnicities? We have been in some black homes where all the dolls were white—this is not a great idea. Kids need to feel good about who they are. They need to feel at home in their own skins. Raising a child to have a positive identity about being black is a first step toward raising a healthy black child. Black children have to know that they occupy an important place in the world. If you devalue them because of their hair or skin color, they'll devalue themselves and their children.

Watch your language.

Do you use the N-word or other nasty terms to describe black people in general? Do you use such words when you're angry with black friends and relatives? If you are going to raise kids in a home where the N-word is commonly used, you will certainly corrupt your children's view of themselves. What we're saying is that if you feel bad about being African American, your kids will too. After you deal with this, you'll be better able to provide the nurturing atmosphere your child needs without the interference of racial hang-ups.

What children most yearn for is having their needs, for food, warmth, clothes, cleanliness, sleep, cuddling, and interacting with parents, met with words and music in a loving and caring tone. Show them how precious they are.

CALL-OUTS

Shalonda Triblett, of Kansas City, said it well: *The main thing is to use your resources and to be a loving parent. If you truly don't love that child and don't show that child that you love him, he's going to be lost forever. Parents are the first teachers. And if you don't show them the love that you have to give, then they're not going to be able to give it to anyone else. If you can't show them that I love you enough to show you the right way, then they're not going to be able to successfully be productive citizens of society.*

I myself was an adopted child at birth. I didn't even meet my birth mother until I was thirteen. And that was an issue for me. That was a battle that I had to overcome. But with love, I did that. I had my demons to fight too, you know? I went through the rebellious stage and all of that. But it all began at home, because I knew I had that love, and because my mother taught me right from wrong, I rose above it.

The child's world should be peaceful. Hold a child when he cries. Comfort him. Don't scream at him. Try to discover what is wrong. Remember that within your four walls it is your job to protect. And you cannot protect the child if you're afraid of him or her or if you're feeling guilty and you want to buy things to compensate. You can't protect the child if you worry that the child will be upset with you. And, believe us, you're never going to win a "Best Caregiver Award" by yielding to your guilt and giving kids whatever they want. You can buy their attention, but you can't buy their love.

CALL-OUTS

Dr. Lewis King, from Compton, California, talked about protecting our kids: *[One] protection that's necessary is emotional protection. And that comes with love and caring and touch and holding and saying civil things to our children.*

The key word in this social protection has to do with affirmation and not negation. Do we affirm each other, or are we constantly negating each other? Can we approach each other in a civil manner and have a civil discourse with our child, with our spouse, with our friends, with our colleagues? [Finally] children need social protection. Social protection also comes through how we look and behave at home. How many of us at lunch or at dinner talk to each other? Or do we have a TV dinner and forget each other and talk to a boob tube?

UNDERSTANDING CHILDREN IN TRANSITION

A Philadelphia schoolteacher told about a fourth grader who came to her and said, "Miss, I won't be coming back to this school anymore. I don't know where I'm going. But I won't be coming back here. And this is my dolly; I'm going to give her to you because I know that you will give her a wonderful home." Children sometimes understand things in a way that adults never can.

CALL-OUTS

Dr. Charles Collins, of Cincinnati, reported: *One of the things that I just want to talk about is the idea of separation. When children are separated from a family, it is one of the most devastating things that ever could happen to them. When they lose one of their parents, it is just like they've lost an arm or a leg. When we talk about things that we need to look at, we need to look at what systems need to be in place so children won't have as many transitions in their lives. These transitions can be very, very devastating.*

Thankfully, foster parents help fill this void. At any given time, in fact, more than five hundred thousand kids in America are in foster care, and two-thirds of them are black. Foster parenthood is rarely easy. Abandoned children may have trouble not only with their own sense of self but also in their relationships with others, even with those who care.

CALL-OUTS

Randall Weeks, a private practice counselor in Greenwood, Mississippi, spoke to this issue: *One of the problems that many of these children have, and it is in part a result of going from home to home, is something called an attachment disorder.*

In the way of example, if you were to take a piece of masking tape and stick it on the wall, the first time it's going to stick there pretty well. If you peel it off, and put it back, it'll stick, but not quite as well. The more times you put that tape on the wall and peel it off, the less it will stick, until eventually it won't stick at all.

Weeks, however, believes that foster parents can go a long way toward providing children with love they may never have experienced and the kind of bonds that can stick for life. Still, he cautioned, "It takes something very special to be willing to let this child come in, and to give them your love, and your care, knowing that they won't be there forever."

CALL-OUTS

Lori Ross, of Kansas City, on the issue of communication: *Many of these kids have been hurt by the adults who were supposed to care for them. So, sometimes, opening the door to communication takes a whole lot more effort than it will with other people.*

As they begin to attach in their new homes with their new care-givers, they have a whole lot of fear that something that they do or say will cause their caregivers to reject them and send them away again. And so, sometimes, when they have done something that wasn't very good or they have some feelings of self-doubt, they're really afraid to come to you and share that with you.

I think sometimes we have to be that tough-guy parent—tell them that we're going to go for a drive out to the middle of nowhere, and until they speak, we'll just keep on driving because we're more stubborn and more tenacious than they could hope to be.

As with parenthood, it is easy to describe the *problems* of foster par-enthood from afar. But the joys and rewards can only be learned up close and through experience.

CALL-OUTS

Patricia Dozier, of Washington, on becoming a foster parent: *I had a mom who worked real, real hard. I didn't have my father with me, who I wanted with me most of all. He was around, but he wasn't with me, you know.*

I grew up with a lot of hurt inside, a lot of pain inside. The first thing I wanted to do was get away from my mama. I thought that I

---

could live out here in this world and take care of myself. I didn't think that anybody in this world could take care of me. So I was a rebellious child, okay? So I had to go through life learning the hard way.

Left to my own thinking, I got married early. Didn't know anything about marriage either. It wasn't long before I left. I became an alcoholic and an addict, because I didn't know any better. And it was painful. I didn't even know what I was leading myself into.

But life is not about that anymore for me. My life today is a life of giving back. Because see, I've been out there in that world, where I see children walking up the street with nothing to eat on Christmas.

You know, I found my purpose in life, found out that I was here to give it back, to give children that hope, to give them that love, to share a stability and understanding, to listen when there's nobody there to listen to. That's why I am a foster parent today.

Some Ideas on Protecting Your Teens

Adolescents have special issues. They are still kids, but boys will be boys, and girls will be girls, with all that implies.

In the midst of many kinds of change, these kids are searching for their identities and a sense of autonomy. It's often a time of anxiety and impulse. They have a great need to be independent and an even greater need to fit in. They are more likely to look to peers for guidance than to parents. They may challenge your values and choose their own poisons in doing so, but they will be guided through it all by what you've taught them, good or bad.

To the general public—and even some parents and caregivers—teenagers can be scary. As a result, many adults choose not to stand up to those teens who challenge them. In poor black communities, teenagers are at real risk of not getting through this stage safely, if at all. To move on to a productive and successful adulthood, they absolutely need your help.

Whatever you do, don't abandon them.

On the contrary, you must stay heavily involved to help them navigate the many perils that they face—dropping out, getting pregnant, getting shot, stealing, shooting up, getting drunk, getting high, going to jail, catching AIDS or STDs, killing themselves intentionally or otherwise. They need a safe harbor somewhere.

Reach out.

Whether you are a parent or a caregiver, a relative or a friend, lend all the structure and support you can.

Don't hit.

If beating is unproductive for little kids, it can be downright dangerous with bigger ones. They hit back. Hitting may lead to a complete shutdown in communication. In some cases the teenager runs away, which is highly unnerving for you and dangerous for them.

Talk to your teens.

You should praise them for the good things they do and respect the talents they have. Encourage them to get involved in after-school programs.

Work with their teachers.

Contact the school to see how you and the school can help them graduate. Help them find mentors and tutors if they need them.

Know where they are.

You know the kind of trouble they can get into, so help them stay out of it. Know where your kids are and who they are hanging out with. Are they drug dealers, criminals, and pimps? Are they involved in violence? Do they have guns?

CALL-OUTS

A character Dizzy Gillespie once played describes the dangers of having a gun: *Let's say you do not have a gun, and you were at a dance, and a guy steps on your foot, and says to you, "I'm sorry." You don't have a gun, and you say, "yeah, that's okay." But if you had a gun, and you are at a dance, and a guy steps on your foot, and says, "I'm sorry," and because you have a gun, which gives you some kind of magical power that you can't handle—you become a totally different person: you say "What do you mean, excuse me?" It turns from an apology to a debate to a challenge of the person's manhood. Which, by the way, is not the correct definition; demonstrating manhood would mean saying, "Excuse me—it's all right," even if you had a gun.*

Talk to your girls candidly.

Girls should not yield to the seductive talk "If you love me, you will have my baby." Abstinence is an option that can be empowering. Keeping girls on the right path is key. Girls who value themselves and envision a future are more likely to resist antisocial behaviors. Always keep the lines of communication open. That includes talking about sexuality, birth control, and options should she become pregnant. One more thing—girls need to learn to demand that boys wear condoms—latex or polyurethane condoms.

Talk to your boys too.

Condoms don't completely protect against disease, and accidents can happen, but it is still important to use them—every time. Boys need to know how to use them correctly. Girls and boys should know the risk of getting STDs and HIV/AIDS if they engage in unsafe sex. Boys should also be educated about the value and rewards of abstinence.

Draw a line when you have to.

If you know your kids are involved with the wrong people, if you worry about whether they will come home safely at the end of the day, do something about it now. Marshal all of your resources. You have to intervene to preserve their future.

You may very possibly face behaviors so troubling that intervention is no longer a matter of choice. If the child is on drugs, you have to find help at a substance abuse clinic and stick with that child. If the child is arrested, however disappointing, you have to stand by your kid and help with legal entanglements. If he or she is in jail, you should visit and try to steer the youngster to constructive programs on release. If your child is in prison, even if for the rest of his life, you can't give up.

Never give up! Remind that child of your love. Strive to see that no other parent has to go through what you have. Champion violence prevention programs. Try even harder to keep your home nonviolent. Work to help ex-inmates as well. You can play an important role in helping your children and other people's children who have gone down the wrong path.

RAISING VICTORS

Besides helping children develop a positive identity, you must teach them to assert themselves constructively when the odds seem stacked against them. If you express confidence in them, these kids will have confidence in themselves and overcome the obstacles life throws their way.

4

TEACH YOUR
CHILDREN WELL

Our great athletes know how to win. They win with their legs, their eyes, their arms, their bodies, but most of all, with their minds. They know they have to be smart and strong to go up against somebody who thinks of himself as Goliath. And to be strong, they have to work and study and learn.

Too many of us have forgotten this obvious lesson. On our path to victory, we have wandered off course. We were so busy worrying about the white man, we stopped paying attention to the black man. We remember the injustice of how slavers brought our people to America, but we have forgotten the brilliance of our response—how we sneaked around late at night and taught ourselves to read, taught ourselves secret signals to resist, taught ourselves pride and will and love. We have to draw on that history of persistence.

When you walk into a class or a presentation at work, the challenge is to know as much as can be known, not to be satisfied with 70 percent, but to know it *all*. If you're taking a test, there are few better feelings than to open that booklet, look at that first question, and know the answer. You just smile to yourself and move on to number two, and you smile again because you know that answer as well. You know it cold, and you know the next one and the next one after that. It takes work.

When you are finished, you look around and see people still writing frantically. Now, we admit, it is not particularly admirable to glory in the misery of others, but still, you just feel good about what you have accomplished. And you feel even better because, unlike some of your classmates, you worked for it. Unlike weed or alcohol, this is a high that strengthens and smartens and keeps on keeping on.

PASS IT ON

Learning is a high we have known for centuries and one that parents have passed on to their children. As a useful exercise, we all might want to think about our foremothers and forefathers and try to imagine how magical it must have been to learn to read. Reading and writing and math opened doors for them, long shut, and so they developed a love for learning that they have passed on to us. Benjamin E. Mays stated it well: "He who starts behind in the great race of life must forever remain behind or run faster than the man in front."

LIFE LESSONS

Frederick Douglass, on learning to read during his enslavement: *From that moment, I understood the pathway from slavery to freedom. It was just what I wanted, and I got it at a time when I least expected it. Whilst I was saddened by the thought of losing the aid of my kind mistress, I was gladdened by the invaluable instruction which, by the merest accident, I had gained from my master. Though conscious of the difficulty of learning without a teacher, I set out with high hope, and a fixed purpose, at whatever cost of trouble, to learn how to read. The very decided manner with which he spoke, and strove to impress his wife with the evil consequences of giving me instruction, served to convince me that he was deeply sensible of the truths he was uttering. It gave me the best assurance that I might rely with the utmost confidence on the results which, he said, would flow from teaching me to read. What he most dreaded, that I most desired. What he most loved, that I most hated. That which to him was a great evil, to be carefully shunned, was to me a great good, to be diligently sought; and the argument which he so warmly urged, against my learning to read, only served to inspire me with a desire and determination to learn. In learning to read, I owe almost as much to the bitter opposition of my master, as to the kindly aid of my mistress. I acknowledge the benefit of both.*

Malcolm X said, "Education is our passport to the future, for tomorrow belongs to the people who prepare for it today."

Nothing could be more true about the African-American journey from slavery and segregation to success. Education provided the most direct path out of poverty for a people left impoverished and mostly illiterate after emancipation. Education—in trade schools, public schools, vocational schools, community colleges, four-year colleges, universities, and professional schools—has been at the core of our people's progress. Without education to lift us up, most of us would still be struggling at the fringes of society. Given this glorious history, it troubles us that so many black youth are as thrilled about getting an education as they are about getting head lice.

INSPIRE THE CHILDREN

Every child has a brain—we know, sometimes that's hard to believe—and we need to work it. We need to inspire and guide our children to feel the thrill of victory through genuine accomplishment. When they make a mistake, we have to say, "Wait a minute. Don't be afraid. We will help you. The teacher will help you. You work with it. You can help yourself." That's how Edison made lightbulbs. The first time he screwed one in, nothing happened. The second time, nothing. He just kept screwing them in until he brightened the world. It is noteworthy that an African-American inventor, Lewis Latimer, improved upon Edison's work to create a longer-lasting bulb—which made electric lights cheaper and more efficient. And he did not succeed on his first effort either.

The reason we wrote this book was in the hope that it can help your kids brighten the world too. Every last one of our children is gifted in some way. It's just that no one has helped each of them discover and nurture his or her own particular gift.

Without inspiration and guidance, these gifted children can make decisions that are absolutely, incredibly dumb. We know that many of you are as old as we are and some of you are just as confused. You, too, wonder how a young person can say, "I'm not gonna flip burgers, so I might as well go out and sell drugs. And if I get killed, I get killed." Now that boggles our minds, because we didn't come from that. We came from survival. And we want our youngsters to learn as quickly as possible what we learned the slow, hard way.

So why not tighten up the game? We all have some piece of Frederick Douglass in us. As a slave wanting to read, Douglass knew that this skill wasn't going to take him to the White House or even convince the master to let him in the front door of the big house. What was he thinking?

He was thinking of the future. Educated ex-slaves like Douglass made major contributions to the abolition of slavery. He was a powerful speaker and writer. Black Americans have always used education as the chief weapon in their struggle for equal access to American society and civil rights. Education still provides—as Malcolm X said—our greatest hope for the future of African-American people. But illiteracy keeps people in chains—our ancestors in real chains, our children in emotional ones. In either case, people who cannot read and write are more easily oppressed and are handicapped in their fight for freedom. At our call-outs, we met any number of people who understand the power that attracted Douglass to reading, and the pitfalls that await those who ignore it.

Dr. George McKenna spoke out in Compton: *When students leave the Compton Unified School District—I'm not condemning, I'm just giving you facts—and show up at Cal State Dominguez, 90 percent of them have to take remedial English and math. They may average 3.7 GPAs, but we have to ask—did they earn the grade or just get it handed to them? We have to look at ourselves. We can't be embarrassed by that or offended by the one who holds up the mirror. Let's say, "Okay, we know we got some problems." Let's try to deal with them and stop blaming other folks.*

Now, when we underachieve, we compare ourselves to some other underachievers and celebrate being the best of the pitiful. And that, ladies and gentlemen, is a definition of insanity. When you create an alternative reality and believe that where you are is normal, you're insane.

We see a lot of alternative reality in Compton, kids who pride themselves on saying, "I will walk like this, I will talk like this. It won't get me anywhere, but I'm a big man in a small square and I will kill my fellow brothers over land I neither lease, own, rent, or pay taxes on, and call it my turf."

There are invisible children like this walking around Compton every day. They fail their classes, and we don't see them. We may not even look at their report cards. They go nameless. They fall out, while we just celebrate the one or two that got into the UC system.

SAVE OUR SCHOOLS

The worst schools in any community are in neighborhoods where people are poor. These schools often have inferior resources, weak teachers, and low-quality courses. Schools in affluent areas have the best resources. This much is obvious. Affluent parents of any race, who live in cities with poor public schools, can afford to bypass the public school system altogether and send their children to private schools. School systems in most cities remain heavily segregated with high percentages of poor black and Latino children.

These poor students do not have equal educational opportunities, and there is blame enough to go around—schools, parents, and the entire community. Black parents and caregivers, you have a dual task. You have to speak out for better schools, and at the same time you have to speak to your kids at home and support their learning. Sometimes you may have to buck up and make the best of a bad situation. Griping alone isn't going to make your kids any smarter.

You parents and caregivers have to make the best use of whatever a school offers, but the schools need to get their acts together and start educating our children as if they mattered. The cumulative effects of poor schools for black people over the decades is one very good reason why black students underperform. But it's not the only one. Even bad schools produce smart kids. Make sure your child is one of them.

TAKE ADVANTAGE OF EVERY OPPORTUNITY

Problems in teaching poor black kids can show up as early as preschool when children come from homes where there is not a whole lot of learning going on. If yours is such a home, admit it and take advantage of preschool and Head Start programs. A lot of kids who are eligible for Head Start never get there. The fact that you don't have an education should not stop you from trying to help the kids in your charge. If you know a parent who has trouble reading, it is never too late to get that person to a literacy program at your local school or community college. The child's education gives everyone a motive for learning.

You can regularly talk to the children in your care and explain how the world around them works. This helps. You can read to them, which is a time-honored way of teaching children Standard English. They have to learn it. If you can, take your kids to playgrounds, museums, and public libraries. Expanding a child's world increases his knowledge and prepares him for academic challenges—a definite plus for doing well in school.

Turn Off the TV

You definitely don't have to be a genius to know that spending too much time watching TV or other electronic media will slow your child's development. Black kids are more likely to watch five hours of TV per day than white or Hispanic kids. Five hours is too much. Watching doctors on TV isn't going to help them get into medical school any more than watching cowboys will help them ride a horse. Studies show that watching too much TV interferes with school performance, but you don't need a study to know that.

When the kids do watch TV, they should watch something educational, and you should watch with them as much as possible. We understand that when you are busy, the temptation is to let the TV babysit the kids, but even a wall-sized plasma TV doesn't care about your kids, and apparently neither do the people who do the programming.

Random TV watching does not prepare your kids for school, and many of them are not ready when they enter kindergarten and first grade. Teachers report that in poor neighborhoods children often begin school not knowing their colors or the letters of the alphabet. Some have limited vocabularies and little knowledge of numbers. Some don't even know that sheep go "Baaa." There is no good reason for this.

Love Those Little Ones

Poor kids often start side by side with youngsters who know their colors, have a good vocabulary, and can even read and count. From day one, the poor kids feel left behind and may never catch up. As the years pass, they fail to get the attention they need in overcrowded classrooms with overwhelmed teachers and fall further and further behind. What is truly sad is that sharp-eyed teachers can identify the children who will become high school dropouts the day they walk in the kindergarten door. And they often could do much to help kids who are lagging behind.

Unfortunately, some of these teachers shouldn't be in the classroom. For too many of them, teaching isn't a passion. It's a paycheck. They tend to pass the buck to the parents when they deserve their own fair share of blame for the kids' poor performance.

For children who are starting kindergarten without the skills of their peers, their teachers should give them the support and tutoring and even the love they need to get them up to grade level. It is much easier to get these kids on the right track when they are still young. Because they often need social support as well, teachers in the early grades would do well to maintain a network of support across grades so that the children's progress is closely monitored. This would help ensure that the children receive the services they need as they need them.

Studies show that by the third grade in city schools—even for students who were ready for school—there is a slow decline in performance because schools are not building on the students' strengths. Many poorly performing students receive "social promotions" to the next grade level even if they haven't learned one thing about division or multiplication or spelling. When the time comes for the transition to high school, many kids are so far behind and so unmotivated that they drop out.

Kids are even more likely to drop out if they get no support from their parents or caregivers. Being teenagers—and we have all been there—means the tug of their peers and the streets may pull them off course. Many veer into lives of crime, drug dealing, alcohol abuse, premature sex, and violence leading to death at an early age. Many of these young people are bright, mind you, but we lose them to the culture of the streets. We take this for granted, but we shouldn't. We can't afford to lose one of them and should mourn the loss of each one we do.

No matter how thinly stretched you are, you must support your children's education. It will make all the difference in the world for their future. A high school dropout is looking at a lifetime of poverty. A high school graduate will earn double the income of a dropout. And a college graduate will often double that.

YOU'VE GOT TO BELIEVE!

We have heard many inspiring stories from kids in poor black communities who just wouldn't quit. Usually some adult wouldn't quit on them either. Caregivers and parents, you might argue that it's up to the schools to teach your children, regardless of their abilities. This is true to some extent. But it is also up to you to show up at school, find out what the difficulties are, work with your children at home, and keep asserting yourself until the children get the services they need—and until everyone gets the message that the children's education matters. You start out in a cocoon, whether you come out as a moth or a butterfly all depends on how your education has (or has not) fed your development.

CALL-OUTS

Dr. Troy Brown Sr., from Greenwood, Mississippi, knows firsthand just how much education does matter: *I've had a lot of challenges in my life. What I had to come to understand—that I had to believe—is that it was okay to fail. A lot of us have problems with failure. We have no problems with success. But when it comes to failure, we tend not to bounce back from it.*

In school I was a special ed student. There were a lot of things that I couldn't do. And I got to the point where they used to call me "Troy Brown, the dumbest kid in town." But then I had an opportunity to go to a small school called Rust College in Holly Springs, Mississippi. And they didn't require that you have an ACT score, because the ACT score I had didn't allow you to drive a dump truck. And here I was; I was on a college campus and I could hardly read or write. I had to come to an understanding that I had just as much right to be there and to try. I had an opportunity, and I took advantage of it.

I never thought that I would be dean of a university and never thought that I would be down in Louisiana helping those people build that state back together again. But all I'm saying is that my story is not unique. The only thing that's unique about it is that I decided to take responsibility for myself and I decided that I was not going to allow my shortcomings to have an adverse impact on my future. Somewhere along the line, we are going to have to say to our young people that some things are not acceptable. Not trying is one of them. Nothing beats a failure but a try.

KEEP THOSE KIDS IN SCHOOL

We are all worried sick about the high school drop-out rate of greater than 50 percent in many of our cities—with much higher rates for black males than females. In Baltimore, for example, about 75 percent of black males do not graduate from high school. This is preposterous—criminal even.

These problems start early. A recent Yale study found that black students are twice as likely to be expelled from preschool as their Latino and white peers. *Preschool* for crying out loud! But the study also showed that the rate of expulsion could be halved if the teachers had consultations on helping these students. This study, though focusing on preschoolers, shows that interventions help even at an early age. Potential high school dropouts need interventions all along the way.

Dropouts have limited opportunities to obtain anything but the most menial of jobs. And they often reject these jobs—a mistake, in our opinion—to engage in literal dead-end activities like drug dealing and gang-banging.

KEEP THOSE KIDS OUT OF PRISON

As a result of such stupid decisions, our jails overflow with young black male high school dropouts. A year of college at a state school costs the state about ten thousand dollars; a year in jail costs about twenty-five thousand dollars. Educated kids usually pay the state back. Ex-inmates rarely do. Everyone would be better off if we could figure out how to keep students in school and out of prison.

Ex-inmates' life chances shrink because few institutions or programs are prepared to give them the tools and job training to get work and become productive citizens. Many become a burden to their families, and some end up homeless. A good number of ex-inmates develop mental problems, which often go untreated.

Come on, people; we need to do something!

The teacher is often the last mature adult some kids will know before they hit the slippery slope to prison. Their parents and other caregivers may have already given up on them. Teachers have to realize that they may very well be the last stop before a child winds up institutionalized— the last hope even. Prisons will not fix a soul that is hurting or a mind that is wanting. When released, these young people probably will come out at the same educational level as when they went in.

The despair and hopelessness of too many of our impoverished black youths are heartbreaking. We have to inspire them to learn and get an education. We have to prod their parents and caregivers to be even more concerned and involved. We need to spur on their teachers to teach even better and to improve the schools that now allow these kids to languish.

KEEP THE FAITH

Many dedicated African Americans have devoted their lives to improving our schools. We need to encourage them and eliminate the political and bureaucratic roadblocks that have left us with the sad state of affairs our kids have inherited.

We have to copy the methods of successful schools in low-income black communities. Positive examples exist in cities around the country. It is not enough simply to add tougher courses or more homework. Schools succeed best when the entire "school culture" is changed to support success instead of failure.

Education reformers report that the core components of effective schools are: a sense of purpose, clear standards, high expectations for all, a belief that all students can be educated, safe and orderly environments, strong partnerships with parents and caregivers, and a commitment to solving problems. Such a tall order for change requires a deep commitment from black communities, as well as from local governments.

It is extremely important that schools are safe environments and support nonviolence among their students. It is impossible for students to learn when they are afraid they might be shot or assaulted on their way to school or, tragically, *in* the school.

There are so many inspirational stories out there of young black people who have overcome unbelievable hardships to make something of themselves, to succeed. Their train was bound for glory, and it got there. At call-outs in cities throughout the country, black people have rallied to share their stories and to seek inspiration.

As we travel, however, we see too many examples of lost black youth wandering aimlessly through their own personal deserts. We have also found that many of these young people can get back on track and succeed when helping, committed adults provide the intense aid and love these kids require. It isn't easy, but "easy" has never been part of African-American history.

GET THE KIDS A PRO WHEN NEEDED

Students with learning or emotional problems often have trouble in school. They need special help from tutors, teachers, psychologists, and doctors who can help them to succeed. Parents and caregivers, you must also be involved, but you know that already.

> **CALL-OUTS**
>
> Dr. Susan Wilson, in Kansas City, noted the challenges: *Kids who have a short attention span need more structure than the average child. So that means you need to have a schedule for them at home—what you do when—and post it up. And you need to follow that schedule, which is sometimes hard to do. You need to help them slowly develop longer attention spans by giving them something to do with a timer and having them practice paying attention longer. The sooner you can teach them how to use a planner and how to write things down and keep track, that helps.*
>
> *Now, having said all that, there are some kids, no matter how hard we try, who have severe attention deficit disorder. . . . And even if you do all those things and cut out the sugar, they still may have hyperactivity and attention problems. And just like you wouldn't say to a diabetic, "Tough it out and see if you can make it without your insulin," you wouldn't say to a kid who has very severe ADHD, "Tough it out and see if you make it without the medication."*

If you suspect that your child has ADHD, get that boy or girl to see a mental health professional pronto. Teachers should not be the ones making a diagnosis or recommending medication. It is not enough to think your child is hyperactive and have him put on medication. That may or may not be the right thing to do. Other approaches should also be tried. These include learning management skills to work with your child and/or adjusting his school program. Even when your child is on medication, you should combine that medication with other behavioral strategies or the child will continue to struggle. Nutritional and dietary approaches can help too. In fact, healthy nutrition is crucial for proper brain function. You should discuss these alternatives with your health-care provider. Don't be afraid to ask.

FIND HELPFUL ADULT ALLIES

We can learn a lot from the strength foster parents have shown in moving wounded youth from victims to victors. In Cincinnati, we heard from a young woman who had been adopted by a professional sociologist who she had already known for nine years. With the older woman's help, the younger woman's life was turned around.

CALL-OUTS

Krystal Gary has a powerful story to tell: *I'm twenty years old. I'm a senior at Scarlet Oaks Vocational. And I'm taking up nursing. This year I will be going to Northern Kentucky University for cardiac nursing. I never thought that I would be graduating from high school because of the past and everything that went on with me and my history. I would like to tell you a little bit about myself.*

I grew up in Covington, Kentucky. I was born in the projects. At six years old I was given up—taken away from my mother because of her drug abuse. I have been through foster homes, group homes, facilities, jails. I have been in and out. At twelve years old I went to live with my dad after he found out that I was in a foster home. He took custody right away. He moved back to Covington, to Kentucky, but he couldn't be there, because he had to work.

I did not have my mother. My mother was incarcerated. She was on crack cocaine. So I chose the streets. The streets were there for me. It was everything that I couldn't find in parents. It was people who were there to listen. I skipped school. I did drugs, alcohol, shoplifting, gangbanging, hustling, everything. I was in and out of jail for long periods of time. I didn't have any goals for myself. I didn't see myself graduating

---

from high school. I didn't see myself hitting eighteen. I didn't see myself getting married. I didn't see myself going to college.

I was angry. I would fight at the drop of a dime. I was out of control. It wasn't until I got locked up for a year and six months that I really started to think. I didn't want to keep on going down this road. So I started to write. And it became poetry. After I got out of jail I went back to Covington and I went back with my dad, and I knew that I was being put back in the same situation. You've got to move yourself up away from what you know that's not good for you.

You can't expect to change just by yourself. You need somebody there, especially when you're young. These young kids need you. Even though I am twenty years old, and just now graduating from high school, I'm proud because I did not in a million years think I would graduate. I thought that I was going to be dead somewhere. I thought that I was going to be nothing. I thought that I was going to be a crackhead out on the streets. And I'm doing it.

CALL-OUTS

Chandra Mathews-Smith is Krystal's foster mother, and she, too, has a story to tell: *I've known Krystal for about nine years. When I took her in, it wasn't easy. She was angry at the world. But one thing that I knew was that I had to rejuvenate that fire in her. We had to look beyond all of her faults and truly see her needs. That's not easy.*

Our kids need to know love. If they don't love, if they don't know what commitment is, then they cannot feel. No matter what Krystal does in this life, I'm confident that her heart is healed. She has replaced that anger and hatred with a self-esteem and a self-confidence and ain't no stopping her. I know that the single most important factor contributing to her success and any child's success is that relationship with a caring, competent adult. It doesn't have to be the mama. It doesn't have to be the daddy or the auntie. It just needs to be an adult that can make the connection with the child, and be there for her despite it all.

There are over 500,000 children in foster care. There are over 150,000 on a waiting list. Now you want to talk about evidence-based practice? The evidence-based practice consists of us in this room, part-nering together to show these young people that despite all of their faults, we're going to see their needs, and we're going to partner with their guardian, and we're going to partner with the jobs and family services people, and we're going to take them back. And when we do this, that's the ultimate evidence-based practice.

With more than five hundred thousand children in foster care at any given point, and two-thirds of them black, we all have to advocate for a strong and effective foster care system. We should also support kin foster homes. Grandparents, uncles, and aunts need the same kind of financial assistance offered to all foster parents. When parents are unwilling or unable to keep their children, adoption can provide the kids with a perma-nent and stable home. We should see to it that children are not bounced around from one home to another. When they are returned to their origi-nal homes and families, we should make sure that social service workers carefully monitor their return and provide support for families where par-ents have been irresponsible in caring for the kids. There is no greater con-cern than protecting all children from injury. That is our common destiny.

When it comes to participating in your child's education, teachers often complain that parents don't show up.

CALL-OUTS

Hollia Thompson, of Greenwood, Mississippi, told us what can happen when we do show up: *As a parent, we have an obligation.*

Whether you take a child into your home, or whether you brought that child into this world, you took that obligation. And when we don't attend those meetings at school, a lot of times things happen.

I go into meetings with parents and they say, "I thought my child was graduating with a diploma. And now we're sitting there, and the child is in high school, and they're graduating with a certificate."

There is a big difference between a diploma and a certificate. My son LaRon got a diploma. LaRon did go to school. LaRon learned what his rights were. LaRon also advocated for what he wanted. LaRon wanted to do what all children want, what we bring them up to do, and that's leave our homes and go out on their own. So he has now achieved those goals. He did finish school. He did go to a community college, where he pursued paralegal studies. He also took some courses at Jackson State in criminal justice. And he is now living in his own home. If I could leave you with anything, I would say never let anyone make you give up on your dreams for your children. You have to push. You have to advocate. And the word advocate *means "to speak up for, to speak up on behalf of someone else."*

PROTECT YOUR CHILD

Parents, you have to say to your kids, "Okay, where is that homework?" If you don't ask, you aren't protecting them the way they deserve to be protected. The word *protection* means just that. If you have a child in your house and you're not interested in what the child is getting out of school, if that kid is never asked a question about anything he or she is supposed to be studying, you are not protecting that child.

You are leaving that child wide open to stop studying whenever he or she wants to. And school will mean nothing to a child if she doesn't hear from you how important it is. In our day, even if our parents weren't scholars, we knew that they were ready and willing to come "bother" us about our homework.

Bill Cosby reflects on his own childhood: *Even if I didn't want to study, I had to be ready for my father. And sure enough, even if he was half drunk, he would say, "Junior, what are you doing in math?" And at least I would have to pay enough attention to say something to get him off me, because if I didn't, the man was going to say, "Go get the book," and then we were going to be there all night.*

So I had to pay attention. And I'd say, "Dad, you would be surprised. There's a man. His name is Isosceles. He loves his triangle so much that he's worried about the hypotenuse." And my father would say, "That's enough. I'm going up to bed."

On another occasion, my father might say, "What are you doing in science?" And I might respond, "Oh, do you know there's over two hundred veins in a leaf and I can name them all?" He would say, "That's fine with me. I'm going up to bed."

Children need parents involved—all of them. And if you're not doing it, be ashamed of yourself.

There may be many things you can't fix in your schools, but you can make the best use of what you have to get the best you can for your child.

Dr. Arnold Mindingall, in Birmingham, Alabama, reinforced the need for involvement: *Today I read a statement from the late Ed Bradley, when he talked about growing up in Philadelphia. He said that his parents, both his parents, worked two jobs twenty hours a day. But one of the things that they reminded him of was that you can do whatever you want to do, you can be whatever you want to be. So in that statement we have the design for what parents are all about. They have to be a model. They have to live it so kids can see it. And they have to preach it to them.*

At private schools, they don't hesitate to ask parents for their resources. They put their hand out and parents write a check or do whatever. The issue is that parents can provide whatever resources they have. It doesn't have to be money, but they have to be involved. They do have to take ownership of the school. The other idea is that parents have to embrace the idea that the primary responsibility for the education of their child belongs to them.

REINFORCE STANDARD ENGLISH

We've said it before, but we will say it again: we must teach our children to speak Standard English. Are you listening, folks? We know that many African Americans have their own dialect when speaking, and this is all well and good. But when you are applying for a job or a loan or trying to talk your way out of a speeding ticket, it's time to go Standard.

Historically, we as a group have used words and sentences in a unique way, which has been described as Ebonics or Black English. This language style is more pronounced among lower-income black people, but middle-income black people will kick it around as well. Ebonics has its own charm and force as a language and has made valuable additions of words and expressions to enrich the English language. In fact, much of Ebonics is related to the grammar and vocabulary of the languages of slaves who were captured in West Africa; it is a legitimate dialect.

Expressions like "right on," "give me some skin," "give me a high five," not to mention "cool" and "hip" and "jazz" for that matter, all derive from the black experience. No ethnic group in America has had nearly our influence on spoken English, much of it energizing. In music, the use of the black vernacular in the lyrics of blues, jazz, and today's hip-hop are part of the richness of American culture that has been embraced by people around the world. Black people can be proud of their contributions to American language and speech. Again, though, as colorful as this language can be, it can limit the potential of our children to learn to do well in school because schools function on Standard English, not Ebonics.

Sometimes we meet black kids who don't want to speak Standard English. In their world, it's obviously not the coolest thing to do. But Black English in school and on the job gets the user nowhere. Its nonstandard grammar makes communication tricky. Your homies may be able to understand you, but can the Hispanic kid who is still struggling with English? Probably not.

Also, the shaky grammar can project ignorance, even hostility. This means it can make your kids look dumb to many people even if they made a perfect score on their SATs. Some employers, even in fast-food restaurants, may not hire them because the customers can't understand them, or are wary of them, even if they are a wizard with the french fries or a magician on the cash register.

Teachers, it doesn't hurt for you to understand Ebonics, all the better for you to help the kids transform their speech into Standard English. But you have to stay on these kids and make sure that they can at least speak the common language before they head out into the world.

Parents, you need to ride your kids. If you are uncertain of your own language skills, there are all kinds of language programs out there in schools, books, and DVDs that the entire family can use. The payoff will be enormous. Good language skills will enhance your kids' testing ability and their success in school.

Parents and caregivers, it's worth mentioning again that the more you read and talk to your children, the more rapidly they will learn language and be prepared to achieve. Talking and reading to infants and children help to lay down the physical structures in the brain that allow children to develop skills in language. Let's face it—the high drop-out rate for black students is related in part to poorly developed language skills, and this shortcoming keeps getting bigger and bigger over the years.

BACK OFF THE RAP

Rapping—from hambone to the dozens—has been a particularly male form of black cultural expression from the time the first boat docked and probably even on the other side. These language skills play a much bigger part in the identity of black boys than they do for black girls. "Black talk" becomes part of an African-American boy's expression of himself and his emerging manhood.

The problem is that, for black males especially, there seems to be a correlation between a high drop-out rate and a deep attachment to Black English. These kids often feel pressured to know how to rap in black dialect. They feel they "own" Black English and use it with a certain bravado and arrogance. Those who don't or won't speak the dialect are considered not "hip" enough or even "black" enough and may face rejection. When rap became a major form of entertainment in the seventies, some black females joined the genre. But even today, black males dominate rap, hip-hop, and gangsta rap music. While there is positive hip-hop, it is the profane gangsta rap that seems to be strongly promoted. And so we are treated to image after image of young black males spewing angry, profane, and women-hating rap music that plays on the worst stereotypes of black people.

As if poor black kids didn't have trouble enough, they often turn to these rappers, even the gangsters, as role models. Some middle-income males do the same. All these misguided souls, poor or not, saunter through school imitating the rappers and ignoring Standard English because it is "white." Unfortunately for them, gangsta rappers don't design the standardized tests or do the hiring for jobs. And no translator at the UN can tell you what "fo' shizzle, ma nizzle" means. Hanging on to such styles in school can spell doom for these kids.

CALL-OUTS

James Lyons, from Compton, California, reported on a conversation he had after testifying before Congress: *One of the senators followed me out in the hallway and said, "Well, Dr. Lyons, I just don't understand it. You need to break it down to me. Tell me why is it that your folks score at the bottom of every standardized test that's given? ACT, SAT, GRE, LSAT. What is the problem?"*

He wanted me to say that there was just something inferior about us, that all the money that we put into Head Start and Upward Bound and Gear Up is just a waste of time. But you know what I told him? I said, "Our problem is one of priorities. You see, there isn't one question on the SAT or the ACT about Lil' Bow Wow."

We need to recommit ourselves, rededicate ourselves to the pursuit of knowledge. I'm not just talking about getting a degree. But I'm talking about education and educating the mind. You know, we are turning the clock back. There is absolutely no justifiable reason for an African-American student or a Latino student to tell me in new student orientation in the year 2005 that they're still being ridiculed in their high schools because they are studious.

A young man from one of the nearby high schools told me that he was criticized when he was inducted into the Honor Society at his high school. They told him he was trying to act white. I met a young man who wants to appear so regular, so down that he gives his textbooks to a lady friend in his neighborhood so he can stroll out of the school book-free.

We hear stories like this all the time—as if black people are not interested in education. There is the striking story of a young high school teacher in a lower-income area committed to teaching English, particularly English literature. One day she had a meeting with her supervisor, who wanted to know what she was currently teaching. The young woman answered, "Iambic pentameter." The supervisor then questioned her on whether this was relevant to the culture.

Relevant to the culture? What culture? Try telling the late great poet Gwendolyn Brooks that iambic pentameter has no relevance to our culture!

LIFE LESSONS

As it happens, Gwendolyn Brooks was born in the city that launched the *Brown v. Board of Education* case, Topeka, Kansas, and soon afterward moved to Chicago. Although he was a janitor, her father appreciated the value of an education and provided a desk for her and all the bookshelves she could handle. Brooks's mom, meanwhile, took her to meet Langston Hughes and James Weldon Johnson, two celebrated poets of the Harlem Renaissance.

Her parents' encouragement paid off. By the time Brooks graduated from college, she had already published more than seventy-five poems of her own. After graduation, she continued to pursue her craft while also serving as a wife and mother. In 1949, then just thirty-two, Brooks published *Annie Allen,* her second book of poetry. Among the awards that the book garnered for Brooks was the Pulitzer Prize, the first ever given to an African American. Brooks continued writing—and receiving awards—until the day she died in December 2000.

RESPECT OUR ELDERS

Older people, many of whom have spoken out at our call-outs, have great words of wisdom for our youth. Unfortunately, many young people have turned a deaf ear to that wisdom. That was not always the case. Teens once felt obliged to listen when their seniors chose to set them straight on some life issue, critical or otherwise. Today, too often, elders themselves pull back. They fear that black youth will dismiss or even disrespect them. This is too bad. The elders have historically provided the sense of calm and continuity in the black extended family and the larger community. They taught us how to survive and even thrive in a world that could be hostile.

CALL-OUTS

Bill Cosby remembers: *Nobody can say things better than old people, the way old people say them. A young man once shared an anecdote with me about his father, a man of deceptively simple wisdom.*

"Dad, you know, I've thought about becoming a doctor," the young fellow told his father, "but you know what, by the time I'll graduate as a doctor, I'll be thirty years old."

The father looked at his son like he was the dumbest person on earth. "You're gonna be thirty anyway," he said with a wry smile.

The son took the message to heart. I should know. He was my doctor. There's no person I have ever heard who could say, "I worry about you sometimes," with more power than an old person. When that elder says, "You're out there acting a fool. You know I worry about you sometimes," it goes right to the core.

TALK TO YOUR STUDENTS

Teachers and administrators, we have discovered that it pays to talk to your students on a regular basis, even to gather them all for an assembly in the auditorium. If need be, you can hold an assembly every day to go over behavioral problems or other problems in the community.

You can use this as an opportunity to help students sort out their feelings of anger and sadness. You can address teenage pregnancies and introduce the resources for girls who need services. You can talk about what can be done to get your students back on track when they have wandered off. You can teach the kids about their health, about better eating habits, about the proper care and development of their bodies. You can show them the realities of what having a gun can do to them and their future. Too many schools lack the counselors to reach the children who need them.

Helping children understand the impact of violence in the real world can also provide opportunities to teach nonviolence. Too many of our children live in chronic fear of being the victims of violence, and that interferes with their learning.

Assembly time can be fairly brief as long as it is held regularly. Students start the day with the feeling that they are in school, that they are there to get an education, and that people care that they are there. Young people should be given a chance to come up and read, to sing, to recite, to talk about where they are going. A daily assembly helps create a real esprit de corps—a feeling of pride and belonging.

Assembly time is a way to reach everyone at once. Some students will listen, and some will not, but at least they might start to learn. You need to talk to all your students about respecting each other, boys to girls, girls to girls, girls to boys, boys to boys. You need to talk to them about taking responsibility for their anger, for their tempers. You must teach your kids not only good manners but also the cultural value of treating people with respect. Good manners show strength of character that encourages an atmosphere of mutual respect. Schools with this kind of positive climate will produce more student winners in every sense of the word.

There are few more rewarding moments for geezers like us than to meet a young person with manners. After a certain age, we all look a little warily when we see young people coming our way. The spring in their walk, the straightness of their spines, the clarity of their eyes, the glow of their skin, the fullness of their hair—all of this can intimidate an older person. But when they approach us and we hear them say, "Yes, sir" or "No, ma'am" or "I beg your pardon," it reminds us that we are all in this together, that we are all links in a powerful chain. When we hear these simple terms of respect, we can sense that there is education going on in school, that there is work being done at home, and that the culture is in good hands.

DON'T OVERLOOK YOUR COMMUNITY COLLEGE

God bless the community college! In our experience, the community college provides a safe harbor for those who blew off high school and veered off course. The front door of this institution welcomes you like your own personal Statue of Liberty—give us your slow starters, your late bloomers, your high school dropouts, your born-again victors. There are lots of stories here, and these stories come from all over the United States.

CALL-OUTS

Ed Rice, vice president of Student Services at Mississippi Delta Community College, shares one of them: *If you have an individual who wants to go back and get that high school diploma, we can provide a nonthreatening environment. It's more like a drop-in setting. There are no time constraints. It's not where you have to go at six every night. You can go at three. It's basically open to whenever that individual wants to go and practice for that GED exam.*

Tonight we heard from an angry eighteen-year-old, who grew up in two or three different families, who felt abandoned, had low self-esteem, and wasn't even sure what that was. "I'm kind of private," he told us. "I don't want anybody to know that I can't read and I can't write." He asked if we understand where he is coming from.

Yes, we do. We see people like him all the time. We have staff on our campus that work with a variety of individuals, whether it be individuals who cannot even speak English and where English is a second language for them, to individuals who have very little formal education, whether it be third-, fourth-, fifth-grade education. We can help them.

People who feel as if they have no choice need to know that community colleges offer a world of choices. The following are just a few jobs a person can get by attending a community college:

- *Nursing.* With two years' training, a person can earn a salary of $46,000. That's as a licensed practical nurse (LPN). Another two years and that person can become an RN, a registered nurse, whose salary can go beyond $80,000.

- *Auto mechanics.* With a one-year certificate, auto mechanics can start at up to $50,000. They can earn even more once they work up to running a shop.

- *Computer technology.* For those who can repair and program computers, the salary begins at $35,000 to $42,000 and goes up quickly.

- *Culinary arts.* With a two-year certification, an apprentice chef can make more than $30,000. The world's top chefs make CEO-level salaries.

- *Dental hygienist.* They clean and examine teeth, meet a lot of appreciative people, and start at $35,000 or more.

- *Emergency medical technician.* EMTs live a high-drama life and make a decent, steady living. A person with a two-year degree in paramedic training can earn around $35,000.

- *Physical therapy assistant.* After a two-year program, a PT assistant can start at $35,000 and do a lot of good.

To become a victor you have to have a calling, and a community college is a great place to find one.

CALL-OUTS

Bruce Crawford, vice president of Instruction at Alabama's Lawson State Community College, described the vision of community colleges: *The mission of Lawson State centers around providing educational opportunity for all of our citizens, promoting economic growth in the community, and enhancing the quality of life that you have in this city. The target groups that we have are our students who are transferring to four-year colleges, and then we have students who are going directly into the workforce, getting ready for a job or even starting their own career path.*

We also are addressing specialized training for industry and business where we do some specialized training, customized on what they need the workforce to do. We have a center that is focusing on manufacturing, industry-type jobs, training for automotive mechanics, auto body repairs, diesel services for heavy and medium truck industries.

We will help our students with GED training if they don't have their high school diploma. Some training courses are one year and some are two years.

A great virtue of the community college system is that students can go there and be guided by a real human being. Someone will talk to them about their interests and their goals. Let's say a student wants to learn how to fix elevators, make $55,000 a year, $1,000 or so a week. The school can teach him that.

"Look, I went to community college. I didn't have my high school diploma, but they helped me get my GED and find a job." We assure you: parents love to hear that. "Look, I've got a job, and no bullets in my future." Parents like to hear that even more. If our children have goals, then they'll jump over hurdles to reach them.

Bill Cosby role-plays as a foster parent with Chuck Hatcher, Adult Admission Representative from Cincinnati State Technical Community College:

Hatcher: A lot of our students come in to Cincinnati State, especially out of high school, having to take developmental classes.

They have to take English, reading, writing, math, at the high school level.

We spend a lot of time working as a kind of cheerleader, and our students sometimes get discouraged because of it. "You mean I've got to take basic math again?" The thing is, at Cincinnati State, we're open access. A student who has a high school diploma or GED, we can get that student moving. And so that's what we try to do, is to help students, where they are, and get them where they want to go.

Cosby: My wife and I are foster parents. Our foster son is twenty-seven years old now. And he's still in the house. Well, he is enjoying it, but we have trouble getting him out of there because he doesn't have a job, and he gets mad at us when we ask him to go get one. He throws the remote down and he leaves. And then he comes back at dinner time. He doesn't want to be tested because he said he's had enough of that. And he says he's tired of people telling him what to do. But there is something that he likes to do, and I was just wondering what you have at that school for automobiles—anything? He loves the automobile.

Hatcher: What does he love about it?

Cosby: Well, he can take one apart.

Hatcher: Can he put it back together?

Cosby: Well, that was his problem. In fact, he did a little time for that.

Hatcher: Okay. That can be a setback, but it's not something we can't get over.

Cosby: He seems to be ready, but he doesn't really trust people. If we brought him down, is there someone, a human being, we can talk to? Because every place we call, we get, "Do you know the first four letters of the person's name?" And then, "I'm sorry but their voice box is full." Or "Stand behind the yellow line." And we're just tired of standing behind yellow lines.

Hatcher: When we look at people his age, twenty-seven, and they've done some time, they think the world's over for them.

They really feel that, you know, "What in the hell can I do right now?" And so what I say is, "Where do you want to go? Is that remote control attached to your hand?"

Cosby: No, my wife told him that. He threw it just to show her that it wasn't. He's a nice boy. He doesn't misbehave until we ask him to do certain things. But if we take him down to the college, can we get a human being to talk to us?

Hatcher: You sure can.

Cosby: Can we get somebody who won't make him feel like he's stupid? Or who's going to give him a test to make him feel even stupider? Because he sounds like he's ready.

Hatcher: At Cincinnati State, we would ask him to come down and visit. We'd be glad to show him around, show him all the neat stuff, show him what the automotive lab can do. Not only can he take a car apart, but he can also put it back together—and learn how to run the business. It's the two-year associate degree graduates who go into the automotive field. If you go full time for two years, you can actually graduate, if you meet the prerequisites and all the fine print.

Cosby: Now here's the problem. He didn't graduate from high school.

Hatcher: That's easy.

Cosby: He stopped in the third grade.

Hatcher: Actually, he probably would feel at home. We have a GED program through the Cincinnati Public School System.

Cosby: So he can get his diploma?

Hatcher: Sure can.

Cosby: And the word won't be out? Can he do it without everybody knowing?

Hatcher: Well, let me tell you what we say, and it's really neat. One day I was working with some guys in downtown Cincinnati in the Second Chance program. One of them talked to the other one, and he said, "Where are you going with these books?" He didn't know they were GED books. And he said, "I'm going to

Cincinnati State." And the other guy said, "Really? How did you get into Cincinnati State?" He said, "Well, I went and applied." Now, what he's doing is getting his GED. And so he's going to school three times a week, getting his GED. And guess where he's going to go after he finishes school? Over three thousand students of the nine thousand students in Cincinnati State have GEDs.

Cosby: And how much money do you think he could make, once he learns how to take the car apart and put it together?

Hatcher: In this area, the average salary for our associate degree in automotive is in the $36,000 range.

Cosby: Now, what else have you got? I saw a guy with a job. He didn't do anything. He came into our house. He looked around like this, and he said, "I don't have the parts." And we paid him $75 to go back and get the parts. It was the air-conditioning man. Do you have that degree?

Hatcher: Oh, yes. We have what's called an HVAC degree program. It's actually a certification program. There's a shortage of HVAC people—HVAC is heat, air conditioners, all that good stuff. It's not hot in here, right? Well, there's a shortage of people with two-year degrees to go help engineers design and write and draw out the designs for these kinds of buildings.

Cosby: And it's two years?

Hatcher: Two years.

Cosby: How much does it pay?

Hatcher: With their degree, starting out—not somebody with some experience—you're talking in the $42,000 to $46,000 range.

Cosby: And then they could be the manager, huh?

Hatcher: Actually, some of them become owners. That's how you make your money.

Cosby: Now, suppose he gets in there—I'm just going on a miracle now. Suppose he gets in, in that first year he gets the GED and then he goes for something with the car, right? And then suppose he finds out that he wants to be an engineer, instead? What happens?

Hatcher: First off, with our being a community college, we're part of the Ohio Transfer Module. That means that you can take courses at Cincinnati State, your general education courses, the English, the math, the psychology, all those kind of things. You can move on into a four-year program based upon their requirements. For instance, we have a very good working relationship with Xavier, with UC. Actually, 38 percent of our transfer requests from graduates this year went to the University of Cincinnati. Over 85 percent of our graduates this year are going on to four-year programs.

Cosby: Now, I just have one more question. Some of these places have classrooms, there are five hundred, six hundred people. What size are your classes?

Hatcher: Our average is eighteen per class. The non-tech classes tend to be larger. I teach psychology at Cincinnati State, and in my class, it usually runs around twenty-seven to thirty students. The tech classes are even smaller. Our Midwest culinary institute has large kitchens, only sixteen people at a time.

Let's hear it for the community college! People may want to come to this community college and think they can't because they have children and they can't leave them alone. Find some other mothers and buddy up with them—"I'll look after your kids Tuesday night, you look after mine Thursday night." Find a way. This place is waiting for you. If you haven't graduated from anything, if you quit in third grade, if you can't read— community college is waiting for you.

You may think you've made some spectacularly dumb choices and you've ruined your chances. No. You haven't. Come on down to the local community college.

We spent a lot of time on community colleges at the call-outs so that poor youth, even high school dropouts, could see the many opportunities open to them. For people who are worried about the cost, don't be afraid to ask about financial aid. Even if you need to take out a loan, it is well worth it. Students should know, too, that going to a community college is a frequent stepping stone to going on to a four-year college and getting a bachelor's degree. Too often, community colleges do not get enough play when we urge students to get an education. But an associate degree or a certification can land a young person a good job with good pay.

Civic organizations in communities should shift some of their focus away from four-year colleges and emphasize the alternative opportunities. Besides community college, there are also other options for job training like the Job Corps program run by the Department of Labor. Even at the high school level, most city kids have the option of going to a vocational school to learn a trade for a decent paying job without a college degree. At a vocational school they can learn trades in computer technology, automotive, culinary, electrical, construction, and health occupations.

Many young people are discouraged at the thought of a four-year college. Let's face it, not everyone is cut out for hard-core academics. Many people would rather work with their hands and provide services to others. There are plenty of jobs for them out there for the taking. Of course, anyone who wants to aim for a four-year college education should do so. We hear all the time of young people who come into a community college thinking that they want a two-year degree and discover they want to continue and pursue a four-year program. There are a lot of smart kids out there who have just never had either the inspiration or the opportunity to excel. They suddenly come to college and discover themselves. If you know young people like this, get them off the couch and back to their local community college.

CALL-OUTS

Beverly Brown, of Panama City, Florida, shared her story: *My name is Beverly Brown. I returned to Gulf Coast Community College in the fall of 1994. I had just gone through a divorce. I was broke, with no skills. I realized that my life was in a pretty bad state. I was the mother of three young children, with no hope, no dreams, and no plans for the future.*

If you've ever gone through a divorce, or watched somebody go through a divorce, you know how devastating it can be. It leaves you feeling hopeless, like a failure.

I was alone, divorced, and poor with a house full of children when I realized I was in the exact same place as my mother when she was my age. I saw a pattern I didn't know how to change. What was I going to do? One day my mom and I were talking, and I found enough courage to ask her a question that changed my life. If you could do it all over again, what would you do differently?

Her answer surprised me. She responded, "I'd go back to college and I wouldn't stop until I finished." At that moment, I decided I would do just what she said.

Was it hard? Some days were harder than others. There were struggles all the way through. I struggled with money, time, a house full of responsibilities, working thirty-two-hour weekends so I could be free to go to class during the week. I did without a lot of the things that I felt I wanted and needed, but all the time I was learning and growing and becoming the person I was meant to be.

My mom was right. Going back to college was the right thing to do. Not because it prepared me for a job, but because it changed me, and prepared me for a world with endless possibilities.

Beverly Brown exemplifies the inspirational words of the renowned educator, Benjamin Mays: "The tragedy in life doesn't lie in not reaching your goal. The tragedy lies in having no goal to reach. It isn't a calamity to die with dreams unfulfilled, but it is certainly a calamity not to dream. It is not a disaster to be unable to capture your ideal, but it is a disaster to have no ideal to capture."

Our youth must embrace his words as they strive to overcome hurdles to achieve the best education possible in elementary school, high school, college, and beyond.

5

THE MEDIA YOU DESERVE

Okay, imagine that the year is 1915 and you are sixteen with the where-withal to go to the movies on your own. You are fortunate enough to live in New York City where they will actually let you in the movies and even let you sit where you want.

You've heard about this great new movie that has come out called *Birth of a Nation*. Everyone is talking about it. You rush downtown to see it with your buddies. You buy popcorn and some lemonade and wait for the thrills to begin.

But what you see at first makes you real uneasy, and little by little, the film begins to makes your skin crawl. On the screen are all these thug-gish black guys trying to rape white women, and here is the Ku Klux Klan riding to the rescue. The Klan? Riding to the rescue? And worse, the rest of the audience is cheering for the Klan. You just slink out of there before the final credits and take that subway back to reality.

Welcome to the world of American media. It would not get much worse, thank God, but it would be about another forty years before it got much better.

In the 1950s, Sidney Poitier broke through race barriers and began to get some serious leading roles in films, the first black actor to do so. In the 1960s, it was one of us, Bill Cosby, who became the first black per-son to costar in a TV drama, namely *I Spy*. And it was also the first star-ring role of any sort in which the black actor did not play a maid or some kind of Amos and Andy-like buffoon. In the 1970s came *Roots,* the most popular miniseries of all time.

By the 1980s, TV shows like *Frank's Place, The Cosby Show, Roc,* and *A Different World* presented images of African Americans that were authentic and not stereotypical. These shows played an important role in eliminating negative images of black people and instilling a greater pride in black Americans.

In the movies, black actors appeared in a myriad of roles. Top stars emerged. Directors like Spike Lee made powerful films from a black perspective and garnered many awards.

In some cities, black Americans anchored news programs. On national news shows, they held significant reportorial posts. Many good documentaries focused on black history and various aspects of black experiences. A host of good, strong, black role models for children emerged in the media.

And then, just as things were getting better, they began to get worse again. After Hollywood had put most of the silly or ugly stereotypes behind it, it began resurrecting them. Many black sitcoms in the 1990s reverted to buffoonish stereotypes, and black comedians prospered on cable making liberal use of the N-word. In the world of music videos and their movie spin-offs, the imagery grew uglier still.

So now imagine you're a sixteen-year-old kid in 2007 and you're watching thuggish black guys on TV lusting after women, when not degrading them as "bitches" or "hos," and committing random acts of violence. Have you noticed the women are usually light-skinned? This narrow-minded sense of beauty—which favors a European standard over an African one—began in slavery and continues today, causing much pain for darker-skinned women. And when you ask who is now perpetuating these images, you learn that it is not supporters of the Klan but African Americans and "sympathetic" white people who should know better.

And you say to yourself, *Come on, people!*

Watch with Your Children

Parents and caregivers, as you surely know, some of the most negative images of African Americans on TV and in the movies seem to be the most popular among young people—black and white. With both good and bad media out there, you have to help select media for kids that will support their success and suppress their urge to give up or drop out.

Media—books, magazines, movies, computers, video games, and especially television—have profound and sweeping effects on all our lives. Their influence is pervasive. These media have dominated so many homes that some have called them "a third parent," but not a very helpful one. The media are poor substitutes for the positive values that you can provide your kids.

All kids are affected by media, and it is difficult for parents to counteract the media's effects. Nearly all homes in America have TV sets, and a high percentage have two or more. In some homes, the TV is on all day, even during meals. Some of you will freely use the TV as a babysitter without thinking about what your kids are watching. Latchkey kids come home from school and turn on the TV, play video games, or surf the Internet until their parents get home. The smallest of school kids— eight, nine, ten years old—watch some of the most salacious shows. Is it a coincidence, do you think, when TV stations run the *Jerry Springer Show* at three thirty in the afternoon?

With cable, which most homes now have, kids can turn to all manner of adult shows, including those that are extremely violent or sexually graphic. In addition, they casually watch music videos and listen to CDs filled with the kind of imagery that people of our generation did not hear or see until we were adults, if then.

Even some of you with very young children will not monitor what they watch, and every one of you knows that even your littlest kids are at least as handy with the remote control as you are.

KEEP THE TVS OUT OF THE BEDROOMS

It troubles us that some 19 percent of children one and under in the United States have TVs in their own bedrooms. Babies! They can watch whatever they want without your knowing. We know that if each kid has his or her own TV, they won't fight over what to watch. But we also know that you won't sit around and watch TV together as a family. If you want to know—and you should—what your kids are viewing, then putting a TV in their bedroom is a seriously bad idea.

Plus, watching TV in their bedroom may interfere with the kids' sleep, especially if they watch scary and violent stuff. In these instances, children may find themselves waking up with nightmares and feeling weird the following day, not to mention sleepy. Often children watch so much violence, they become numb and immune to its effects, which is not a good thing at all.

When the television is in a common area, however, you can select the programs for your preschoolers. Then, too, you can use your veto power on programs that the older kids might want to watch, and you can stay in touch with what they enjoy. When you watch together as a family, you can talk to each other and comment on what you are watching. You can even make fun of stuff together and live life like, well, a family. How about that?

DON'T LET THE KIDS
WATCH TOO MUCH OF ANYTHING

There are other problems associated with screen time in other forms—computers, DVDs, and video games. Children today spend more time in front of screens than do air traffic controllers. And the weird thing is that we scarcely exaggerate. Children from low-income homes watch more TV than children from middle-income homes, and this can lead to all kinds of problems.

For one, if these kids are spending a lot of time watching TV, they are not playing games on their own or with friends or getting a little whiff of fresh air. For some kids today, the "great outdoors" is that small space between the car door and the front door. It shouldn't be that way. The beautiful thing about nature is that it doesn't care what color you are. Fish don't discriminate—they don't want to be caught by anyone.

Kids learn by doing, using all of their senses. Media screens use only audio and visual stimulation and are generally passive. Kids just sit and watch and turn into little zombies. They don't have to exert themselves and, in fact, begin to count on the TV to keep them amused. They don't use their own resources to learn to have fun and entertain themselves through their own initiatives. Pretty soon, they don't have any resources to use. They may rely so much on entertainment coming from the screen that it becomes habit-forming. They suffer withdrawal and become bored without it. If you're a parent, you know about the hysterics that follow your demand to turn off the TV—even after hours of viewing. It's like taking a crack addict's pipe away.

USE THE MEDIA TO EDUCATE

Educational television, particularly on PBS, has been shown to benefit children, especially those from low-income homes with few books or other educational supports. What your kids learn from educational programs can help to prepare them for preschool and kindergarten. They can learn a lot about many things including numbers, words, colors, and nature.

It's often through preschool television that kids discover the multicultural world that surrounds them. They explore songs and dances from different cultures, which can be both fun and enriching. They see different forms of native dress and customs, which help them develop respect for other people's cultures and lifestyles. This kind of exposure also helps prevent them from developing prejudice toward others at an early age. Indirectly, you may even learn more about tolerance when challenged by your children.

Don't Forget TV's Limits

For all its virtue, educational TV is still TV, and too much is still too much. We also have reservations about "edutainment." Music can mesmerize young children. They can begin to associate learning not with doing but with sitting passively in front of a screen. Too much song, dance, and other entertainment may create problems in your child's ability to learn in a real classroom without such diversions. These kinds of habits and expectations may interfere with learning later in school, even in the elementary grades.

The fact is that children who watch a lot of TV do worse in school than those who watch less. Those who engage in other activities such as reading, games, and creative play learn best. Kids who associate learning with entertainment may be turned off by the necessary but often unexciting routines of school. They may expect the teachers to "sing and dance" to teach them. Times tables, anyone? Not likely. There is no amusement in that. Kids may resist demands made upon them and refuse to put their own effort into the learning process. When teachers require their participation, these kids may not know how to participate. In the city of Bikini Bottom, SpongeBob SquarePants never asks them to join in.

Keep the Kids Engaged

One of the complaints we commonly hear from kids of whatever age is that school is "boring." But boring in relation to what? The Power Rangers? Our suspicion is that it is boring compared to the intense entertainment they are exposed to very early in life. Many kids have become entertainment junkies because the media have become such relentless pushers of addictive junk.

That much said, teachers, you need to keep your students active and alert. You don't have to entertain them, but you do have to engage them. Schools can be more inviting when the physical environment is pleasant, but you should demand student participation regardless of the environment.

In the classroom, your kids need to write, spell, and do math, not just watch videos or computer screens and hear the sounds of numbers and words.

Parents, you, too, need to roll up your sleeves and get these passive little people engaged in active learning. You and your kids should actually sing the songs on educational TV programs, not just listen to them. You should point out colors and explain numbers every chance you get: "How many buttons?" "What number is the big hand on?" "What's the difference between a 3-point shot and a 2-pointer?" Sports are rich with numbers. So is shopping for that matter. When at the mall, talk to the little ones about how much things cost and have them give the bills to the cashier and count the change. As we said, children learn best by doing. TV can only teach when parents and children watch together and talk about what they are seeing. Watching together is important for any number of reasons, not the least of which is getting to know your kids and keeping them on the right track.

COOL THE VIOLENCE

Here is something we all know: there is too much violence on TV—even on cartoons. Child-care professionals believe that kids who are exposed to a lot of violent media are more likely to use violence. The older they get, the more they see, the more violent they get.

TV shows and movies almost inevitably make their violent actors attractive, whether they are the good guys or the bad guys. In the spirit of equal opportunity, the bad guys now include women. Young girls may be imitating these images; the amount of violent crimes committed by girls is accelerating in America. Girls now make up 29 percent of juvenile arrests, up from 23 percent just fifteen years ago. Inspired by the likes of Lara Croft, the video game butt-kicker turned movie icon, girls are less hesitant to do a little bullying and butt-kicking of their own. "You've come a long way, baby," said the TV ads, but in this case, the wrong way.

Too often, the media present violence as the primary way of resolving conflict. It is surely the most dramatic way, the most manly (and now womanly way) to resolve differences—with guns blazing. Plus, it seems to be satisfying, thrilling, and fun. Media provide the violent scenarios that swirl in the unformed heads of our young when they carry out crimes of violence. Violent media seem to play on the myth that "boys will be boys," encouraging youths to act out their every aggressive impulse. This myth cannot be used to excuse violence.

Despite what TV network executives want us to believe, the truth is that hundreds of studies link violent media with increased aggression. Stop for a minute and think about where kids learn about guns—how they work, what they do, whom to shoot at. Unless you've got a rifle range on your block, the answer is probably media: TV, movies, and video games.

We have seen parents bring children as young as five or six to R-rated movies filled with profanity, violence, and sex. On one occasion, we saw a mother slap a little girl to shush her when she cried out in fear at a bloody shooting scene. Some parents don't realize that screen violence can traumatize their kids and cause anxiety and nightmares. Worse, media violence gets more intense and gorier by the year. You can forgive a city kid for not knowing that chain saws were actually designed to cut tree limbs. There is overkill—all puns intended—and violence is everywhere, even in the movie trailers shown in otherwise innocent venues.

ACCEPT THE RESPONSIBILITY

With violence and killing so prevalent, and its horrors so apparent, you have the responsibility to monitor the effects of media violence on your kids. For one thing, we know that the media glamorize violence—much of it gratuitous—and make it seem appealing. Many people get an adrenaline rush from watching violence, similar to sex. Media executives build on this reaction by linking images of violence and sexuality in the same scenes, particularly where women are raped or murdered.

Guns can be powerful phallic symbols, and even if young gangsters don't know what the word *phallic* means (representing a penis), they know the testosterone rush that comes when they "stick it" to another person.

Excessive media violence plays a role in societal violence, but it is hardly a complete explanation. Many other factors—like poverty, fatherlessness, motherlessness, unemployment, and the easy accessibility of guns—contribute to the violence epidemic. Still, media violence is like a pollutant; it amplifies the toxic atmosphere that gives support to violence, and it undermines efforts at violence prevention, particularly among young people.

Studies show that being exposed to a high level of media violence may make your kids numb to it. Producers of movies, TV, and video games try to dampen this effect by making violence "fun." You've heard kids laugh in the movies at gory, violent scenes as if it were fun, and then they go out and commit violence in the same spirit. *Fun?* If you're a parent whose son has a colostomy bag on his hip from a gunshot wound in the gut, you know just how much fun violence can be. You just can't accept this reality and do nothing.

Exposure to media violence also heightens feelings of paranoia. You or your kids may begin to feel there's more violence than there actually is and withdraw. Even if you live in a relatively safe neighborhood, you may be barring yourself in and walling the world out because of the media's paranoia-generating coverage of murders, mayhem, and massacres.

If you get the sense that news programmers are pleased—privately, of course—when they have some sensational murder to report that adds excitement and attracts viewers, you are probably right. There is a lot of truth in the cynical comment about TV news coverage: "If it bleeds, it leads."

WALK AWAY

On TV shows and in movies the true impact of violence is often not shown. For example, people are murdered or killed, but you rarely see the bloody damage, or if you do, it is quick and glamorized as part of the excitement. Viewers seldom see the aftereffects of nonfatal violence—the paralysis, the blindness, the brain damage, the lifetime dependency. Nor do they experience the emotional damage—the broken hearts, the shattered lives, the abandoned children. As a result, young people who commit violence for the short-term thrill have little appreciation of the long-term harm they inflict on themselves and others. This "reality blind spot" may make it easier for them to pull the trigger. It is up to you to tell them otherwise. Although we are all exposed to the media, it is our poor black and Latino youth, without much in the way of direction or hope, who are the ones most vulnerable to the message that violence is the answer. Better, they think, to go out in a blaze of glory than to wither away into a life of poverty and obscurity.

One of the more common reasons given by black youths for shooting each other is that they were "dissed" (insulted or disrespected). How sad is that? How fragile must their egos be to risk years in the pen to protect what they see as their honor? Remind these wounded souls that when the other guy has a gun, the manly thing to do is to walk away. A boy's real commitment is to his parents and his family and his future, not to his momentary street credit. But that's almost never the message the media give.

Don't Fall for the Stereotype

Crimes committed by black youth are overreported on the news—frequently they are shown in handcuffs, spread-eagled, or being frisked for suspected criminal behavior. These images reinforce stereotypes that lead to racial profiling by ordinary citizens as well as by police, especially since they are rarely balanced by positive portrayals.

Such attitudes may cause law enforcers to fear black youths and—in too many cases—to resort to the excessive use of force. Every year there are reported cases of police brutality against our people, many of which turn out to be true. This, in turn, sours relations between police and poor communities. The loss of rapport between the police and the community further contributes to alienation, anger, and violence. As should be obvious, media can have a major influence on destructive attitudes in our society—especially in children and youth. Keep that in mind.

RESPECT YOURSELVES

Minister Farrakhan said that this gangsta mentality is leading our children into the valley of death. He was not being metaphorical when he said "valley of death." There's no return ticket on that trip. Does anybody stop and say, "We understand that and we will not go there"? Or do you just keep on keeping on?

The enemy—namely the bad guys in the gangsta rap industry and their white enablers—is calling this a "culture." This so-called culture promotes the moral breakdown of the family. It deliberately influences women to become pregnant before they have finished their education and influences men to shuck their responsibility when this happens.

Those who defend gangsta rap claim there is no harm in profanity, no harm in vulgarizing women, no harm in dropping out of school, no harm in blaming the system for the disaster they have made of their own lives. They don't fight the mess that they have inherited. They glory in it. The gangsta rapper is saying, "I am somebody because my mother is a drug addict, and I don't know who my father is. I have been in three or four foster homes, and I have been in trouble, and that is okay because the rappers are saying that's who I am."

The truth behind this kind of antisocial swagger is that swagger is all there is. It is no more than a cover for a life of sadness and frustration. In the climactic scene of the film *8 Mile,* Eminem disses Papa Doc, his black opponent in a freestyle rap showdown, for being named "Clarence" and having "two parents." The wound is lethal. Eminem prevails. In the world of hip-hop, to be educated as Papa Doc was, and to live in a suburb with both parents, is to be less "black" than even a white guy. But neither in the film nor in real life is there any accounting for what happens the day the music dies.

What is particularly troubling is that parents will buy gangsta CDs and give them to their children. Little kids now listen to women-hating, violence-promoting music that their own parents gave them. That's something of a seal of approval, don't you think? What effect, we wonder, can this be having on young black children's views of their families and communities? How well are gangsta videos promoting a dead-end life of crime to our children that can lead them only to the cemetery or the prison cell? This is pathetic. There is no better word for this phenomenon. Black people, including parents, are victimizing their children and undermining their chances to be victors.

Caregivers, parents, please! Come to your senses. You should never buy or allow your children to buy CDs with the "Parental Advisory: Explicit Content" label. Talk to your kids about what this music does to our culture. Knowledge is power.

DON'T IMITATE THE SLAVE MASTERS

Among its other charms, gangsta rap promotes the widespread use of the N-word to sell CDs among people of all ethnic groups. In fact, the audience for gangsta rap is made up predominantly of white youth, who get a vicarious thrill from participating in a black thug fantasy, including the degradation of women. Black youth, as well as some misguided adults, have defended the use of the N-word, suggesting they are somehow making it a positive term.

Don't fall for that nonsense. The N-world is a vile symbol of our oppression by slave masters. It was the word that empowered lynch mobs and emboldened them to mutilate black bodies. Remember Emmett Till, the fourteen-year-old boy lynched in 1955 for whistling at a white woman in Mississippi? The N-word may have been the last word he ever heard. You don't honor his memory by trivializing it. You can't change its meaning by saying "nigga" instead of "nigger."

How many times have we all heard angry black kids denounce their black foes in the most vile and derogatory fashion: "I'll kick your ass, nigger" or "You nigger son of a bitch." There is nothing cute about this. The N-word still has a negative connotation, which suggests both self-hatred and the projection of the same hate against other black people, including the "bitches" and "hos" who represent their mothers and sisters. We wonder if much of these kids' rage was born when their fathers abandoned them. These wounded youth need true nurturing, and yet they work as hard as they can to erect walls of hatred to shield themselves from what they so desperately need.

Yet, as our youth are being swept up in decadence and glorified self-hatred, we do almost nothing about it. Mind you, we are not opposed to rap as an art form with its rhyming music and strong beat. It's an extension of black music, from blues, swing, and jazz to rock and roll. The difference from the rock and roll beat is that rap sounds aggressive—almost angry—even when it is not profane. This form of hip-hop style may indicate a new assertiveness on the part of black youths, but it encourages self-assertion in ways that are self-defeating, self-degrading, and finally, self-destructive. The use of racist language in gangsta rap has created a permissive attitude, even encouraging white shock jocks to express their racism as so-called comedy. It undermines the righteousness of the attack on white people and others for their language when black artists wallow in the same garbage.

We need more constructive rap that will encourage black youths to feel proud and positive. There are rap songs that encourage self-help, but by and large the big media push self-destruction. Black adults, young people, civil rights activists, churches, and fraternal orders need to speak out more against music that degrades black people. In fact, activists should investigate and protest record companies that produce and promote gangsta rap to teenagers in general, but particularly to black youth. More than 90 percent of the radio stations and other retailers that market hip-hop and associated products may be white-owned, but we provide most of the product and buy way too much of it.

LIFE LESSONS

For years, veteran rapper Master P admits to having been part of the problem. He was that indeed. The lyrics of his raps were pure sex and violence. Some samples: "Why you lean when you walk, look mean when you talk / Keep that green in the vault—we some gangsters, nigga." Or some of the more printable lyrics on the sexual front: "Man she mean, she shakin' like a tamborine / Booty bustin' out her pants and seams / So that may be why her cheeks bounce like kids on trampolines."

In May 2007, however, Master P shocked the hip-hop industry with his pledge to form a record label "with 100 percent clean lyrics." In launching Take A Stand Records, Master P and his son, Romeo, are boldly breaking the mold. Now he is ready "to be part of the solution." The label will record only those artists who promise to serve as role models. Said Master P, "There's too much negativity out there—enough with the stereotypes. Hip-hop is a movement, and it is time for it to move forward." We hope he sticks with the plan and succeeds. It won't be easy.

We're pleased that more and more black leaders are speaking out against the degrading forms of hip-hop. During a call-out in Birmingham, Alabama, a young person acknowledged that older people put down hip-hop and rap music all of the time but rarely provide alternatives. What, he asked, might they be?

CALL-OUTS

Attorney and singer Lauren Lake answered: *I've been a singer for many, many years. And I have sung hip-hop and rap and everything*

---

else. And what I want to say is that there are many alternatives. You can still love hip-hop and rap. You just don't have to accept the negative images and the negative songs that are out here. There are tons of positive rappers out here.

There are tons of rappers out here trying to speak conscious words, and yet their record companies don't push the button on them the way they do on some of the other negative rappers who continue to then use imagery and things that only work to oppress us even more. So, it's not like you can't love a genre of music. I've sung with rappers, I've done rap videos, everything. But I'm from a different era.

And that's why I said the train has left the station, and we can't keep up. There used to be a day when rap was enjoyable music. And if you just are honest with yourselves, you have to say, if this is what you're intending to listen to every day of your life, what are you gonna really get out of it? If you listen to those lyrics, where are you going to go?

And most of these rappers are rapping about money and cars they do not own and they never will. They don't have any money. They never had any money. And they won't have any money because they can't read and understand the contract that they sign. You know why? Because they didn't finish school, and they didn't listen to their parents, and they're out there doing a whole bunch of nothing, singing about a whole bunch of nothing, and giving you a whole bunch of nothing in return. Be smart. You can love music without loving ignorance.

CALL-OUTS

A young male in the audience responded as follows: *I'm from the hip-hop generation. I grew up listening to hip-hop. I grew up listening to rap. The point that Ms. Lake made that was very powerful was the idea that there is very little positive rap today that actually builds up the African-American community. The rap today, in large part, perpetuates the very thing that we need to get away from, the images of African-American women being objectified sexually.*

The images of African-American males being portrayed are as gangsters and thugs. These are things that we have to defeat as a people, and we can defeat them economically. We buy positive records, and that's what will be put out. The main thing is not to be controlled by what the media and what these huge recording companies pitch to us as music or as what we should be listening to.

CHILL THE SEX

Too many programs—where do we begin?—use sex as a way to capture an audience. Today, even during the so-called family hour, TV shows are so loaded with sexual innuendos, suggestive situations, and foul language you'd think you were watching the adult after-hours channel. Few of these shows say one word about love. The industry's idea of a relationship is—"You see me. I see you. You want it. I'm going to give it to you. We're both hot. Now let's do it."

Where is the courtship? Where is the tension? Where is the romance? Where is the tenderness? These questions may seem old-fashioned, but the new-fashion shows very little respect for the female. Mothers and fathers used to protect their daughter's virtue or at least tried to. The boy had to respect the girl and honor her parents. This did not always happen, to be sure, but there was at least the expectation of it, and the media reflected that expectation.

It used to be that at least there was one parent who was embarrassed if the child misbehaved. We're at a stage now where even the parents don't get embarrassed. We heard of one thirteen-year-old girl whose mother caught her having sex. The mother said, "Well, at least you waited." It's that bad.

Music videos are the worst. They are so loaded with sexual gyrations and writhing bodies you'd think Dionysus (the Greek god of sex, wine, and drunkenness) was the new head of programming at a major cable channel. The only image of women in these videos is as sexual objects. In hip-hop and rap music, particularly gangsta rap, the language is laced with sexual profanity and the crudest of sexual images. Girls are reduced to "hos" and "bitches." Boys are reduced to pimps.

If we stay together as a people, we can't lose. But when we mess with each other, that's when we have cause to worry. We're letting our girls dress up like prostitutes and sluts. We're letting our boys dress up like pimps and prisoners. When did people get so deranged that they decided to model clothes after thugs and convicts? And when did we get so stupid that we bought them? No one really wants to raise children like this.

It is even more amazing that girls, young black girls, routinely dance to music that calls them "hos" and "bitches." Have they lost their little minds? When we ask them how they can demean themselves in this way, they say (in denial) that they don't listen to the lyrics; they just dance to the beat. Oh, yeah? And we used to just read girlie magazines for the articles.

Come on, girls! You're not fooling your parents. You're singing along. A child who can't recite the first word beyond "I have a dream" can recite every word of Young Gotti's *Same Day Different Sh*t* CD, especially his hit tracks "Make That Ass Shake," "I Get High 2," and "Shoot 'Em Up." An evil trifecta—sex, drugs, and violence—all on one action-packed CD. What more could your preteen ask for? Rap is what they hear and see. This is not good.

Here's a brief example of the lyrics from popular rap group the Ying Yang Twins "Wait (The Whisper Song)." And these are pretty run-of-the-mill:

> *Ay bitch! Wait 'til you see my d****
> *Wait 'til you see my d****
> *Ay bitch! Wait 'til you see my d****
> *Imma beat dat p**** up*

Mary J. Blige, a popular black singer who turned her life around from drugs and alcohol abuse, said in 2006 that some rappers were smart but "they'd rather keep it gangsta than get real with themselves. I know people who have never been out of Yonkers. Where they live, gangsta is the mentality."

Gangsta rap and the media in general promote premature sexuality and even unsafe promiscuous behaviors among our young. The sexualized images on TV, music videos, soaps, and cable are pervasive. To make matters worse, kids have painfully easy access to porn on cable TV and the Internet. The kids themselves, girls especially, tell us that TV shows encourage them to have sex. But amidst all the cheerful encouragement, there is very little said to them about the responsibilities and risks, including pregnancy, that come with engaging in sexual activity.

CALL-OUTS

Alvin Brooks, former mayor pro tem of Kansas City, described kids learning about sex from the media: *One of the things I'm finding in working with young people is that they're not being taught by their parents or other adults in their lives about the birds and the bees. They're learning it from their peers, from the streets, and TV.*

There is nothing now that you need to imagine. It used to be when you'd go to the movies, just about the time folks got ready to kiss, it would fade out. Now you see everything, even on the sitcoms and not just on cable, but on the regular commercial stations.

And I don't think we take enough time to talk to our young girls and young boys about what womanhood and manhood are all about. I'm convinced it takes a man to talk to a boy, a woman to talk to a girl. Now, am I saying that a man can't talk to his daughter or a woman can't talk to her son? No, I'm not saying that.

I'm saying, though, that it's good if a man can tell a boy about manhood and a woman can tell a girl about womanhood. Now, I don't mean someone that's just a grown-up boy or grown-up girl. I mean a woman or a man.

Recently, a woman called me about her son, and she said, "I got this problem, Mr. Brooks." She told me that there's a girl who's run away from home, and her mother won't come get her, and she's pregnant. I said, "How old is she?" The woman answered, "Twelve."

I said, "Oh my goodness, twelve years old. How old is the boy?"

She said, "Fourteen years old, and he's my son. And the girl is staying at my house and the mother won't come and get her."

So here you are. Those of you who are working with teenagers and teen moms know that there are eleven- and twelve-year-old girls that are getting pregnant, who have come into womanhood. The boy is just three or four years older, and is much older sometimes. But who's taking the time to tell these girls about what it means when they come into womanhood?

And when that boy reaches a point to where there is a sperm there, who's talking to him? They get their information from their peers. And we sometimes feel embarrassed about talking about it. You know what I'm talking about. And I don't want to see a show of hands, but how many of you have sat down and talked to your son, your daughter, about manhood or womanhood? I suspect if we told the truth, only a few of us have done that.

PROTECT YOUR YOUNG ONES

Little is said about the use of contraception and condoms not only as birth control but also as a protection against sexually transmitted diseases, including HIV. HIV/AIDS is epidemic in black communities. Although African Americans comprise 13 percent of the American population, they represent about half of new HIV infections. As is evident, young people can't afford to take sex lightly because there are considerable risks of disease and teen parenthood. And yet the media encourage kids to have sex as though it were no more dangerous or complicated than dodge ball or jumping rope.

Folks, you must pressure the media to wake up and smell the carnage! Educational programs can help protect your children against the bombardment of sexual messages, but not for long. Once the kids get beyond *Sesame Street,* they enter a media neighborhood where no one will help them distinguish between lust and love. The same marketers who exploit the sexual awakening of our teenagers show up at AIDS benefits as though their hands were clean.

At this point, you can appreciate why pundits have called media a member of the family, but too often media show up in your living room like a disturbed relative with lots of dirty pictures to show and an abundance of bad advice to give. Earlier we discussed the long hours children (and adults) sit and watch their TV screens and whatever shows up on it, not to mention their video game and computer screens. We know it is very hard for you to monitor your children's use of media. The temptation is to use TV as a babysitter, a practice that is very hard to change. But victors have to make the effort. Victims don't, and they never do.

CALL-OUTS

Shirley Harrington, of Washington DC, talks about what media could do to help us on the path to victory: *I'm a product of the sixties from Mississippi. And one of the concerns I have right now is that no one is harvesting our experiences to pass them on. People have talked about some kind of a center where freedom fighters and folks in the struggle can start passing on how we train more people, how we get more young people involved because the struggle does go on. It starts with all of us. We have to work with more black media and other media people who are more sensitive to our better half, so that we can come up with a better image of ourselves.*

The media is killing all of our communities. We need a lot more ways that we can talk about the thousands and thousands of great programs that are right here in the District of Columbia, all the great churches that are doing great work for our community. I know we have the black radio, the black television owners. But some kind of way we've got to do a better job of telling, so people can know the good stories and know the good coalitions that are already being developed.

WATCH YOUR HEALTH

Another problem with watching too much TV is that it can make you and your kids fat. Advertisers bombard you with junk food ads, especially on children's programs and black shows. These ads are very seductive. They suggest this food is good for you—ummmmhhh!—and will make you happy, so bring along the whole family.

Fast-food outlets create clever lures to seduce kids and families into buying their unhealthy food. It's known as "tie-in marketing." It works like this: A toy based on a popular movie is put inside a fast-food meal and then advertised to children. Children are told the item is "free" if they buy the special high-fat, high-calorie, and low-nutrition meal. Kids then beg their parents to take them to the fast-food restaurant to get the special toy. The whole family ends up at the fast-food haven, and they all waddle down the path to obesity together.

WARN YOUR KIDS

Children do not appreciate what an advertisement is doing until they are about eight years old. Younger kids tend to believe what an advertisement says. If an ad suggests that eating hamburgers will make them feel like a king, they want the crown. So don't be surprised if they start nagging you. Advertisements actively encourage them to nag, as if they needed any more encouragement. If you yield to the kids out of frustration or guilt, the ad executives consider their marketing a success.

The billions of dollars focused on ads and marketing to kids is, to say the least, exploitative and often adds to family stress. It also teaches children values that foster materialism. Children are trained very early to be consumers, to become brand conscious, to ignore value for the sake of status. In Sweden and Norway, the governments were so troubled with this type of exploitation that they outlawed direct marketing to children under the age of twelve on television. And in Great Britain, corporations are restricted from advertising high-fat, -salt, and -sugar foods on or around TV programs that cater to children under sixteen. The United States clearly is not doing enough to rein in the commercial misuse of children. Don't be shy. Tell your congressperson.

Unfortunately, corporations are powerful, and some are more interested in profit than in people's health. Tobacco is a case in point. For years companies denied that lung cancer was linked to smoking, despite overwhelming scientific evidence. Smoking causes lung cancer! Tobacco execs continue to play down the contribution smoking makes to other diseases, and they continue to market their products to adults and teenagers as though it will improve their lives. Hip-hop artists, revered by black teenagers, market certain brands of cigarettes in black magazines. It's only recently that laws have been enforced to stop the sale of cigarettes to children.

Hip-hop artists also promote the sale of liquor in black magazines. The number of ads young African Americans are exposed to in magazines has actually gone up, even while it has dropped for the population in general. Alcohol advertising was included in *all* of the top-watched programs among black youth. Researchers are increasingly finding that young people who are exposed to alcohol marketing are more likely to drink alcohol and to drink heavily. That's the whole point of the ads, isn't it? The earlier kids start drinking, the more likely they are to become alcoholics as adults. Alcohol also plays a major role in street violence and car crashes.

Media marketing is effective in making people want material things. Otherwise, advertisers would not advertise. Advertisers aim to make us consumers who want to "better" ourselves and "keep up with the Joneses." It works. We have a consumer driven economy, which affects many of our values, especially if material values are unbalanced by spiritual or communal ones.

The products you buy contribute to your sense of worth and status. What you own becomes very important to your self-esteem. A brand-name sneaker or starter jacket means so much to some poor black kids that they will kill for it. Knowing how desperate these kids are for status, marketers often use black sports stars to advertise their overpriced gear. We suppose that it is a sign of some progress that black people have become trendsetters worldwide, but your kids pay a high price for it in every way.

We have all heard stories about folks who are living in poverty but who will spend their last dime to buy overpriced sneakers to appease their nagging children. Money that could have been used to purchase good food or books or educational supplies just isn't available anymore. These parents think they are showing love for their kids, but love can't be bought. They would all be better off spending time together in a nurturing relationship. That only costs time, and you don't have to go to a loan shark to get that.

SHIELD YOUR KIDS

Parents and caregivers, you are the ones who have to help your kids see through the shallowness of the ads that inundate them. Don't let them become selfish and materialistic. This "I have it and you don't" mentality can destroy a family and a community. It can erode a sense of sisterhood and brotherhood. It can undo a child's dreams. If you want to build communities with more caring and cooperative people, you have to shield yourselves and your kids from media images that promote the opposite.

First, you have to be media savvy yourself to protect your children from harm. We all know too many people who ignore the TV rating system for programs, so you have to know the rating system and use it even though it is not perfect. You have to learn about the V-chip that allows you to program your TV to block shows not appropriate for the children. The TV industry does not publicize the V-chip because it hurts their bottom line. It helps yours. More importantly, it helps your kids grow up wholesome and healthy.

There is also software for computers to prevent your kids from logging on to adult sites on the Internet or accessing chat rooms. The Internet can be a wild place. You're the new marshal in town. You've got to tame it. For starters, make sure your kids know enough not to give out personal information on the Internet and never to meet in person anyone they meet on the Internet. Creeps and pedophiles prowl the Internet with a variety of false identities. Just as you would not let these whack jobs go to your kid's bedroom in person, don't let them go there virtually. Keep your computers in a public place and monitor what the kids watch.

TRUST, BUT VERIFY

There are many good educational sites for young children. Some of the educational programs that teach about colors, numbers, geometric shapes, and vocabulary may be more effective than TV because they engage your child. Children may be learning by doing on the computer, but time on the computer should be limited just as it is for TV viewing. Computers are no substitute for real play and interactions with others in learning activities.

Many poor families do not have computers at home, but local libraries and schools have them for public use. Even some Head Start schools have computer time for preschoolers as part of a common learning experience. While many educators believe it's just fine for children younger than six or seven not to have computer time, others are concerned about black youths falling behind youngsters who were introduced to electronic technology in preschool. Many children in poor families do not have access to the latest technology at home. Libraries help, but the "digital divide" between the rich and poor still exists.

If you don't use a computer yourself, you may feel helpless both in understanding and reviewing what your kids are doing. You would benefit from at least some training, particularly since computer literacy is becoming necessary to obtain jobs even at lower levels. In our information age, where cell phones and handheld computers are becoming common, schools and community colleges need to help black communities to keep up with the growing use of technology.

Those who use cell phones and the Internet, kids especially, will be bombarded with advertisements just as they are on TV. We don't believe most children need cell phones. But we understand the security value of staying connected to your kids through the phones. This is another medium, however, that you have to monitor. Ads on children's cell phones can completely bypass any type of potential parental control.

The best way to keep connected with your kids is not by cell phone but by solid interpersonal relations in the home. Children need to understand the effects of media in their lives, and you have to tell them. To foster a positive attitude, you need to screen out the sex and the violence and the porn and teach your kids how to decode the stereotypes that devalue black culture under the guise of "entertainment." You should also request media literacy courses in schools and community centers to help them navigate the turbulent media sea and stay off the rocks.

Television and other electronics are not likely to disappear, and few people would want them to. But we can raise our voices for better programming and content. If we don't like how a show depicts black people or exploits our kids' weaknesses, we should not buy products from the sponsors. This is the best way to bring about change. It is also important to write letters of complaint. In the meantime, use the media's positive *and* negative dimensions as tools to educate and uphold the best in social and family traditions. Take an extra moment in the car, at the dinner table, or just sitting around the house to talk with your children—to share your values, to teach, and even to have some fun laughing and complaining together about the worst and best on TV.

As a people, we have created a disproportionate share of the media content people all over the world see and hear. Although some of it is excellent, much of it is not. Let's make it better.

6

HEALTHY HEARTS
AND MINDS

Kansas City has become corporate America's favorite test market. Kansas City is the Peoria of this generation, America's most representative city. If it plays there, it will play anywhere. All the better to turn to a resident of Kansas City for a summation of the nation's health.

> **CALL-OUTS**
>
> Dr. Bernard Franklin, on the health issues facing the black community: *It is even more challenging for us to excel if we're not taking good care of our bodies and our minds. When you listen to the statistics, think about the kinds of food you're eating, when you last exercised, and when you had a health checkup.*
>
> *There are many among us who do not have health insurance and face barriers to getting affordable, good-quality health care. But there are some things we can do to change those horrible statistics. Let me just list some for you. African-American men live an average of 7.1 years fewer than white men. Forty percent of African-American men die prematurely from cardiovascular disease versus 21 percent of white men. The rate of homicide deaths is six times greater. The infant mortality rate for African Americans is twice that of white*

babies. African-American women have a higher rate of breast cancer, despite having the same rate of mammography testing as white women. One in four African-American women over fifty-five has diabetes. The death rate for HIV/AIDS is seven times greater for African Americans than white people.

Forty-four percent of African Americans are considered overweight, and 21 percent are obese. The obesity rate has doubled over the last three decades for preschool age children and tripled for children six to eleven. Half of these obese children will stay obese as adults. Many experts believe the biggest factor in the increase in obesity is high-fructose corn syrup, the sweetener found in sodas, energy drinks, fruit drinks, ketchup, and many other products. The average American is consuming sixty pounds a year of this.

Only 25 percent of us are consuming the recommended daily intake of fresh fruits and vegetables. Junk food and other highly processed foods are usually poor in vitamins and minerals. Nutrient deficiencies such as iron, B vitamins, essential fatty oils can cause learning problems. More than 60 percent of American adults do not get enough physical activity to provide health benefits.

In children twelve to seventeen years of age, the overweight factor increases 2 percent for each additional hour of TV viewed daily. Starting in adolescence, girls' physical activity declines 7.4 percent per year, while boys' activity decreases 2.7 percent per year. Lastly, many of our health issues that could be prevented with better diet, more exercise, and frequent health checks are just left by the wayside.

So, think, think about what you're putting on your plate. Think about what you're putting on your child's plate. Mrs. Huxtable said it best. Food is medicine, both good and bad. Is it a bag of fast food that's adding to the profit margins of the big corporations and robbing our health and longevity? Well, the way many of us are eating is about the same as eating rat poison or arsenic. Let's not assign blame or point fingers, but let's work together to address the critical issues that face our community, our families, and our children.

THINK HOLISTICALLY

As you probably know, it is difficult to separate general health from mental health. Mental health affects the way we feel, the way we act, and the way we think. They go together. They play off each other, in good ways and bad. People with diabetes, for instance, are more likely to become depressed, and people who are depressed are more likely to get diabetes. Stress and anxiety disorders can lead to heart disease and stroke, but heart disease can bring on stress and depression. Stress, anxiety, and depression can weaken the immune system and open the door to physical illness and chronic diseases. Although the mind-body connection is ever present, the mental health component often gets short shrift if any shrift at all. So when you think of your health, think holistically. No one can understand your body the way you do.

Even though medications can be extremely expensive, clinicians trained under the Western medical system tend to think first in terms of medication. When people take a whole-body approach, however, they often improve not only specific health problems but also their general well-being. As you have surely discovered, modern life can be more than a little stressful. If you don't know where February's rent is coming from or the money for January's heating bills, life can be a whole lot more stressful still.

Eating well and taking care of your body can help ease the stress and prevent illness. Stress management techniques—meditation, deep breathing exercises, simple exercise—can be enormously helpful in getting through tense times. When your own best efforts aren't enough, there are non-Western approaches such as acupuncture, yoga, and herbal medicines that can be helpful. You'd be surprised just how much we can learn from the Eastern traditions. These folks have been exploring the mind-body connection for centuries.

CALL-OUTS

Dr. Hillary Wynn, in Panama City, observed: *I don't know how many people know that about half of the people with diabetes also have depression. How many people knew that? Is that surprising to anyone? Chronic illness affects your immune system. Chronic illness affects your perception of the world and yourself and things around you. The immune system and your psychology, your nervous system, communicate with one another.*

People's immunities go down with chronic illness. Immunities go down with depression and chronic mental illness. So the key is whole health—spiritual health, mental health, and physical health. If you remove one piece, then you're not meeting your full potential, and you are potentially dangerous to the people who are close to you.

DON'T BE PASSIVE ABOUT YOUR HEALTH

One of the major barriers to the well-being of any group of people is not having access to good health care. People who are hobbled by illness shoulder all kinds of stresses and burdens, which makes it that much harder for them to get ahead. After all, it is very hard to get a new job or return to school when you are unwilling or unable to get out of bed in the morning.

As you probably know, there are some diseases and conditions that hit black people hardest, such as hypertension, diabetes, HIV/AIDS, and prostate cancer. Some of these diseases you can limit if you live right, and some we can eliminate altogether. We have a lot of power in our hands.

You can do a lot to prevent illness if you get the care you need for you and your family when you need it. This is not always easy, especially if you don't have private insurance or any insurance, and you have to use over-crowded and understaffed facilities in the neighborhood. Long waits are discouraging. Indifferent health-care workers are annoying. The paper work is aggravating. But forget about the inconveniences. This is your health on the line. Don't be passive about protecting it. Good health is too fundamental to your well-being to neglect it for any reason.

CALL-OUTS

Dr. Lewis King, in Compton, California, talked about how to help our children: *The first protection is the protection that comes under physical circumstances—physical protection. And that speaks to the issues of health, nutrition, and safety. Are our homes ones that we can consider to be safe from toxic environments, including humans who are toxic? Are our homes filled with nutritious substances to allow the body and the brain to grow? Do we practice good health habits like drinking six to eight glasses of water a day and eating foods that are not compromised by excess fats and sugars?*

So the first protection we need to look at and address is physical health. That includes things as simple as walking from here to home, walking around and getting some exercise. The second protection comes in the form of emotional health. That's very much misunderstood because the concept that most people talk about is emotional control. You should never control emotions. You should regulate them. There is a real distinction here. Prisons control emotions. Violence controls emotions. What we have to do is to consciously and rationally regulate our emotions ourselves.

The overriding message in this chapter is that we must be active about taking care of our health and mental well-being despite the inequities that remain in the health-care system. For instance, when cost is a major barrier we need to enlist people with the know-how to get insurance through government programs, or to get free care at public hospitals and clinics. We believe all Americans should have health insurance, but millions do not. A universal health-care system would improve health care for everyone. This would be a boon to black people, who make up approximately 20 percent of the nearly forty-five million Americans without health insurance.

OVERCOME THE PAST

In the past, some physicians suggested the reason for different rates of disease between black and white people was due to innate or genetic differences. In a number of illnesses, in fact, ethnic groups may have certain genetic vulnerabilities to particular diseases. There are a few that are specific to certain ethnic groups, such as sickle cell anemia, which mostly attacks people of African and Mediterranean ancestry. Historically, though, the major reason for different health outcomes stems from discrimination in medical practices. Discriminatory practices have been eased, but not entirely eliminated.

What follows is a summary of some of the injustices our ancestors suffered. We cite these to give you an appreciation of what they endured to survive. They did not struggle, however, so that our young people could throw their health away. If we understand what they went through, we might be inspired to take care of ourselves and get ourselves to the doctor when we need to and ought to, despite our historic and often justifiable distrust.

Some older black people have had firsthand experiences with the "separate but equal" health-care institutions in the South. To a certain degree, these negative experiences have shaped black perceptions of the health-care system to this day. To quote Martin Luther King Jr.: "Of all the forms of inequality, injustice in health care is the most shocking and inhumane."

Back in the day, black people often found themselves in segregated clinics and rundown hospital rooms where necessary equipment was frequently old or absent. Their wards were often understaffed and underserviced. If a shortage of supplies and medicine existed, they had better have brought their own bandages with them. Care was limited and provided by black doctors, usually general practitioners, and even these doctors were in short supply. If they so chose, white doctors could refuse to see black patients, and could treat them indifferently even if they did see them. In short, segregated medicine would never make an American history highlight reel.

For much of this period, all medicine was something of a gamble, but for African Americans the odds could be a whole lot worse. They were sometimes singled out for life-threatening research without their knowledge or consent. This practice did not end all that long ago. In Texas from 1956 to 1962, for instance, esteemed white professors at a medical school took black babies who were wards of the state and withheld an essential fatty acid from their baby formula to see what effect it would have on their health.

These researchers had earlier conducted the study on dogs and found that they developed skin problems. The black babies without the normal formula also developed skin lesions, as well as other health problems. After these initial findings, a larger "controlled study" was undertaken using additional black babies, who again received the defective formula. They developed lesions, and a few babies died, but their deaths were attributed to other causes.

As you might suspect, these studies were conducted without informed consent from the parents. No one knows how withholding this necessary fatty acid affected other areas of the infants' growth and development, and no one seemed to care much. Because of such abuses in the past, research on human subjects today requires informed consent and review by an Institutional Review Board that follows strict federal guidelines. But you can't erase these experiences from our cultural memory overnight. They created bad feelings about the medical-care system that resonate to this day.

The Texas experiment is one example out of many of medical abuse. Another common practice was the involuntary sterilization by tubal ligation or hysterectomy of black women without their knowledge. So common, in fact, were these operations, and so frightening, that women called them "Mississippi appendectomies." Since they were often misled about the exact nature of the surgical procedure, black women and men developed a distrust of white physicians, especially in the South.

This distrust was reinforced by the public exposure in 1972 of the notorious Tuskegee Syphilis Study conducted by federal agencies on poor black people. Government investigators began the study in 1932 on Alabama black men who had contracted syphilis. There was no real cure for syphilis at the time the research started, and the researchers wanted to study the natural course of the disease and its complications.

A deep ethical problem arose when antibiotics were discovered in the 1940s to treat syphilis, but the doctors, wanting to preserve their experiment over its natural course, kept the drugs away from their subjects/victims. The study ran for more than forty years without the subjects' consent or even their knowledge that a treatment was available. None of the doctors intervened, and men died who did not need to. When the media exposed the study, distrust penetrated deeply into black communities.

Ordinary black citizens know of this study, and it is one of the reasons we as a people can be suspicious of doctors and hospitals. Even with solid new protection for patients against unethical or unauthorized research, many of us fear doctors may be doing research without our permission. Such suspicions can make us fearful of medications and procedures and cause us to keep an unhealthy distance from hospitals and doctors.

African Americans still wonder if doctors and nurses harbor prejudices that translate into poor care for black people. The cultural memory of segregated medicine has generated a legacy of distrust. Things began to change only after the passage of the Civil Rights Act of 1964. Even after that act was passed, Southern hospitals moved very slowly to desegregate. Some argued that they were running the best system for both races. It wasn't until black communities turned activist and sent complaints to the federal government that the hospitals were forced to respond.

Even after the hospitals were desegregated and the signs for "white" and "colored" were removed from waiting rooms, black patients were afraid to sit on the "white" side. They believed that the doctors and nurses would be angry and not give them proper care if they sat on the "white" side. Surveys show that we still don't trust the health-care system unquestionably. For that reason we are much less likely than white people to volunteer as research subjects.

Suspicions also keep some of us from seeking care, which is ultimately harmful to our health. One of the reasons that certain cancers are so lethal is that too many of us wait too long before seeking help. The problem is compounded because many poor black people do not have adequate health insurance or ready access to health facilities. The legacies from the two-tier system of health care during segregation still have remnants in our health-care system nationwide. The black poor suffer more inequities than middle- and upper-income groups because of additional biases against poor people that are so prevalent in America.

Protect Our Children

One barometer of the health of any population is the infant mortality rate. The black infant mortality rate remains high, as it has for decades. Although the rates for all groups have fallen over time, the black rate runs at least twice the rate for white babies. One of the reasons for this difference is that poor women do not have the same access to prenatal care and delivery as middle-income women. Even if they have access, they may not have the know-how to take advantage of it properly.

The high rate of teenage pregnancy doesn't help much either, as teenage pregnancy is more likely to lead to premature delivery and at-risk births. Complications during pregnancy in women not receiving prenatal care may also result in increased deaths for mother and child. That's why it is so important for all women to receive good prenatal care and why it is important for you to make sure that the young women in your charge do just that. Healthy babies are much more likely to survive and thrive, and black babies on their way to being victors need a good start.

Seize the Day

Another measure of a population's well-being is the life expectancy rate. Around the turn of the twentieth century, life expectancy for Americans was forty-seven years overall and thirty-three years for black people. We have seen spectacular improvement across the board to seventy-seven years on average, but black rates still lag. The life expectancy at birth for white males is seventy-five; for white females it is eighty; for black males it is sixty-nine; and for black females, seventy-six.

Although black women outlive white men, black men don't live as long as they could or should. Despite great medical advances, they are not getting the attention they need.

The top seven causes of death in the United States for African Americans (both men and women) are:

1. Heart disease
2. Cancer
3. Stroke
4. Diabetes
5. Accidents
6. Homicide
7. HIV/AIDS

Okay, we all suspect that black people don't always get the same care and procedures for the same illnesses as white people. Even when willing, physicians may not provide culturally competent care, which can hurt the rapport between doctors and patients of different backgrounds. In fact, given historic fears of not being treated kindly or with understanding, African Americans may avoid physicians and clinics altogether.

Knowing all this, it still doesn't make any sense to ignore your health. When you put off seeking treatment for things like cancers and diabetes, you flirt with disaster. Once again, the word *victim* shows up. Here, too, we have to examine that if there is a presumed victim, at what point do we say to that person, "Here's how you begin to help yourself. Here is what you need to do so that we can move forward."

For instance, we all know people who are grossly overweight, diabetic, and have high blood pressure and breathing problems. The person looks like a victim—the labored breathing, the sad face, the anger, the self-pity. At some point, though, we need for this person to take care of the problems that he can take care of himself, and we all know that the proper thing for him is, number one, to begin to eat properly.

We can help. When he gets around friends or family and starts playing the victim, we cannot indulge him any longer. We need to get him into a position of getting better, stronger, more active in his mind, and in his life. His forebearers did not go hungry so he could eat himself to death.

There are many things that we can all do to improve our health even in a medical system that is not completely free of bias. For instance, if you devalue yourself psychologically, you will devalue your body as well and you will be more likely to engage in dangerous behaviors that put your health in jeopardy.

Many of us are too passive about our health. Through community programs and as individuals we can make changes to support our own health and the health of black children. There has to be action on two fronts: improving the health-care system, for which we need the help of policy makers; and at the same time, becoming personally proactive in supporting healthy lifestyles.

We can play an important role in closing the health gap and eliminating what some call the "black health deficit." Government agencies and the National Medical Association (an organization of mostly black physicians) are actively at work on these issues. These groups are trying to encourage healthy lifestyles. But there is also much we can do to improve our health and that of our families.

TEACH YOUR CHILDREN WELL

Here is something you already know, but a little reminding doesn't hurt: one of the simplest things you can do to get your kids healthier is to have them eat better. How about a cooked breakfast to start the day! This beats giving your child a couple of bucks and sending him to the corner store. These kids are going to buy what we would have bought if someone had given us a dollar or two—a cola, a bag of potato chips, some Twinkies or Ring-Dings or whatever they are selling today.

A kid who comes to school on a donut and a soda loaded with caffeine is starting the day off stupid and probably a little jumpy. So don't give your kids money and expect them to buy something nutritious. They won't.

Fortunately for the two of us old guys, no one in our day had a dollar to give. Ironically, kids today are not so fortunate. Many are left unprotected and undirected. Parents, if you can, make a lunch, even if you have to do it the night before. Do so and explain to your children what they should be eating. The cafeteria won't train your child. You can. We're talking about parenting here. We're talking about not leaving your child unprotected.

In our homes, we need to balance our meals—breakfast, lunch, and dinner, and then maybe a snack. We need protein. We don't need a thousand kinds of rice and then some mashed potatoes and other starches. We understand—the potato tastes good. The potato hasn't an enemy in the world. But there are too many carbs here. Some of us have eaten ourselves into high blood pressure, high cholesterol, high triglycerides, and even diabetes. Come on, people! We can do better.

SLOW DOWN ON THE FAST FOOD

The fast-food places don't help. We line ourselves and our children up there as though we were eating from a food bag. There was a time when we had to sit down to eat, and many of us of a certain age remember getting whupped just for being a few minutes late. The beatings might have been excessive, but the message from our mothers was clear: "I don't care what ball game you're playing. I didn't work all day and cook this good meal so you could miss it."

Families should eat a variety of fruits and vegetables, including dark leafy greens. Focus on eating whole grains instead of highly processed foods, like white bread and white rice. When buying dairy products, choose the low-fat options. Eat lean meats, chicken (without the fatty skin), and fish. Avoid frying your food; healthier cooking methods are roasting, broiling, grilling, and steaming.

It is important to get plenty of Omega-3 fatty acids, which are good for the heart, brain, and other organs. Fish such as salmon, mackerel, and sardines are good sources of Omega-3s. Be sure to drink plenty of water, and go easy on the caffeine. And cut down on sodas, which have little nutritional value. Also include 2 percent milk in your family's diet to help develop and maintain healthy bones. Goat milk is a good substitute, particularly if you have trouble digesting cow's milk.

The government has created a new food pyramid, which is more specific to different age groups. Check it out. The pyramid can be found at www.MyPyramid.gov and is a good source of information on how to eat well. One more thing while we have your attention: ask your physician if a daily multivitamin and fish oil supplement should be added to your diet.

WORK TOGETHER

It's not easy for people living in low-income neighborhoods to get fresh produce and meat. The local supermarkets in these neighborhoods tend to be overpriced and underwhelming when it comes to quality. That is, if there is a supermarket at all. Public transportation is not a great way to do your shopping—we understand that—so if at all possible, get a ride from a friend. Your kids deserve healthy food, and you will appreciate the bargains.

Some communities have started community gardens on empty lots as a way to work together to produce fresh, healthy food that everyone can enjoy. Another way to bring fresh food into the community is to support farmers' markets. These markets are a great source of fresh, locally grown food. They improve the quality of the food in the neighborhood and support the environment at the same time. Churches and other neighborhood organizations would do well to think along these lines.

Eat Together as a Family

When thinking about ways to eat better and grow together as a family, don't overlook the family dinner. Back in our day, families ate together— even if we didn't have much to eat. Eating with your children encourages healthy eating habits and also improves communication. We know you have busy lives: parents working long hours, children busy with school and activities. So make it a point to eat together at least several times a week. This can help keep the family connected and the kids in shape. And whatever you do, turn off the TV! Otherwise, you'll eat too much and talk too little.

Watch Everyone's Weight

Kids are simply getting too fat, and there is no excuse for it. We all have to pitch in and do something about it. We know that obesity causes psychological and physical harm, but it's hard for any of us to change behaviors. Saying, "Turn off the TV and exercise" is easier said than turning off the TV and exercising.

What black people eat and how much physical exercise we get is in large part under our control. We can work together in our communities to create a more exercise-friendly environment. We can put demands on our local government to increase police presence to make being outside safer.

We can encourage churches and mosques to host gyms and fitness clubs. We can advocate for public pools and safe playgrounds. On a more immediate basis, we can get together and form walking groups to encourage each other to get our bodies moving.

One more thing: watch that soul food. Good as it tastes, soul food can be extremely high in fat. We are talking about lots of fried food like pork chops, chicken, and fish—not to mention vegetables seasoned with fatty ham hocks. Soul food dinners also contain an abundance of carbohydrates: macaroni and cheese; candied yams; potatoes, including potato salad; biscuits; and sugary desserts like cake and pie. Our mouths are watering as we describe this food, but we would be better off saving it for special occasions.

Now, as you know, in the time of slavery, black people got the leftover scraps of food to make into their meals. This is where "soul food" comes from. There is a little history here to savor. We understand that. But there is no history at the fast-food chains.

Today, unfortunately, many of us supplement our traditional soul food diet with junk food from fast-food restaurants. Because these foods are cheap and convenient, poor people consume high-fat, high-calorie meals in great quantities. Food chain advertisements are heavily promoted on black television shows and on billboards and posters in black communities. Our ancestors worried that their children would go hungry. We have to worry that ours will get too fat. The risk of obesity is now greater than it has ever been before, especially since we don't burn off a lot of calories sitting in front of a TV screen. The fast food that we all eat—especially those burgers high in saturated fat—we can do without altogether.

PASS ON THE SALT

Did you ever think that soul food is so good that it can't be good for you? If you are salt sensitive—like many black people—you are right. Too much salt for some people can lead to high blood pressure, stroke, and heart failure. Black people are 30 percent more likely to die of heart disease than white people and 40 percent more likely to die of stroke. Again, this is a disparity that African Americans have the power to alter. So pass on that salt. You won't even miss it.

KEEP A LOOKOUT FOR DIABETES

We all know someone with diabetes. It is a chronic illness for which there is no silver bullet. It demands a holistic approach that focuses on prevention and good medical management and requires a whole lot of self-discipline. Type 1 diabetes usually comes on at a young age. It may be hereditary in part, but doctors do not know what causes it. People with Type 1 do not produce insulin.

Type 2 diabetes usually comes on later and is affected by family history as well as by being overweight and exercising too little. Type 2 diabetics may have insulin resistance, but as time goes on, less and less insulin is produced. Children as young as ten are now developing Type 2 diabetes, largely because of obesity.

If you are suffering from diabetes today, you are much better off than you were a generation ago in terms of treatment. But you have to take care of yourself. Once diagnosed, you should ask your primary care doctor for a referral and go to a specialized clinic for diabetes management if it is at all possible. These clinics provide more comprehensive and holistic care and closer monitoring.

You may not even know that you have diabetes. If you have a family history of diabetes, however, you should be closely monitored. Blood sugar levels should be followed to detect pre-diabetes; treatment can slow or prevent the onset of full-blown diabetes. In fact, everyone should be screened, especially people who are overweight. Discovering diabetes early can prevent the complications that occur with uncontrolled diabetes. Studies show that diabetics who maintain good control over their blood sugar can avoid complications and prolong their lives for many, many years. The complications from uncontrolled diabetes can seriously diminish the quality of life—or even end it. The physical disabilities that can result cause physical and psychological pain and hardship.

It is not pretty. Untreated diabetes leads to heart disease, strokes, kidney failure, leg amputations, and blindness. The price is high for ignoring this quiet monster. In our community, where diabetes is epidemic, we should make a pledge to ourselves:

- To lose weight and try to maintain a healthy weight

- To cut down on high-carb, high-fat, high-calorie food

- To get exercise regularly—walking helps

- To get off our collective behinds and stay active, even around the house

If you are under a doctor's care, you should be sure to have a glucose monitor to check glucose levels daily, or as the doctor prescribes. If you're on medications, take them regularly. If you need to take insulin, you need close management from a physician or a nurse practitioner. And to check your overall control of your blood sugar, you should see your physician at least twice a year to get a special blood test called A1C that measures blood sugar control over the previous two to three months. You need regular foot and eye exams as well.

Family members should learn about diabetes. Managing diabetes takes discipline and reordering of lifestyles and eating habits. This, too, takes a village, at least an extended network of family and friends who get involved to aid the afflicted family member. Helping diabetics to keep appointments is important. When a young person has diabetes, they may need a great deal of adult help to keep the disease under control. There is information at diabetes clinics or through the American Diabetes Association, and online as well.

REMEMBER MR. TOOTH DECAY

When talking about health, too many of us, including health-care workers, neglect to talk about teeth. But good oral health should be part of any larger conversation about health. Tooth decay, for instance, may not be the most serious disease in childhood, but it can get nasty. If untreated, it leads to infections, mouth disease, and damaged or lost teeth.

What is more, damaged teeth don't look very good. In our world, let's face it, it pays to look good. For better or worse, cosmetic problems create barriers to getting a job and forming social relationships.

As in other areas of health care, dental care for the poor has been difficult to obtain. More than one hundred million children and adults do not have dental insurance, either privately or publicly. With public coverage like Medicaid, getting access to a dentist is not guaranteed. Often dentists may refuse publicly insured clients because the reimbursement rates are too low. Poor people may not know how to find dental care when it does exist, and some may avoid dentists out of fear of pain.

We know old memories die hard, but modern techniques have made dental procedures much less painful and more comfortable than in your grandparents' day or even your parents'. A little minor discomfort is certainly worth it to protect your teeth and avoid painful mouth diseases. Educational programs to raise awareness help too.

It would also be helpful, of course, if health clinics and hospitals had dental services on-site and not separated in places that are hard to get to. For children, a visit to a pediatric dentist could be part of the scheduled routine when the child goes for a well-child visit. The easier it is for parents to get to the dentist, the more likely they are to bring their children for proper dental care.

Poor children are less likely to get sealants that protect against cavities or to get instructions in oral hygiene. Some kids have never been told that they should brush their teeth twice a day—once after breakfast and once before bedtime—and floss once a day. Too many of them don't know what flossing is—or brushing for that matter. Make sure that the kids in your world—grandkids, neighbors, students—do know. Don't take this for granted.

The purpose of fluorinated water is to protect against cavities by strengthening the tooth enamel. Recently, some people have raised concerns about fluoride. If you have concerns, be sure to talk to your dentist. There are some dentists who question fluoride's safety. But there has been more than fifty years worth of research monitoring fluoride in the water. Reports show that fluoride in the water is especially helpful for those without access to regular dental care. It helps to prevent one of the most common childhood diseases—dental decay—which is five times as common as asthma in five- to seventeen-year-olds. Fluorinated rinses and toothpaste with fluoride are also helpful. But be careful. Fluoride products, even toothpaste, should not be swallowed. In high quantities, fluoride can make you sick—especially small children.

Even baby teeth need to be cleaned and monitored. Tots should see a dentist by their first birthday and then have regular checkups. Later, school-based dental health clinics are convenient and effective, as are off-site programs that provide services to the public schools. Dental schools often offer an additional resource by sponsoring clinics for low-income patients. The fact that the dentists are still in school shouldn't worry you. Parents in cities with dental schools should look for such programs.

As seems to be true for many diseases, African Americans have a higher risk for contracting cancers of the mouth and throat. They are also at higher risk for gum disease, particularly smokers. Tooth decay doesn't just hurt the teeth. The infection can get into the blood stream and infect the whole body. Even young people can lose all of their teeth, and dentures aren't cool in anyone's book. While Medicaid may cover some dental care, it isn't covered in all states. The costs associated with dental care can be formidable for poor people, so they often do without.

To improve oral health for poor people, many issues related to public policy have to be addressed. While the whole country needs more dentists, there is also a problem with the distribution of dentists. Many do not practice in poor neighborhoods. The steep cost of dental school (more than fifty thousand to sixty thousand dollars a year) does not encourage even more sacrifice after graduation. Plus, there is not a lot of scholarship help available for low-income students pursuing a career in dentistry. A little scholarship money could go a long way. Because of the shortage of dentists of color, white dentists do much of the work in black communities, but often without training in cultural competence. We should encourage this type of training.

The neglect of dental service for the poor requires that we turn activist on the dental community. Beyond good health, a nice set of teeth also supports feelings of self-esteem and confidence.

CONTROL YOUR CANCER RISKS

One good way we can lower our risks is by getting regular checkups to detect cancer and by seeking help without delay. Because of awareness programs, black men are finally catching on that checkups for prostate cancer are a good thing. These exams aren't exactly fun, but they only last a minute, and the same cannot be said of cancer, which is a major killer of black men.

Doctors don't know all the reasons, but black men are more likely to contract and die from this cancer than white men. Black women also must go for regular checkups to detect breast cancer and cancer of the reproductive organs in particular. With early detection and prevention, many black lives can be saved. To win the battle with cancer, family members have to join in and push your loved ones to do the right thing.

SPEAK OUT ABOUT HIV/AIDS

We may not hear about it as much, but HIV/AIDS certainly hasn't gone away, especially not in black communities. African Americans, who make up 13 percent of the United States population, account for about 40 percent of AIDS cases since the epidemic began, and today they account for almost half of the new cases and about 56 percent of the deaths.

HIV/AIDS is one of the leading causes of death among black women between the ages of twenty-five and thirty-four. HIV/AIDS rates among black teenagers have risen, now accounting for 65 percent of new cases, and rates among black women are also about 67 percent of new cases. This is a tragedy. We must be more active in the battle against AIDS. We have remained too silent for too long because of the shame and stigma attached to this disease.

Early educational programs were not particularly effective. One reason was that some black people, who distrusted the medical system in the first place, helped spread rumors that HIV was created by white doctors in a conspiracy to infect black people.

In the beginning, too, many of us believed AIDS was mostly confined to white homosexual men. After all, that is who we saw on TV and in the magazines. But times have changed, and attitudes are beginning to change as well. Drug users who share needles, and black men who have sex with men on the "down low," have brought the disease into the everyday community through heterosexual relations. People are waking up to the risk.

A large number of African Americans may be engaging in risky behaviors because they don't value their own lives and the lives of others as much as they should. As a result, prevention efforts, including safe sex and needle exchange programs, have lagged in black communities.

Come on, people! It is time for us to take care of ourselves. If you are having sex and haven't had a condom separating you and your partner, you better hustle down to the clinic and get tested. You owe it to yourself, and you owe it to the community. Pregnant women with HIV/AIDS need to talk to their doctors about how to protect their babies from becoming infected.

Women, if your man refuses to put on a condom, you should refuse to have sex with him. Period. This isn't a guy you want in your life anyhow, let alone in your bed. If need be, buy some condoms for him. They don't have to come in bright colors, but they must be made of latex or polyurethane (an alternative for people allergic to latex). Both partners should be sure to read the instructions on the package. Condoms do not provide 100 percent protection against AIDS or pregnancy, but then again, umbrellas don't provide 100 percent protection against the rain and we still use them.

Unfortunately, you cannot always expect even a regular partner to tell the truth about his or her other sexual contacts.

The Black AIDS Institute, located in Los Angeles, California, is making pioneering efforts to check the spread of HIV/AIDS among African Americans by using innovative education and prevention campaigns. Faith-based and black civil rights organizations should also get behind these efforts to curb lethal, self-destructive behaviors.

As is obvious, AIDS has been a major strain on black communities already struggling with a host of other problems. We have heard people say they don't want to talk about AIDS because they can't take on any more burdens. But silence will only make this burden heavier. This is one disease we can't talk away. No one has to get AIDS. Every case is avoidable. But we cannot continue to deny what is a reality. If our people stepped up their activist educational efforts and avoided high-risk sexual behaviors, we could make an immediate difference. Get your local clinics, settlement houses, and churches involved in the battle.

RESPECT YOUR LUNGS

We should also fill the battle lines against asthma among black children. Black children and young adults are roughly three to four times more likely than white people to be hospitalized for asthma and two to six times more likely to die. Many black kids with asthma show up much more often than they should in emergency rooms.

If you're a parent or a friend of such a child, you know how hard it is to keep a home free of allergens, especially older homes and apartments. But there are things you can do, like listening to advice from doctors and nurses on how to respond to an asthma attack, and promoting stop-smoking programs to help others break the habit. You should never expose children to second-hand smoke. There are many good reasons for breaking the smoking habit, but the health of your kids is the best of all. And you should always educate your kids about the risks of smoking. Just because the billboard says you should smoke doesn't mean you have to. We must pay attention to the surgeon general's warnings: lung, mouth, and throat cancers; heart disease; stroke; and emphysema are all strongly linked to tobacco use. We all have some control over whether cigarettes will kill us or our kids.

RESPECT YOUR MIND

Substance and alcohol abuse affects all segments of American society, but such abuse particularly takes a toll on poor people of any ethnicity. Abuse of drugs like heroin, cocaine, crack, or marijuana leads to addictions that will damage your physical and mental health. The same is true for alcohol.

Addicted individuals hurt their families, become a burden on the community, and are more likely to engage in violence and other criminal activity. A great number of people end up in jail because of the illegal activity associated with drug abuse. And then, if they do not get help after being released from jail, many return to a life of drugs, mental illness, unemployment, and often homelessness. You're right. This is not an attractive picture. Let's do something about it.

While we know that crack possession is more stiffly punished than possession of powder cocaine, and we see the bias in these numbers, we also see what crack can do to a community. Junkies and drug dealers can destroy a poor neighborhood. They add more than their fair share to the high rates of crime and the senseless homicides among our kids.

These druggies not only hurt the community, but they also hurt themselves—even to the point of death. An untold number of such overdoses may actually be suicides of people who can scarcely tell the difference between life and death in the first place. If overdosing weren't worry enough, drug abusers are also in extreme danger of contracting HIV/AIDS from contaminated needles. This is one of the main ways that HIV/AIDS has been spread among black people, along with a whole rash of other diseases such as hepatitis. We're told that needle exchange programs can be effective in decreasing the spread of disease, but we know that getting off the needle altogether is more effective still.

Alcohol also contributes to the spread of HIV/AIDS, and you know why. When people are drunk, they are more likely to do things they regret—like engaging in high-risk sex. They also regret driving into bridge abutments or calling the Kung Fu master on the next bar stool a punk. Lethal drunk driving tragedies are far too common. You don't have to give up responsible drinking to avoid these problems, but you do have to give up the abuse of alcohol.

Chronic alcoholism has life-threatening effects on a person's mind and body. In both men and women, alcoholism can produce dementia and cirrhosis of the liver that can end in death. Alcohol abuse increases the chances of contracting cancers of the mouth, gastrointestinal tract, bladder, and other organs. Alcohol misuse in pregnant women is particularly tragic as it can cause harm to the unborn baby, including mental retardation. Alcoholism also costs a lot of money.

Excessive drinking disrupts families, triggers family violence, and leads to some of the worst parenting on the planet. It may look fun and sexy on the billboards, but there is nothing fun about the detox tank and nothing sexy about the DTs (delirium tremens).

To the degree we can, we should protect our kids from ads that promote drinking or smoking. We've got to educate them. The corporations aren't about to. Often low-income communities are saturated with liquor stores and billboard advertisements for liquor. Some black activists have protested and had billboards removed. Others have put pressure on municipalities to stop licensing so many liquor stores in black communities.

We have to expand these efforts and other education and treatment programs in poor communities. About 25 percent of those admitted to publicly funded substance abuse programs are black. But treatment programs are only effective in about 40 percent of the cases, and many of those later relapse. We need to do a better job with our substance abusers.

LIFE LESSONS

For seventeen years music great Ray Charles was bedeviled by his dependence on heroin. After his third arrest in 1965, he decided it was time to put the devil behind him. As was shown in the movie *Ray*, quitting was not at all easy. The addiction had wormed its way inside him and had to be rooted out. But with the help of friends, family, and community resources, Charles persisted and succeeded. There are some musicians who believed they could not succeed without drugs. Ray Charles proved them wrong. He went on to enjoy good health and an enormously productive career for almost forty more years.

There are some questions we need to ask. What types of twelve-step programs, such as Alcoholics Anonymous, would work best with black people? How can the better ones be modified to be culturally sensitive? Would predominantly black groups work better for black substance abusers? Some reports indicate that clinicians who are in tune with their clients' cultural values are more likely to succeed. Training in cultural competence is helpful for those treating substance abusers. But whether the counselors are sensitive or not, we must all do more to reduce substance abuse and drug dealing in our communities.

If your kids stay in school and believe in their futures, they are less likely to be lured into mind-bending drug abuse. That is a given. Our activists—and we should all be activists—must demand new public policies and initiatives to treat substance abuse in poor communities. We all have many burdens that will not disappear in the temporary "high" of drug sedation. In the end, substance abuse only creates more obstacles to success for our youth. You can't become a victor if you are always stoned.

LOSE THE GUNS AND THE RAGE

Homicide is the leading cause of death among young black men. That's crazy, but it is true. Suicide has increased as well. We sense that many black youths who are acting violently are sad and depressed. One of the symptoms of depression, particularly in adolescents, is extreme irritability and touchiness, which easily leads to fights in the home or street. This irritability, of course, is associated with feelings of anger that are also connected to feelings of mistreatment.

Physical punishment, child abuse, domestic violence, and psychological abuse fuel much of this anger in black kids. Rap music feeds the rage. Too much of it has an aggressive, confrontational tone even when the lyrics are positive. But in gangsta rap, the aggressive beat and harsh speech projects anger. Anger is so strong among some black kids that it is seen by some as a mental-health problem. Kids who suffer from attention deficit disorder, post-traumatic stress disorder, and conduct disorders are ripe for anger disorders when they experience additional stresses and blows to their self-esteem. It is important that these youths get the mental-health treatment they need.

CALL-OUTS

Dr. James Kelly, of Cincinnati, responded to a question asking why teenagers are so angry: *Quite often anger is a mask for hurt and for pain. And part of what you have to be able to do is really talk with that young man about where he's hurting, and where there's pain. Because we have learned over the years that people won't respond to our hurt and to our pain, but they will respond to our anger. So we act out our anger. We live out our anger. So I would encourage you to really spend some time with him, and find out, you know, where he is really hurting.*

Many of the people in jail for violent crimes are victims of child abuse and neglect. Fifty to 75 percent of young jail inmates have a diagnosable mental disorder. The number of young offenders in need of psychiatric care is astounding. Yet few mental health services are provided. And even then, there is an overreliance on medications. Whatever their value, those drugs won't necessarily help these inmates navigate life after release from prison.

FACE UP TO MENTAL HEALTH ISSUES

The history of mental health treatment for black people, especially in the South, is even less honorable than the history of physical health. Although treatment has obviously become more equitable, many mental health workers today fail to see how the legacy of racism contributes not only to genuine stress among black people but also to resistance to those professionals who treat it.

As we see it, the truth is that being black in America aggravates all mental health problems that black people experience. Psychotherapists need to consider the stress associated with being discriminated against and rejected—or the fear of the same. Ideally, therapists from all backgrounds will free themselves of bias. If they do, and the word spreads, hesitant African Americans might become more receptive to mental health care. This is easier said than done, we know, but the cultural memory of black America cannot be overlooked.

Mental health is not a popular subject in black communities. We are a strong people who survived slavery and Jim Crow. Mental illness is seen by many black people as a sign of weakness. Some of us are in complete denial about mental illness in regard to ourselves or to the people in our lives. But we can't wish it away. Mental health is a serious issue for black people.

In a 1999 report on mental health, Dr. David Satcher, then U.S. surgeon general, observed that although the rate of mental illness was higher among black people than white people, African Americans were less likely to seek out and have access to care. And sometimes they didn't trust getting care from white therapists because of fears of being misunderstood.

Many black people still fear involuntary and unjustified long-term commitment to mental hospitals although there are many laws in place today that protect the rights of patients. Such fears could be lessened if there were increased awareness and open discussion about mental illness, which is as real as any other health problem. Until we face up to the problem, depression, anxiety disorders, schizophrenia, and bipolar disorders among black people will continue to burden us.

Come to grips with depression.

Although less likely to report depression than white people, those black people who do suffer are more likely to face severe and more disabling bouts of depression. Despite the severity, they are much less likely than white people to seek treatment. Some black people may see their illness in a religious context as a troubled relationship with God and seek spiritual counseling instead, which may help in some cases. Some black ministers have joined with mental-health agencies in order to refer patients and collaborate in their care. A few churches provide professional mental-health services on the grounds of the church itself. We think this is a good trend because people trust the church and will seek and accept help when the church has said it's okay to have mental-health issues.

Preventing youth suicide is an especially important challenge for the church, mental-health programs, and families. Since suicide is often connected to clinical depression, it is important that we recognize it as a serious problem and be on the alert for symptoms in ourselves and others. We should urge anyone at risk to seek help. The major symptoms of depression are important for people to know:

- Ongoing sad, anxious, or "numb" mood

- Loss of pleasure and interest in activities, including sex

- Restlessness, irritability, chronic anger, or mood swings

- Sleeping all the time or not much at all; waking up in the middle of the night or very early in the morning

- Reduced appetite and weight loss, or increased appetite and weight gain

- Persistent physical symptoms that do not respond to treatment (such as chronic pain or stomach problems)

- Lack of attention to personal hygiene and appearance

- Difficulty focusing, concentrating, remembering, or making decisions

- Fatigue or loss of energy

- Feeling overly guilty, hopeless, or worthless

- Thoughts of suicide or dying

In addition, people with bipolar disorder (manic-depressive illness) often show severe mood swings—moving from depression to euphoria.

Former Surgeon General Satcher suggested that it is best to think in terms of risk factors and protective factors when considering mental disorders. For suicide, risk factors include:

- Previous suicide attempt

- Mental disorder

- Co-occurring mental and alcohol- and substance-abuse disorders

- Family history of suicide

- Hopelessness

- Impulsive and/or aggressive tendencies

- Barriers to accessing mental-health treatment

- Relational, social, work, or financial loss

- Physical illness

- Easy access to lethal methods

- Unwillingness to seek help because of stigma attached to mental and substance-abuse disorders and/or suicidal thoughts

- Influence of significant people—family members, celebrities, peers who have died by suicide—both through personal contact or inappropriate media representations

- Cultural and religious beliefs

- Local epidemics of suicide that have a contagious influence

- Isolation, a feeling of being cut off from other people

If you spot a pattern of likely symptoms, you do not have to sit around and wait for the worst to happen. You can strengthen the protective factors in the sufferer:

- Help find effective and appropriate clinical care for mental, physical, and substance-abuse disorders.

- Restrict access to highly lethal methods of suicide.

- Arrange for family and community support.

- Support ongoing medical and mental health-care relationships.

- Share skills in problem solving, conflict resolution, and nonviolent handling of disputes.

- Encourage cultural and religious beliefs that discourage suicide and support self-preservation instincts.

By the way, the emotional problems associated with suicide can also lead to homicide. Often there are no ready cause-and-effect answers to the motives of either. Many of the same risk and protective factors could be applied to both homocide and suicide. So keep your eyes open, not just in your home, but on the street as well. We need to actively support violence- and suicide-prevention programs to lower the number of tragic and needless deaths in our communities.

Seek appropriate treatment.

Many black people go to hospital emergency rooms for mental crises. It might be because there is less stigma in going to an ER than to a facility or department labeled "mental health (or psychiatric) clinic." People with a mental crisis are in great pain and require immediate attention. This is the kind of attention they feel they can get in the emergency room from the doctors on duty better than they could at a sluggish and bureaucratic mental health center. Other names such as "family health center" or "wellness center" may be more inviting to people who might feel stigmatized by going to a mental health clinic, even when it accepts walk-in patients.

A growing number of mental illnesses are now thought to be traceable to disorders in brain function and genetic predispositions. People with a family history of depressive disorder, bipolar disorder (manic-depressive illness), or schizophrenia are more likely to develop such disorders, particularly in stressful environments. The understanding that these illnesses may represent a chemical imbalance in the brain is increasing. It helps us all see the problem as a disease, which is less stigmatizing than a "mental disorder." We can view our affliction or that of a family member much the way we would an illness like high blood pressure or diabetes. We can set aside the notion that mental disorders are related to poor character, moral frailty, or personal weakness. This is a big step forward.

ENCOURAGE CULTURALLY COMPETENT CARE

To undo the legacies from the past, we would encourage all health facilities to be more welcoming to black people. America has a long history of valuing a white life more than a black life. Those of us who have felt unwanted and rejected need to be reassured. We need to believe that health personnel really care about us. Friendliness and respect from staff members are certain to make us more comfortable about accessing health care. A movement in the medical field to have health personnel trained in culturally competent care is now under way.

The goal is to improve understanding and communication between patients and health professionals. The first step for a practitioner in becoming culturally competent is to take a look inward. We all have a perspective, a lens through which we view the world. That lens influences our subconcious assumptions about people—whether they are poor people, people of other races or ethnicities, the other gender, a different sexual orientation, people from different religions, or people with disabilities.

Once we examine our own biases and stereotypes about other groups, we are better prepared to interact with others with a more open mind. Such training may lessen the health workers' bias that leads to the lapses we have been discussing. The state of New Jersey has passed legislation to require physicians to have courses in culturally competent care as part of their requirements to get a license to practice. It would greatly benefit all of us if other states followed suit and included other licensed health personnel such as nurses, social workers, and psychologists. Loud, active voices coming from black communities may facilitate these important policy changes for the better.

Our health is a two-way street. If we are to ask more of the health-care system, we should give more in return. If we ask for their respect, we should give them ours. We should also take an active part in changing lifestyles, behaviors, habits, and attitudes that imperil our health. We can play victim all we want, but it does not make us one bit healthier. In health, as in life, we can and should be victors.

7

THE HIGH PRICE
OF VIOLENCE

When watching *Birth of a Nation* in 1915, the year the movie premiered, our imaginary sixteen-year-old would have seen the whole spectrum of pre-civil rights stereotypes on epic display. Black people were criminally minded, stupid, violent, oversexed, and prone to sexual assault—particularly of white women. If this sounds a lot like the behavior of many Southern white people, there is good reason for that. It was.

In the South, white people often projected their own violent behavioral patterns onto black people. In fact, it was extremely rare for a black man to rape a white woman; one historian has said that the likelihood was about equal to her chance of being struck by lightning.

Plus, the stakes were scarily high. Even the *imagined* rapes of white women in the South could lead to widespread lynching of black men. It was the infamous murder of fourteen-year-old Emmett Till in 1955 for whistling at a white woman that galvanized black communities and woke up much of white America to the continued possibility of such barbarous behavior even in the era of television and integration.

The high rate of crime in some black communities today may have its roots in Southern culture, but we can't lay it all on the South. Poverty, fatherless homes, and the lack of good parenting all aggravate it. The angry kids who come out of these homes are all the more vulnerable to the pull of the streets and the lure of crime. When introduced to the criminal justice system at an early age, they often grow hardened and even more tied to the kind of self-destructive behavior that sends them back to prison. This, in turn, leads to mind-boggling rates of incarceration for black men.

At last count, about 2.2 million Americans were in jail, one of the highest rates in the industrialized world, and the number of black males among the incarcerated ranged between eight hundred thousand and one million. When they are let out of jail, there is little for them to do productively, and their opportunities in life range from few to none. In turn, feelings of hopelessness, fatalism, and nihilism lead to more crime and often death at an early age—by suicide or homicide.

Crime and killing in black communities confirm, in the minds of many people, that black men are prone to violence. That word *prone* suggests that black males have a natural leaning toward violence, but there was little that was "natural" about the brutalizing impact of a culture based on slavery, both for black and white people.

LIFE LESSONS

Although he failed to legislate against slavery, as he was a slave owner himself, Thomas Jefferson saw its corrosive effects up close: *The whole commerce between master and slave is a perpetual exercise of the most boisterous passions, the most unremitting despotism on the one part, and degrading submissions on the other. Our children see this, and learn to imitate it . . . The parent storms, the child looks on, catches the lineaments of wrath, puts on the same airs in the circle of smaller slaves, gives loose to his worst passions, and thus nursed, educated, and daily exercised in tyranny, cannot but be stamped by it with odious peculiarities. The man must be a prodigy who can retain his manners and morals undepraved by such circumstances.*

People who are treated violently by an oppressor are more likely to try to gain power over others by controlling them with the use of violence, even within their own group. It is interesting that many black parents who use physical punishment on their children call it a "whupping." High levels of violence—child abuse, domestic violence, sibling abuse, personal assaults, and homicide—continue to plague our community centuries after the slave master put his whip away. Come on, people, we can do better!

CHANGE THE THINGS YOU CAN

In the days of the Klan, evil dwelled outside and rode in. Protection, meanwhile, came from within the neighborhood. Now the attack comes from within the village. This change, as you know, is not necessarily for the better.

The Klan pushed our people together. Today's violence pulls us apart. Often we know who is doing the attacking, and yet we are rendered mute for fear not only from the people who committed the crime but also from their family and friends. To be a silent eyewitness in our own village is to know a level of frustration even our ancestors did not know. We feel isolated among our own people and no more empowered than our ancestors did. This attitude of "don't snitch" is not limited to incidents of violent crime in poor communities. It is a pervasive attitude in America. Employees refuse to speak up when shoddy building materials are used; administrators do not report illegal financial reporting; doctors don't report colleagues who put patients at risk. We need to change our societal values to ones that build community rather than destroy it.

As a parent or caregiver, you can help change the village, one household at a time. You must protect your children—meaning you must know where they are playing when they leave the house, whom they are playing with, what they are doing, how you can reach them. You know how much violence is out there now—loud arguments, profanity, shootings, stabbings—and you don't want your kids to be part of it. You know how real the threat is and how constant. You know the sounds you hear and the sleep you lose.

We know how much we are asking of you. But we all know, too, that to be victors, your kids can't be victims and they can't be victimizers. We do not have control over all of the elements that encourage violence in our community, but we do have an obligation to examine factors that we can control. Yes, we do. We are not an inherently criminal or violent people, but we commit and suffer a disproportionate share of crime. It is important to understand the legacy of slavery, but it is even more important to transcend it, to break the psychological shackles that still bind us. Our high rates of poverty, lack of community supports, and self-defeating behaviors can be changed, and must be.

Black communities and families—if inspired to positive action—can do a lot to reduce crime and violence. We must have the creative help and cooperation of law enforcement and the criminal justice system, but we must ask for it to get it, demanding it if need be.

AVOID EASY ANSWERS

Throughout history, adults have often feared teenagers, and they continue to do so today. One woman told us, "I hear the statistics, and I read about these young men who are being arrested and sentenced every day. Yet it seems like you lock up seven and ten pop up, ready to do whatever silliness or seriousness there is to do to get arrested."

"So with all of the numbers," she added, "with all of these people I've been reading about who are being incarcerated and how they're building more jails, I don't see how that's true when I look out and I see so many who seem to be in the same place and same position, like locusts."

When did they start putting armed guards in the hallways, do you remember? When did they escalate to metal detectors at the schoolhouse door, do you remember that? When did they put bars on the doors and windows? When did schools turn from a place of innocent learning to an armed camp, and why? These are questions that we have to ask and keep asking until we have answers.

FACE THE FACTS HEAD-ON

Here are some unfortunate facts: Black youths are six times more likely to die from homicide than white youths and seven times more likely to commit a homicide. During the last thirty years, close to 50 percent of the homicides in the United States have been committed by black people, mostly black men, and 94 percent of the victims of black killers were black. Is this crazy or what? Homicide, in fact, is the leading cause of death among black males between the ages of fifteen and twenty-nine and has been for decades.

There has been a drop in the overall rate of homicide among black males in recent years, but the likely reason for this is that so many more black men are in prison. In California, for instance, the state prison population increased sevenfold just in the last twenty-five years. Although homicide rates among young black men have decreased, black males under eighteen are more likely to kill than those over twenty-five.

Too many of you have heard and seen on the news a reporter stand in front of yellow ribbon and say without emotion, "Well, today a young black man was shot and killed." And you just look at him and you think, "Well, another day, another brother. Stuff happens." No. Nothing "just happens." We make it happen. We can make it un-happen.

To get beyond the numbers, talk to the coroner. Ask the coroner what's the age, the average age, of these deaths, these shootings. Ask him what it feels like to pick up the heart of a fourteen-year-old child who's been blown to pieces by a bullet. Most of the victims aren't even old enough to vote. And it's not only the police killing these young men. They're shooting each other. This is insane. We cry and we bury. But we do little.

CALL-OUTS

Dr. Marie Pierre-Louis, in Washington DC, chief medical examiner for the District of Columbia, reported on the deaths she had seen: *It is not easy for us to see your body on our autopsy table. To have to crack open your chest with shears, sew up your skull, see your brain come out. It hurts. Sometimes your head is just like a bag of bones, a bag of stones, and it takes a lot of effort to reconstruct your face so your parents can recognize you, so we can give your body back to them. Sometimes you survive for years, in a wheelchair with sores all over your back that do not heal completely. Someone has to clean you. Someone has to feed you.*

Education is very important. And you have, yourself, to make the decision to say no to this violence, to remain in school. Because, you see, if you don't get that high school certificate, if you don't get a certificate from college, there is one waiting for you at the Office of the Chief Medical Examiner. It is the death certificate.

The homicide problem is so out of control that some pundits have suggested that these killings are part of the "culture" of the black poor. Gangsta rappers glorify violence to young black teens. Many—in a twisted way—may feel they gain status among their friends by shooting someone even if they go to jail for years or even for life. Some teens have been killing themselves with firearms instead of killing others. As a result, the suicide rate has risen among young black males in the past three decades to approach the rate for all young males combined.

GET THE GUNS OUT OF YOUR LIFE

Homicide and suicide have a lot in common. They are both forms of violence in which guns are often the weapon of choice. We can't allow this. Parents and caregivers, you need to ask your child, "Do you know if there's a gun in this house? Is there a gun outside of this house? Is there a gun someplace where you can get it?" You have got to know, and you have to let your child know the terrible consequences if he ever pulls that trigger. And on your end, if you have arms in the house, you better make sure that they are locked away where even Houdini couldn't get at them. Too many young children play with guns found in their homes and accidentally shoot themselves or others. No grief can match that of the parents responsible for their own child's death.

Unfortunately, however, parents and caregivers often don't know their kid has a gun when they should be keeping tabs. How afraid must you be of your child to allow this? Worse, some of you—and you know who we mean—keep unsecured guns in a home with a kid you know is ready to do harm. And there are more than a few such kids in our world. They are symptoms of the fatalism and hopelessness rampant among poor black youth.

STOP THE CYCLE OF VIOLENCE

If your child gets a gun, puts it to somebody, and shoots, he kills the person and takes two important brains out of society: the victim's and his. Those are two young men who will never see manhood as it is meant to be. Today, a kid who loses a fistfight does not need to endure the embarrassment of losing or even experience the satisfaction of coming back and evening the score. No, now when his friends say, "You can't let him do that to you," he gets a gun and returns with revenge on his mind.

Where is the thought behind all of this? Who is the victim in this situation now? And how do we stop a cycle of violence that would be foolish if it were not so often fatal? The fact is, if we don't stop it, no one will. A gated community does no good if the problem is within the gates. It falls to us to grab that kid who is hurt and angry and say, "You've got to stop. You've got to think. If you blow this kid away, two of you will be gone."

There is no winner here except the devil. There is no honor in this at all. The shooter's first emotion after he blows somebody's brains out is,

Damn, I have to get my sorry behind out of here! Very few of them stand and raise their fists and say, "I've done it!"

Too many kids don't really understand until it is too late how brutal gun violence can be. And our culture is much too accepting of violence as an appropriate response. We should be building on Martin Luther King Jr.'s legacy of nonviolence as a peaceful way of resolving conflicts.

CALL-OUTS

Curtis Boyd, an investigator for the Jackson County, Missouri, medical examiner's office, emphasized what guns are doing: *We deal with dead people every day. I'm going to make it graphic. That's my job. Let's talk about a person who has been shot, we'll say with an AK-47. It's a very popular gun on the streets right now. Say that someone has been shot, say in the head. Sometimes the entire area may be open, flayed open— blood, brain matter, tissue, hair sticking all over the place. It's not good.*

Over the last three years, there's been an average of 128 homicides in our county. Of those 128—47 percent are black males. And I say that, 47 percent doesn't sound like a high number, however, only 25 percent are white males. But then you also have all the other ethnicities that we deal with. So 47 percent, almost half, have been black males.

The need to stop hurting our children and ourselves has been eloquently expressed as a primary concern in black communities. A nonviolent way of life would make black communities sanctuaries where all felt protected, including the children. To make this happen, black people have to rein in their anger and recognize that abuse and violence are not part of the solution for the problems we face today. Our ancestors must weep when they see the black poor so entrapped by their rage. African Americans need to help and support each other to end the epidemic of violence in our communities.

Few people have witnessed the results of the violence in the community the way ER doctors have. Their lives are awash in its consequences.

Dr. Kenneth Davis Jr., who worked in the University of Cincinnati Hospital, is one such doctor: *I'm here to talk about violence, because that's what my work is. I deal in people who suffer all kinds of trauma. In recent years it's been handgun violence. We've seen the number of shootings in this city triple in the last three or four years. Handgun violence is the leading cause of death of our young men, between ages sixteen and thirty-five.*

We're seeing shooting victims as young as three, five years old these days. It's getting worse. Why is it getting worse? One of the problems, we think, is the drug trafficking. Talking to colleagues of mine in other cities like Los Angeles and New York, they say the only way you're going to solve the problem is get rid of the drugs. Otherwise, the shootings will continue. What do we do to stop this?

For every person who goes to the coroner, there are three more that I see. For every homicide-related shooting, there are three other people that are shot and survive. And those are the ones you don't see. And it's not like on the videos. I have a fourteen-year-old boy who was shot in the neck. He's paralyzed from the neck down. He's on a ventilator the rest of his life. He cries every day. But you don't see him, because he didn't go back home.

One of the things that we're going to try and do at the university hospital is initiate a violence intervention program. Ninety-five percent of the shootings that we see are African-American young men. While we have them in the hospital, we're going to try and intervene to break the cycle. Whether it's to try and intervene in the justice system to help them negotiate that or to see if we can get them out of the environment that's caused the problem.

We will see if we can help them in terms of education and job opportunities that will change their lives so that we don't see them again. Probably close to half the people we see are people we've seen before. So we're going to try and break the cycle.

Breaking the cycle of violence is an important step to take. Young victims of violence naturally want to retaliate, and they need counselors, parents, and caregivers to help redirect them from "evening the score." This scenario is repeated in too many gang- and drug-related killings. One way to break the cycle is with violence prevention programs in schools and community agencies—starting early—to teach children anger management skills and nonviolent methods for managing conflict.

Parents and caregivers, you know that this teaching must also be coming from the home. That's where the responsibility begins. That's where the responsibility also ends. If your son murders someone else's child, your life, as you know it, will be over. It will be as forever wretched as the victim's parents'. One single bullet can ruin a hundred lives.

SUPPORT THE SURVIVORS

As many of you know firsthand, a killing leaves the families of homicide victims filled with overwhelming grief, and they often have nowhere to turn for help. These families need support to get back on their feet. Extended family members and churches can help. But mental-health services, including bereavement groups, should be available to people who have lost a loved one to violence. The pain associated with the loss of a child lasts a lifetime. Some survivors help heal by channeling their grief into an active fight against the causes of violence in their communities.

We should listen to the voices of those who have lost family members to murder. They have a lot to share.

CALL-OUTS

Kenneth Barnes Sr., of Washington DC, shared his experience: *I was asked to say a couple of words on behalf of homicide victims and their families. For those of y'all who know me, nine years ago, I walked across this stage. I'm a graduate of UDC. I was getting my master's, I had retired on disability, and I decided to go on toward my doctorate and I was accepted at Loyola College in Baltimore. Around my third year, I got news that no parent wants to hear, and that was that my son had been shot and murdered. He owned a clothing store in Washington DC. He was shot by a young man, seventeen years of age. And this young man, we later found out, had killed at least two other people of which the authorities were aware.*

What we need to understand is that there's an epidemic taking place in America, and that epidemic is death by gun violence. And it's killing young African-American males. Where are our leaders when it comes to talking about this issue? We don't hear it.

The price paid by families of those who are murdered is incalculably high, and no amount of money, no amount of time, can offset it.

CALL-OUTS

Vicky Lindsey, in Compton, California, knows this all too well: *If there's anybody else in here who has lost a loved one to violence, come on and step up here with me please. I want you guys to understand what it's about.*

This is my son. He was seven years old when his brother, my son, was murdered. He was murdered right after Compton High's homecoming football game, November the 9th, 1995. Now let me tell you guys something. I want you guys to see us, and not be us, because it hurts. It hurts every single second of every minute of our lives.

And I was a working single mother. I did twenty some years at MTA. I was a bus operator. I worked. I was off in the community doing community organizing.

I've been doing it since '88, you guys. So if I can do it—I want you guys to understand it can be done. And they talk about single mothers can't raise men. He was the best man that I ever had. So now his brother has to take his place. He's our height now, but he stepped up to the plate when he was seven years old and he became the man of the household, you guys. He became the man.

Don't Abandon the Drug User

As you well know, drugs and alcohol fuel a whole lot of the violence we see around us. The angry young people who abuse drugs and/or alcohol need our help and the help from a variety of community agencies.

Our young people challenge themselves in ways they will later regret. They put alien substances into their bodies, knowing that they could enter what Louis Farrakhan called "the valley of death." Worse, they can take their unborn children into the valley of death with them, and if not death, then the valley of squalor or the valley of suffering. Youth being what it is, they will risk their bodies and minds to achieve something as short-lived and stupid as a "high." And they will pursue this high despite having been warned against it and having seen the consequences in the addictions and deaths around them.

Once addicted, our young people begin to resemble the living dead, like the kind you see staggering around in the movies, but not nearly as entertaining. On the way to the valley of death themselves, they are capable of dragging a whole lot of people along with them and destroying the lives of the people they leave behind. At this stage, no one else around them matters. But then again, we could say that no one much mattered when they began this absurd journey.

Those of you who have had to live with junkies know what it is like. When they come to visit you, you know how inventive you have to be in hiding anything of value. We know of one set of grandparents who feared the visit of their grandchild—and with good reason. On one visit, the kid tracked down their cash reserves to a zip-lock bag hidden among the wet clothes in their washing machine and, of course, took it. He was that desperate. This is not the way extended families are supposed to work.

Drugs challenge families in any number of ways. One is the situation where the mother or father is a dealer or user. In these cases, the child sees and understands that a crime is being connected to his or her life that will sooner or later take his parent away when that parent is hospitalized or killed or arrested. A child growing up in this world grows up without the protection that so many of us have come to take for granted. This child leads a life of such total anxiety that he or she may never recover, but that child is absolutely worth saving.

Cases like these demand a great deal of behavioral forgiveness. The grandparents and other friends and family, even the great-grandparents, have to become involved.

CALL-OUTS

Lamont Taylor, in Cincinnati, shared his personal account of drug dealing: *My mom had me when she was fourteen. So she had to quit school. But I was fortunate that my mom gave me a couple of things—good principles and values. As I got older, about nineteen or twenty, I met a few guys, and they were major drug dealers. They liked me; they trusted me. And they would share things with me out of confidence because they knew I wouldn't have confronted them. I didn't want any part of it.*

As time went on, we saw friends get killed. You've got to take a look at yourself and say, Is this the actual life that I want? *If I forgot to tell you, I quit school in eleventh grade—bright kid, just that once I left school, it was over.*

And so I met this lawyer. He sat down and really gave me a long speech about how he transitioned his life. He did really well for himself. I didn't really listen to him then, but it stuck with me. And as time went on, I had to realize that it was time for me to walk away from that.

Now, I oversee the staffing for hundreds of restaurants in five differ-

ent states. I learned to be street smart and street tough, I had to keep that, and not let that go, but use it in a different form when I'm sitting in a boardroom so that I don't come across in an arrogant way, or as an angry black guy. You know, you have to learn to be emotionally intelligent.

Recovering drug abusers have powerful stories to tell. Their moving testimonies bear witness to the fact that recovery is possible.

CALL-OUTS

Kennett Pilgrim, of Panama City, Florida, told of her journey: *I was born in Panama City, Florida, 1952. I am a native. I was an only child. I had every advantage that any person on the face of the earth could have. And yet I am an addict. And that is what I am. Today I'm a recovering addict. My mother said when I turned thirteen I went berserk. I don't know, but things were not going right.*

I got clean one day before my daughter turned thirteen. That was in July of 1993, and I've been clean for twelve years. But before I got clean, school was a very easy thing for me. I became a registered pharmacist, and pharmacy and addiction don't really mix, okay? It was not a good thing, and it's only by the grace of God I'm not sitting in the penitentiary today. You know, a loving God would not have me self-destruct. I had a self-destructive disease that was terminal.

The worst thing about it is I'm a female. Well, that's not really the worst thing, but it is. You know, as a female addict, we have a stigma, you know, as a prostitute—and we're doing this, we're doing that. Yeah, I've done all those things.

But I'm not what I'm going to be. I'm still a work-in-progress, and I know that . . . I have a master's degree in counseling and human development today. I'm also a licensed mental-health intern.

> *I went to treatment in 1993 at a place called AWARE (A Women's Addiction Recovery Effort). Today I'm the supervisor of that program.*

Often, people are pessimistic about the value and successes of drug treatment programs. But as you can see from these stories, treating drug addictions can be successful and can help bring healing to black communities.

LOVE THE CHILD LEST HE SEEK LOVE IN THE STREETS

When children who are searching for confidence don't get it from a parent or caregiver, they often look for it in the streets, in the gangs. Joining is easy since gangs don't ask for much in the way of a résumé or a formal education. They just want your soul, and every kid has one of those—at least when he or she signs up.

CALL-OUTS

Oscar Bolton III, in Kansas City, talked about his experience: *One of the things about me—as a young person, I thought I could build a perfect family in the gang because my family was falling apart, due to drugs, alcohol, and those things. You know, both parents were on crack cocaine. These are supposed to be my leaders, you know, and one thing about young people, we are looking for heroes.*

In the gang we had to sell drugs in order to stick together. And so I thought we were building this perfect family. And I realized that what we were doing was really endangering ourselves. You know, I've been shot three times.

And as you can see, the family that I thought I was building, this perfect family with the gangs I thought I was building, has come home to my biological family, and they're firing, and you know, the shooting started.

One thing you're going to understand about gang members is they are young people who don't have a voice. Nobody speaks for the gang members. These are our sons, our daughters, our children. These are God's children. And how dare we leave them alone like we leave them? And then we expect the violence is just going to stop.

The disregard that gang members show for their own black lives and those of others may be a form of suicidal behavior. These young people are continually putting themselves in harm's way. They often carry guns and provoke confrontations that lead to their own deaths. This is sometimes called "victim precipitated homicide," which in reality is a kind of suicide. "Suicide-by-cop" is another example of this kind of suicide—provoke the police until they shoot you. Studies report that there are similarities in the underlying emotions of suicide and homicide victims and perpetrators. For example, these victims share feelings of hopelessness, low self-worth, isolation, and devaluation of their own lives and the lives of people who look like them—other black people. A motivation for homicide may be as simple as "He dissed me so I shot him."

Low self-esteem can cause a kid to do things that are physically and mentally self-destructive. These are lost, mixed-up youths. Kids who are depressed, angry, or suffering from mental illnesses need to get counseling. They may cry out in desperation, but they do not know how to ask for help and too often reject it when it is offered. They'd rather kill to gain a modicum of self-respect than come in from the cold. We must not give up on them.

Violence prevention programs and other attempts by community leaders to work with gang members have had limited success. What compounds the danger to our kids is that cities have been unable or unwilling to stop the easy flow of guns to children.

> **CALL-OUTS**
>
> Alvin Brooks, a former police officer in Kansas City and a lifetime fighter against crime, reported: *In 1964 there was a whole different group of young folks. I was a detective assigned to work with gangs and incorrigible youth and runaway youth. Anything that young folks did at that time I was assigned to work with. I don't know whether I could be as levelheaded today.*
>
> *In fact, some of the times, I didn't even carry a gun as a detective. But I would probably have three or four of them plus a bulletproof vest today. But it was a different mentality. I also taught school. And when I went into the classroom with a group of kids, it didn't take me long to determine what kind of parent each one of those children had.*
>
> *Students don't have a chance to bond with teachers, or teachers bond with parents where you don't have a relationship between teacher, child, and parent. It's just not there. Because of the fast life, because of the socialization process that takes place in this nation, we don't have the opportunity to bond with family, to bond with teachers, to bond in the community, to bond with our neighbors.*

RESPECT YOUR CHILDREN FROM THE BEGINNING

Many of our children are abused and neglected in ways that are painful to face. A number of them will become failures, dropouts, prisoners, and killers. We cannot let this happen to our children. We need to eliminate all forms of violence from our homes and families. Children are precious and deserve the best—not the worst—of what life has to offer.

When we talk to police officers, we ask them the ages of the youngest boys they are now arresting. One black officer in New Jersey told us that he recently had to apprehend some seven-year-olds who were bashing out car windows. The parents came and picked up all but one.

"I'm very good at making these kids cry," the officer told us, "but this one, I couldn't touch him. Nobody came for him. When I told him I was going to drive him home, he would not tell me where he lived. He just sat there in the car and didn't say anything."

Finally the officer got an address out of the boy and drove him to his home, which, in fact, looked more like a shack. He walked up to the house with the boy. The boy pulled the door open, and right there, a foot from that door, was his mother on the mattress having sex with a man. The boy walked straight past them as if they weren't even there and sealed himself off behind a curtain.

Seeing the cop, the man got up and took off with his clothes in his hand. The officer then explained to the mother, high on weed and alcohol, what her son had done and what official steps she had to take to address it. The mother signed the one form she had to sign, pulled the covers over her head, and left the son standing mutely behind the curtain. This was all the home the boy knew.

We hear stories like this all too often. They are enough to break your heart. One other police officer told us of catching an eight-year-old trying to bust a window and grab something.

"This one wouldn't even talk, wouldn't say anything," said the officer. So he drove the boy home. The kid had a key. He turned it and opened the door in a low-income apartment complex. The boy walked in with the officer. His mother was on the sofa. The boy looked at her, kept walking, then turned and said to the officer, "She dead, ain't she?"

The officer looked at the boy's mother, and she truly was dead. The needle lying on the floor beside her gave silent witness to the cause. If this wasn't disturbing enough, the boy walked to the cupboard, pulled out a box of cereal, put cereal in a bowl, poured in some milk, and while watching the officer minister to his dead mom, ate the cereal.

We need to help these children. If we don't get involved, then they're going to have to figure out life for themselves.

CALL-OUTS

Dr. Lewis King, in Compton, California, commented on the consequences of abuse: *What happens is that when a parent either commits abuse and neglect against a child or substance abuse, there's a rule that allows the courts to refer the case to a number of centers.*

We have a center called the Place of Family. And in some weeks, they run as many as forty groups of sixteen each of parents referred by the courts. So this is not a small issue. It's a major issue. Working at the King/Drew Medical Center, as early as 1974, we were seeing about three cases a week of sexual abuse of children under the age of seven.

In a study of the youth prisons, one of the profound findings is that 87 percent of the juveniles have been abused either physically or sexually three or more times before the age of twelve. So it's a very major issue. This deep, profound pain is not being addressed by our communities,

You have to begin to address this concern. You have to begin to listen to these kids. Many times, these kids are acting up because of hysterical pain, deep loss, deep feelings of not being secure in the society that has brought them into the world.

Survivors of abuse tell heart-wrenching stories of how they overcame their past and achieved in spite of their histories.

CALL-OUTS

Francine Still Hicks, in Kansas City, is one of them: *My twin sister and I grew up in the projects. It was tough, but at the age of eight we started being molested by a family member for three years. I'm fifty-two. My twin sister's fifty-two. It took her until fifty-one to be rid of this evil-doing inside of her, this harm, this crime. I knew one day I was gonna be rid of it. Even as a young lady, the smells, the touching, you still sense it.*

I think we should tell our children when they are little: Let nothing—

---

neighborhood, anything, drugs, anything, molestation, anything—
hold you back in life. Do not allow it to enslave you. Stand strong. Be
adventurous.

CALL-OUTS

Belinda Wiley, in Kansas City, has survived her own trials and tribu-
lations: *I describe my life as a mountain because it's the highest thing*
that you can climb. I grew up without a father. My stepfather abused me
mentally, physically, and sexually. And my mother couldn't nurture me
after that had happened to me because they ripped me from her arms. So
she couldn't comfort me. She lived in one city, and I lived in another.

I stayed away from my mom for two years. And when she got me
back, I was angry. My abuse got swept under the rug. No one ever
talked about it. It was forgotten. So what I said is—Okay, I'll forget
about it too, but it was embedded in my soul. It was embedded in me.

So I grew up with hatred, low self-esteem, didn't think nothing of
myself. I dropped out of the ninth grade, started having children at a
young age. I was a baby having babies. You know, there was nobody
teaching me how to become a mother. I had to learn it for myself. So I
grew up angry. I started acting out. But I didn't know it. And then to
top all that, I had a drug addiction, became addicted to crack cocaine.
You know why? I was angry. I looked for a way out, and that was
the way out. There was no one I could talk to, not even my mother. I
didn't have a good relationship with my mother. I was angry at her for
letting somebody come into my room late at night. But I overcame.
God gave me hope. My children gave me hope. Everybody's predestined.
But it's up to you.

I stand here boldly, right now, and if you ask me where do I see
myself, I will tell you, I will obtain a PhD in psychology. I will write
me a book. I already got the title. It's called Mountaintop. *And as I'm*

> *getting educated, I would educate the young ones. You have to be*
> *taught in order to be able to teach. You have to be taught first. Then,*
> *you can teach. So I have to get my education first.*

REMEMBER OUR IMPRISONED

In 1954, the year of the *Brown v. Board of Education* decision, about ninety-eight thousand African Americans were in prison. Today, there are nearly ten times as many black people in prison. In 1995, 16 percent of black men in their twenties who did not go to college were in jail or prison; by 2004, 21 percent were incarcerated. According to the Sentencing Project, 32 percent of the black men born today will go to prison at some point in their lifetime. In 2005, 4.7 percent of all black men were in prison, compared to 1.9 percent of Hispanic males and 0.7 percent of white males.

The culture of imprisonment devastates black families and communities. We must make an all-out effort to keep our kids out of jail and step up efforts to rehabilitate inmates while in prison and after their release.

Imprisonment affects the whole community. When young black males are taken off the streets, a lot more females than males will graduate from high school. The same is even truer for college. And as this phenomenon continues, what are we as a people going to do? We look to the family as a foundation for a community, but a family requires males. And when a male is in prison, he is useless, and when he comes out, he's a felon. So he can't vote, can barely get a job. He likely can't even read. And you know what happens to adults when they can't read well and they don't write well and they can't find a job? They end up back in prison.

They don't have to go back, however. They don't have to repeat their mistakes. Listen to the stories of some men who went to prison and were still able to turn their lives around.

CALL-OUTS

Walter McMillan, of Compton, California, is one of them: *This poem has always inspired me. It's by Langston Hughes, called "Mother to Son."*

Well, son, I'll tell you:
Life for me ain't been no crystal stair.
It's had tacks in it,
And splinters,
And boards torn up,
And places with no carpet on the floor—
Bare.
But all the time
I'se been a-climbin' on,
And reachin' landin's,
And turnin' corners,
And sometimes goin' in the dark
Where there ain't been no light.
So, boy, don't you turn back.
Don't you set down on the steps.
'Cause you finds it's kinder hard.
Don't you fall now—
For I'se still goin', honey,
I'se still climbin',
*And life for me ain't been no crystal stair.**

That was one of the first poems I decided to memorize while I was incarcerated in central juvenile hall.

My mother was on drugs from as long as I could remember. I can remember being taught how to sell drugs by my mom because at one

---

*"Mother to Son," copyright © 1994 by The Estate of Langston Hughes, from *The Collected Poems of Langston Hughes by Langston Hughes*, edited by Arnold Rampersad with David Roessel, Associate Editor. Used by permission of Alfred A. Knopf, a division of Random House, Inc.

point, she was selling drugs. Around fifteen years old, I decided to get involved in a gang, and I got into some trouble.

And I went to central juvenile hall and then from there, I went to a juvenile camp, which is a facility for juveniles. I did a year in there. I got out, went back to the same neighborhood. And a month and a half later, I was back in jail. That time I did four years in the youth authority.

The second time, I sort of realized that this is just not a life that I wanted to continue to live. So I started working on my high school diploma and my GED in central juvenile hall. I got that and I went on to the youth authority up north.

I started my college courses while I was in there. And I got released and I went to El Camino Community College, then transferred to the University of Washington and finished my undergraduate degree there.

I'm also involved with the organization called Inside Out Writers. We go to all the juvenile detention facilities. And we teach creative writing classes to at-risk youth, and we're going into the youth authorities and the camps as well. And one of the things that I want to stress to some of these kids is that you have to believe in yourself.

CALL-OUTS

Eddie Spencer, in Greenwood, Mississippi, revealed a slice of his life: *This mug shot right here is not from a fair. This is when I was just getting ready to turn seventeen years old, standing before the judge. And the judge was telling me, "Eddie Spencer, if that man dies, you will get the death penalty."*

And my friend, I know that I had experienced a lot of things, but when I was standing before that judge, my whole life, at that moment, flashed before my eyes. But thank God that the man did not die. I received ten mandatory years in addition to fifteen years for another attempted murder because Eddie Spencer never dealt with his anger. And a lot of people told me, they say, "Eddie, you are just like your dad."

A young white catfish farmer came into the prison one day a week and taught me how to read. And do you know that a lot of the folk, when they saw me, they saw me misspelling words. Some of you all are saying I'm mispronouncing words. Some of you all might be saying you're still doing that, Eddie. But a lot of them laughed at me. They say, "Oh, you big dummy, you special ed and everything."

I also decided that I wanted to continue my education—I ended up going to college in Mississippi. I never will forget. They said, "Eddie, we don't take peoples like you with the previous education training like yours." And what they were trying to say is, "We don't take ex-convicts and everything." But I found myself saying, "Would you please give me a chance?" And they gave me a chance.

God allows people to give Eddie Spencer a chance. Those chances continued to take place in my life—even at this moment right here. Every time I walk in my office, I say, "Lord, look at what you have done." I serve as the associate pastor at a 98 percent white church.

CALL-OUTS

Norman Askew, in Birmingham, added his unique perspective: *I'd like to thank the pastor who saw the same vision that I had about four years ago about doing a group from the program that I work with. And now we've got about fifty young African-American males every Tuesday night here at this church, to empower them to be better citizens. We also have about twenty-five young men that we teach fatherhood to every Monday night.*

I've been through hell and back. But when I was in prison, doing a forty-year sentence, there was a Scripture that really struck me. And I grabbed hold to that Scripture. When I was in prison, I couldn't read and write when I first got into prison. I was almost forty years old. But I got my associates degree, my GED, and a social work degree while I was there.

And while I was there in prison, fourteen and a half years, my name wasn't Norman Askew. It was 21098. I had to overcome that. You become institutionalized when you do fourteen and a half years.

Our drug program has a graduation program, and we have graduated over three thousand people there in the judge's court. The amazing thing I realized when I was in prison is that there are no failures. God didn't create any of us to fail. All of us are supposed to be successful.

Gabriel Ballard, speaking in Birmingham, was a student at Jefferson State Community College, sixteen years old, almost seventeen. He was taken from his mother and raised by his biological father. But right now, Gabriel is participating in a community leadership program for poor youth and has proven to be a great leader for the group.

CALL-OUTS

Gabriel Ballard spoke his mind: *I'm not the real success story. I think my parents are, because they had to deal with me. I made certain decisions like smoking, getting in trouble, getting locked up. I took seven bullets from a twelve-gauge. That left two buckshots in my arm, two in my spine, and three in my leg with a broken femur bone. And they hurt. If you ain't never experienced what a cap does, you don't want to experience it. My daddy, he gave me his key for a reason. He has his key to the city, representing what he's done for the city of Birmingham. But every city is made of communities, and it starts in your community.*

And I had a key to the community. And since all the trouble I've been in, I'm recently the youngest enrolled in Jeff State, and I work

> *with this mentoring group that my dad started called Propel and we go*
> *mentoring young kids.*

Former prisoners can be powerful speakers. Programs like the Exhoodus Tour and others can bring their message to kids while there is still time to redirect young lives. These programs seek to break the cycle of violence and recidivism by having ex-prisoners speak. They share the success stories of reentering society following prison sentences and becoming positive forces for the community. Their honesty and real-world wisdom encourage young people to make better choices than they did. We need to expand and encourage programs like this. Rehabilitated ex-prisoners have a great deal to offer to African-American neighborhoods.

FIGHT BACK IN THE COMMUNITY

A good example of ordinary citizens taking action against the violence in their community occurred in Kansas City. The group in question calls itself the 24th Street Non-Violent Marchers. It was started in response to the high amount of crime in the area.

CALL-OUTS

Joyce Riley told how the group came together: *We had experienced nineteen young African-American men dying within one year's time on our street, three of them within one week. My grandson was in a drive-by killing about two and a half years ago. I was highly upset. I was hurt, confused, and I asked why, why won't someone do something about all this killing, all this crime going on around the neighborhood?*

So then, my spirit told me, Why don't you? So I took to the streets.

I called my police department. And I said, "I need some help. What can we do for you and what can you do for us?"

The major I talked to answered, "Do what you want to do. Do what you think you can do, and we'll be with you." We took to the streets, and we've been there two and a half years now, each Friday night, rain, shine, sleet, or snow. We march there.

We used to march every time there was a death on the street. We did a candlelight vigil. There wasn't nothing wrong with that, but it wasn't getting anything done. You do a vigil, and you go home. So there was more to it than just a vigil. If we wanted the crooks, the criminals, the gun-carrying thugs off the street, we had to go in there with them, and that's what we did.

We marched right in the middle of the drug dealers, the killers, the murderers. They weren't going to run us out, and we weren't going away from them. So we stayed out there. They threatened us. They came by. They did all the mean things. The men came down when the women were marching and did their private stuff, but we weren't going to run. We were there to stay, and this wasn't only my doing. But this was the vision of God.

He said, "Go, Riley. You can do it. I'm there with you." And at this time, we weren't afraid of the drug dealers, the guns, nothing. I think we were just too crazy, really, to be afraid. So we stayed out there since—this is almost three years. We've had one homicide in that area, on those streets.

Activists like Joyce Riley are making a difference. We need action on many fronts. We need advocates to fight for more psychiatric services for prisoners, for more drug abuse and alcohol programs, for more treatment and rehabilitation programs once prisoners are discharged, for more support programs to help inmates with their parenting skills so that the next generation does not repeat the sins of their parents. We would have healthier children as a result.

In short, African Americans need to care more about each other. A couple of decades ago, a group of nationally known psychiatrists said the number one mental-health problem in America was that people did not care enough about each other. Caring is about loving, nonviolence, and giving. At the least, it means not hurting and abusing one another.

When African Americans are committed to something, they make it happen. The civil rights bills did not pass just because white people decided it was an idea whose time had come. We made it happen. We have the power to put our youth on the path from victims to victors. The testimonials in this chapter demonstrate the great capacity of resilient black people to overcome hardships and move onward to success.

CALL-OUTS

Charles Ramsey, former chief of police in Washington DC, has seen it all: *Let me just give you a picture of some of the issues that we're confronted with. First of all, let me start by saying that we've got more decent kids than we have bad kids.*

That fact often gets overshadowed because we focus on the negative, and rightfully so, because we do have a serious problem out here. But we have to continue to support those youngsters who are trying to do the right thing. We also have the reality that we have a significant population of young people that is totally lost. Some are lost because they want to be lost. They have chosen a particular path.

There are others lost because of circumstances, but the bottom line is they are out there. They have no direction, and, unfortunately, they create a subculture of violence. If it doesn't impact you today, it will impact you tomorrow. There is no escape from it, absolutely no escape from it.

Juvenile crime in the District of Columbia is starting to rise again. It had been going down, but we had rises in two major categories. Robbery was up 37 percent, and weapons violations, up 30 percent. And I'm talking AK-47s, Tech-9s, semi-automatic weapons in the hands of fourteen-, fifteen-, sixteen-year-olds in many instances. One out of every three people we arrest for robbery is a juvenile. We have a serious problem on our hands. So far this year, we've had fifty-two homicides; 92 percent of the victims are black. And even though we've not closed all those murders, I bet everything I've got that 92 percent of the offenders are black because black on black crime is the single most problematic thing we face as a community. And we've got to start thinking about it and doing something about it. We are killing ourselves.

We've got to start thinking of real solutions and stop making excuses for it. We have to fix this problem ourselves, all of us collectively—all of us. More police is not the solution. We're not going to arrest our way out of this problem. Some folks need to get locked up. I've got absolutely no problem with that. But we have to try to starve this system at the same time. We've got to keep people out of the system, keep them from turning down the wrong path.

That's the real solution. That future doctor, president, or elevator operator may not be dead. They just may be doing time in some penitentiary somewhere because they went down the wrong path, got locked up, and squandered their lives. Their lives are gone too. We have got to do something to stop it, and the time is now.

Come on, people!

8

FROM POVERTY
TO PROSPERITY

At the end of the day, there are a few critical questions that we have to ask ourselves.

What will it take to pull our people out of poverty? What will get us to contemplate a life with brighter dreams? What will inspire us to pursue the future as if it mattered? How will we learn to respect ourselves and help each other? What will it take for us to become entrepreneurs and to run businesses that will serve the community, not destroy it? We ask these questions only because we think there are answers, real ones, attainable ones.

We are talking about black people in poverty. If you fit that description, we are talking to you. How do you get out of poverty? What must you do to get your mind cleared, your spirit healed, your dreams refocused?

As you probably know, certain people tell us that we are picking on the poor. Many of those who accuse us are scholars and intellectuals, upset that we are not blaming everything on white people as they do. Well, blaming only the system keeps certain black people in the limelight, but it also keeps the black poor wallowing in victimhood.

Do you pick on someone, especially someone you care about, by telling him what he should not do? If we said instead, "Sorry for speaking out of turn. Go ahead and sell your drugs in the neighborhood," would that be a sign of love and affection? How is this going to lift the community out of poverty? How does the selling of street drugs lift anybody's community out of poverty? Our youth have this idea that they can grow as rich as drug dealers, but they are more likely to grow old in prison, or grow dead, than grow rich.

Drug dealers are entrepreneurs of a sort but of the worst sort imaginable. In the best-selling book *Freakonomics*, authors Steven D. Levitt and Stephen J. Dubner ask the basic question, "Why do drug dealers still live with their moms?" The answer is that most drug dealers are lucky to make minimum wage. They work under terrible job conditions, like standing on a street corner all day and talking only to crackheads. On average, they will get arrested six times and wounded on the job more than twice. The chances of their getting killed are one in four, making drug dealing fifty times more dangerous than lumberjacking, the most lethal legitimate occupation.

Real entrepreneurs grow their customer base. Drug dealers bury theirs. Good businesses help create middle-income neighborhoods where everyone can relax and feel at home. The drug business destroys these kinds of neighborhoods. The whole business is senseless and terribly sad.

We hear people talk excitedly about how, yes, the authorities are building new jails for our sons. Is that pathetic or what? Here's our thought: take about one hundred well-behaved young black students, walk them by your local county jail, and when they get right to the building have the kids all laugh. And when the authorities ask, "Why are they laughing?" you say, "Because they built this for us, and we are *not* coming!"

Right now, unfortunately, our young people are coming. What they watch on TV, what they listen to, how they dress, how they think—all of this conspires to lock them into poverty. The way they are raised does not help either. We've got to face up to the fact that without a father these kids begin life sad, and the sadness turns to frustration. They begin by disliking other people as they do themselves and simply not caring about others or themselves. This anxiety goes deep. We can't repeat this often enough: we need to look at ourselves and stop pretending we don't have a problem.

Former mayor of Cincinnati, Dwight Tillery, commented on the depth of the problem: *I want to share with you some data. The city of Cincinnati is 42.9 percent African American. Many neighborhoods in Cincinnati have jobless rates as high as 60 percent. African-American men are three times more likely to be unemployed than white men. The high school graduation rate in Cincinnati for black males is 25 percent, compared to 43 percent for white males. Black males are disproportionately characterized as mentally retarded. Both male and female black students are up to eight times more likely to be suspended.*

Males are four times more likely than white students to be classified with developmental delay, females almost three to one. Expulsions are fourteen times greater for African-American males and seven times more likely for females. This is what we're working with.

GET ALL THE SCHOOL YOU CAN GET

There are many causes of poverty among African Americans, some direct and some indirect. Here is a partial list: institutional racism, limited job opportunities, low minimum wage, mental illness, physical disabilities, drug and alcohol abuse, lack of a high school diploma, incarceration, and a criminal record.

When we look at this list, we can see that institutional racism is just one factor among many. Many of the issues that the black poor struggle with are similar to those that the poor in America struggle with, regardless of race. Most poor people suffer from a lack of resources. They lack the power to get the attention they need. They lack the ability to pull themselves together as a community and to wield meaningful political influence. They rarely have access to good schools, health care, and job opportunities that provide a living wage. The result is a limited supply of realistic job opportunities, particularly for poor black people who have not acquired the skills to take advantage of the opportunities that do exist.

These are not excuses. These are simply hurdles to jump, and they can be jumped. People jump them all the time. One of the most important things for you and those you love is to graduate from high school or to get a GED through community college or job-training programs. A lack of basic education severely limits your life options. No one can stop you from getting educated other than yourself.

CALL-OUTS

Dr. George McKenna, in Compton, California, commented: *There are invisible people in Compton. They are the uneducated and undereducated who have gone through the one institution that they've all got in common called schools. And when they come out unemployed and unemployable, schools are responsible. Now when I say that, my fellow schoolteachers often say, "Are you blaming us?" I don't care if you're blamed or not blamed. The question is responsibility. When I rode in the back of a bus, I knew who to blame for that.*

We used to blame it on white folks. But I knew who was responsible for getting me out of the back of the bus. I don't stop blaming them. I still blame them. But I'm also accepting full responsibility so no matter how much they oppress me, it's my responsibility to stop them. And I learned this from a very spiritual point of view. Martin Luther King Jr. said, "I owe it to my oppressor to stand up and take the whip out of his hand because if I keep him from beating me, maybe he'll get to the Promised Land too."

Take Any Legitimate Job

Parents and caregivers, have you heard a kid say, "Well, I can either flip burgers or go out here and make some real money selling drugs"? When you hear that, do you stop that child and say, "Wait a minute, fool. You don't flip burgers for the rest of your life. You flip them to become the manager of the place. You flip burgers to move from manager to owner of the damn franchise"?

You have to say this to your kids more than once. So do their teachers. If the kids give you lip, ask them to identify a middle-aged, home-owning drug-dealing grandpa with a family that loves him. That will keep them quiet—and busy.

Please remind your young people that there is no shame in hard work. All work is honorable and makes a contribution to society whether that work is as a janitor or an astronaut. An unpleasant job usually leads to a better job as young people develop working skills that are useful on any job, including the ability to work with others and be punctual. The unemployment rate for black people is twice that of white people—this has to change.

The truth is that if we all showed more respect to blue-collar workers, there would be less rejection of so-called menial jobs by our youth. If there was less rejection, kids would see that one job leads to another as the worker gains experience and basic workplace skills such as cooperating with others, taking orders, and keeping regular work hours. By not giving up hope and persevering against the odds, many succeed. During the call-outs, we were deeply moved by the many inspirational stories we heard.

CALL-OUTS

Delores Jones, in Kansas City, shared one of them: *By the time I was seventeen years old, crack cocaine became an unwelcome visitor in our home. I remember coming home and trying to turn on the electricity, and it was not there. I remember wanting to run bath water and I could not. I remember wanting to put food in the refrigerator and I could not. I remember searching my purse for money that I had worked for at the age of sixteen, and it had been stolen to support the person's addiction.*

And so, by the time school was out, I didn't have the opportunity to go to a historically black university, because the funding wasn't there. The person wasn't there to help. But I did have an opportunity to go to school. And I chose to attend Donnelly College in Kansas City on 18th Street. And I also decided that things don't have to be ideal for me to keep going. See, my first car was from a junkyard.

In 2004, I earned my master's in social work, and I am working to complete my clinical license to be a therapist with my own practice. I don't understand why it happened. All I understand is that I made it. I didn't make it by blaming somebody else.

Avoid blaming someone else. Understand what is within your realm of control, which is your ability to speak up and identify what you need, outline a plan to get there, identify what and where you want to be. Write it down. Say it out loud. And if you don't know, somebody else does.

Most importantly, do things you are good at. Just because you're struggling doesn't mean you're stupid. Just because you're down doesn't mean you're finished. You ain't finished. You got it going on. Roller-skate, sing, do something, talk, but talk in terms of where you're trying to go, and lastly, always say thank you. Always say thank you. Pray. Praise God. Give thanks. Give back. But never, ever, ever give up.

MAINTAIN YOUR INDEPENDENCE

Families below the poverty line do benefit from government assistance such as food stamps, minimum health insurance, and subsidized housing. If you are struggling, you should make sure to take advantage of these programs. They are referred to as "assistance" for a reason—they are meant to assist you in getting through hard times. But hard times are not supposed to last a lifetime, and you deceive yourself if you don't think you can take steps to pull yourself out of poverty.

The high cost of childhood poverty is tragic. It is estimated that children who grow up poor cost the country five hundred billion dollars a year. Poor people do not contribute sufficiently to the economy, and the health and criminal costs that grow out of poverty are enormous. Experts argue that we can counter poverty levels by extending the earned income tax credit to more low-income workers. But don't overlook the word *earned*. If you don't earn it, you don't get it. Our children are in great need, and we cannot afford to squander any opportunities.

BEWARE THE TRAP

If you are not working and your only paying job is to stand in line so that the government can sustain you, then you are not contributing to your community, especially if you think that this will be your life's work. If you are honest, you know that you don't have to do anything productive because you have found a way to live off the government unproductively.

Beware! This is a trap. There is a cost to all of this. You have to give up on your brain. If you go to school and get a degree under these circumstances, you cannot use that degree to work. You cannot use your mind to go into any kind of business, unless you are going to do it in a dishonest manner and take a chance on getting caught. At some point, you have to choose between a life of the mind and a life on the dole. You can't have them both.

Now there is also a belief that when you are fully dependent on the government you are worth nothing. So if you are worth nothing, you believe that nobody cares what you do, that there is no value in the government spending any money to keep your accounts honest. We don't mean to embarrass anyone who's already yielded to this mode of thinking. Unfortunately, however, there are too many such people of all races, colors, creeds, and sexes who have.

People who plan to depend on the government for support as long as they can get it think they are playing a game with the system. To play this game, you have to lie to yourself about who you are and what you are doing. You no more want to be blamed for taking the bait than white people want to be blamed for setting the trap. So no one chooses to see what is going on. Thanks to this kind of blindness, there will not be a solution until you size up your part of the equation and solve your way out of it.

STAY OUT OF DEBT

There is another kind of poverty trap, and that is called debt. If there are any financial advisors reading this, you've got to help the people in your circle stop running up their debt with credit card purchases. Credit cards will surely drive them into poverty if they are not there already.

All of us have been heavily conditioned by advertisers to want things. Advertisers play on the need for status and self-worth. People who don't have enough of either—in our own minds, that's just about all of us—are very vulnerable to such hype. The clothes make the person, they say, or the car makes the person or the big-screen TV makes the person. None of it is true. Character makes the person, and character cannot be purchased.

Too many people try to buy self-worth. They never quite can, so they have to buy more and more stuff, and there is always some corporation out there creating "new" and so-called better stuff for them to buy. *Come on, people!*

People in debt are not fully free human beings. They are enslaved by the money they owe. They tend to be sad and confused and hopeless. They see no way out. Any money that is coming in is already promised to someone else. They can envision no unburdened future and often surround themselves with others who see no plausible way out either.

Their weariness and sadness often find an outlet in anger, and that anger inevitably looks for scapegoats. Other than sex, financial conflicts cause more family strife and domestic violence than any other issue.

How does this cycle of indebtedness and sadness and anger happen? It often begins innocently enough. Let's say you borrow money, and you do not read the contract. The contract says that the lender is free to add on to the interest rate any time it wants to without notifying you. You buy a television or clothes or things for the home on the credit card without knowing—or without wanting to know—just how much interest you are paying per month for the pleasure. You may not want to think about the burden of it, but it weighs on you. It shackles you. It holds you down and back.

You may find momentary relief by buying something and foregoing the payment due on one or two bills. But the interest burden just grows heavier, and you grow wearier because one day you know that someone will come and take your stuff away. We repeat, you are not a free human being.

We know a man who is quite used to disguising his voice. So when the collection agency calls, he pretends not to be at home. He also refuses to find out his credit rating and how much he owes to anyone. This is like driving without reading the road signs. You can go as fast as the next guy, but he knows enough to stop at the stop sign.

We all need to read the fine print on the credit card contracts and understand the amounts of interest that we'll be expected to pay. Debt keeps people down, makes them feel as overburdened and unfree as a black sharecropper on a Southern plantation. Real money is money that is not already spoken for. We all want to have money that we can do whatever we want with, and that kind of money does not spring miraculously out of a credit card.

Break the Chains

To avoid the pain of indebtedness, we must escape the hamster wheel of materialism. It's hard, but we don't have to keep chasing "things" at the expense of relationships with our families, our friends, and our community.

Too many of our kids admire thug rappers, with their bling bling and fancy SUVs. Too many think that status comes from things. Too many think that they can possess those things by any means necessary, including drug dealing, pimping, prostitution, and violence. Well, kids, if the repossession man can strip you of everything you value, you don't have much.

No one, however, can repossess your soul or your self-respect. Work on these things, and you will sleep a lot better at night. Work on these things, and it is much more likely that you will save enough to buy a home of your own and raise a family.

CALL-OUTS

Lauren Lake, speaking in Cincinnati, commented: *Many of you know me as an entertainer and a singer and everything else. I sang with them all, traveled and toured. But I am honest enough as a black person to say we've gone off the path a little bit, and let's bring it on back home. An economic power base—that is it. We make the least and spend the most. Boy, we can spend some money.*

But what are we spending it on? Sneakers and jeans? How about homes? How about building businesses? How about using that same twenty dollars you spent on shoes and invest it in something that you love to do and make a business out of it? It is possible. Now, lastly, we've got to take this helplessness and this hopelessness and wrap it up and put it into the dumpster. I don't want to hear another young person tell me they don't really know what they want to be because they can't—because the white man's gonna hold me back.

I don't want to hear it. I don't want to hear it. All this hopelessness and helplessness can go away, and we need to make sure it does. Now, we need to focus. This is our power and our privilege, and I know you look at me and you say, well, how does this little girl know all that? Well, I'm not all that little.

GET CONTROL OF YOUR FINANCES

What follows are some guidelines to help you to get your economic life under control.

- Make a list of everything that you owe. While it can be scary to see it all on paper, it also allows you to take control and make a plan.

- Stop charging anything you don't absolutely need.

- Pay *something* on all your bills. By paying even five dollars a month, you are showing good faith, and you may prevent costly penalties down the road.

- Once you know what you owe, work to pay off the smallest bill first.

- Take any extra money you get, no matter how little, and use it to lower that bill. It's easier to pay off a one hundred dollar bill than a one thousand dollar bill—and the satisfaction of achieving the goal of paying that off will give you a much needed boost.

- After you've paid off one bill, use what you would have paid on that and put that amount toward the next bill. It may be slow, but if you commit to getting out of debt, you will make it. Once you've freed yourself from these burdens, it will be much easier to manage your future.

If you feel you need outside help, some churches and community organizations offer programs to assist people like you. If there isn't such a program in your community, work to create one. Consumer debt is a huge problem for Americans. Credit card companies are thrilled to have you buy things you can't afford on credit. When you do, you spend an average of 35 percent more than if you had paid cash. Programs to help people get out of debt can be helpful by teaching people to set up realistic budgets and by helping them to stick with it. Community agencies can also help spread information about services—for instance, a food bank that can provide food so you can pay the rent.

HELP THE POOR HELP THEMSELVES

If you are willing to assume the responsibility for productive work on your end, the government and private agencies should take up the slack on their end, and you can remind them of this. Tell them to increase the minimum wage and to make serious investments in the educational systems in poor areas where schools are typically underfunded. School funding is usually based on the property tax revenues, which are higher in affluent suburbs than in poor city communities.

This disparity affects many poor neighborhoods regardless of ethnicity. Because of a lack of resources, many schools in poor neighborhoods cannot offer adequate college prep courses, which would increase a student's chances not only of gaining admission to colleges but also of getting scholarship help.

What battles should be waged to level the playing field? For one, you can demand that your state and federal lawmakers find ways to fund education that are fair to all people in the state. For another, you can support civil rights organizations, like the NAACP and Urban League, in their efforts to offer tutoring and scholarship programs. You can join groups like the Boys and Girls Clubs of America, Big Brothers Big Sisters, and 100 Black Men that work to educate our youth. You can also spread awareness of the fraternities and sororities that have programs to tutor and support poor students from all backgrounds.

> **CALL-OUTS**
>
> Timothy Watkins, speaking in Compton, California, made a plea for us to rise to the challenge: *I stand before you tonight a conflicted man because so many things that I hear and know I don't really believe. So many things that I hear about our responsibilities to one another and how we behave toward one another. All of the intent in the world that is undermined and compromised by intentional poverty. And that we suffer the symptoms of poverty and we talk about all the things that*

we've talked about here tonight. And what we're talking about are the symptoms. If we had our way, the platform that our ancestors built would be the one that we thrive on. Rather it's the descendants of others that thrive on that platform.

Many of us think that we're poor people when there can't possibly be such a thing. The potential of human beings is unlimited. And we're rich with potential. We have to decide what we're going to do next. That's the challenge. And we're not all going to move in the same direction. Not all of us at the same time, not all on the same subject.

We are the justice. We are the power if we choose to exercise it. If we're waiting for someone else to tell us what to do and how to do it, it really ain't going to happen. If we'll lead, we'll find that the leaders will follow, and they'll find a way to support what we do.

Spread the Word about Education

We have said it before, and we will say it again: *education is key for poor people.*

Although many individual black people have achieved high-profile success in the worlds of sports and entertainment, this kind of success does little to help the masses of black poor. The odds against black youths succeeding in these endeavors are overwhelming. And even when they do succeed, many fall into an economic freefall when their career ends because they have never bothered to get an education. Education holds out more hope for the ordinary African American than any career path.

While black entrepreneurs helped to shore up the middle-income base, if you review the history of black people in America, you will see that it was primarily our forefathers and foremothers getting an education and earning advanced degrees that opened the doors to middle-income salaries for millions of black people.

Today it is even more true that a degree helps our people get better and higher paying jobs. Currently, on average, a person with a master's degree earns fifty thousand dollars; a person with a professional degree earns even more; a person with a bachelor's degree earns thirty-six thousand dollars; a person with an associate's degree from a community college, twenty-seven thousand dollars; a person with some college, twenty-one thousand dollars; a high school graduate earns nineteen thousand dollars; and a high school dropout earns ten thousand dollars.

Do the math. Getting an education has a direct monetary payoff even in the face of residual forms of discrimination. And we have made progress. In 2005, 1.1 million African Americans over age twenty-five had advanced degrees—such as a master's, PhD, MD, or JD—compared to about 677,000 in 1995. The doors of opportunity are no longer locked, and we have to walk on through.

COMMIT YOUR HEART TO THE EFFORT

Consider what an amazing feat it has been for our people to rise up out of poverty. After emancipation, nearly all black people lived in poverty. In 1968, 35 percent of black people lived in poverty. In 2004, 25 percent lived in poverty, and the "poverty" of today, materially at least, is more comfortable than it was for our ancestors. But still today, the wealth (assets) of the average white family is eight to ten times that of black families. Despite all the challenges, we have survived—and we can do even better if we put our minds and hearts to the task.

Sometimes we blame too many of the problems in low-income communities on poverty. Many social scientists suggest that crime, violence, poor school performance, family breakdown, and a lack of community effectiveness are due to poverty. There are connections and relationships between poverty and social ills. But unfortunately the poor hear too many messages that they are victims and that there is very little they can do about it except wallow in it.

When a kid takes a human life and says, "Poverty made me do it," he sounds much too much like those folks in times past who would claim that "the devil made me do it." This victim posture—gussied up with words like *disadvantaged* and *at-risk*—leads people to deny personal responsibility for self-defeating behaviors. Such attitudes overlook the great advances made by black communities when they have adopted the philosophy of self-help even as they fought racism. We have too many examples over the centuries of black achievement under hardship to deny our own capabilities and to embrace a victim mentality.

N.B.

As the Reverend Jesse Jackson Sr. used to say, "No one can save us from us but us."

We want allies in government and business, but we also need to be self-reliant in as many ways as possible, particularly when there are problems in the community over which we do have some control.

CALL-OUTS

Dr. Janet Clark, in Compton, California, told her story: *I earned my doctoral degree in 1999. But I want to give you some dates so that you can see that the journey just wasn't an easy one, but it was a journey that makes me proud and makes me proud about the thing that I'm able to share with you and young people each and every day.*

By 1968, at twenty-one, I had two children and had flunked out of college altogether. In 1968, I was raped at gunpoint. A man grabbed me in the parking lot behind my apartment. I got very angry. I wasn't in college, I wasn't doing anything with my life, but I was so angry that I just decided that either I was going to make something out of myself or I was going to continue to struggle.

I was in an abusive relationship with my husband. Proud as I was, I wouldn't go back home, and he had me go on welfare. Now, at that time, they had a working mother's budget. It was a budget that allowed you to go to school, that allowed you to stand up and be strong, but at the same time, it was a bridge from where I was to where I wanted to go. With two children in tow, I went to the welfare office.

In 1973, I got my BA degree. I was able to get promoted on the job, and I was told that if I got promoted, I'd lose my welfare check. Guess what I chose? It was fifty dollars less a month, but it was dignity that I had. I was fortunate because where I worked there was a guy who recognized my potential.

So if I can leave you with anything, there are people around you wanting to help you, willing to embrace you, willing to support you and motivate you. But the most important part has to come from within you.

SUPPORT LOCAL BUSINESS

One way to help create jobs in black communities is by encouraging the development of local businesses and supporting them once they're established. Local businesses are convenient for neighborhood employees and also give young people a bird's-eye view of jobs that can be had. If these businesses establish partnerships with local schools, each institution serves to benefit. And black youths will be more motivated to learn when education has a direct reward in the workplace. What seems like a dead-end job "flipping burgers" may become a stepping stone to store manager or someday owning the establishment.

Some people sympathize with young black people who accept self-defeating behaviors. We hear them say, "What else can you expect?" That thinking is a slap in the face to the millions of African Americans who have come from poverty to achieve at every level of American society. Any argument that says crime, drug-dealing, or pimping in the black community is acceptable contributes to the crises in poor black communities. Too many kids who refuse to work a legitimate job end up working in a prison laundry.

> **CALL-OUTS**
>
> Dr. George McKenna, in Compton, California, commented on our own responsibility: *Let's say, okay, we know we got some problems. Let's try to deal with them and stop blaming other folks. I know New Orleans. You have this mayor who stands up and says, "You drug dealers and dope addicts and thieves and hoodlums better not come back." But why threaten them now? He knew they were there before Katrina. Why did we just tolerate it?*
>
> *We just say, "It's okay to be pitiful," so much that it sounds normal after a while. We ought to want to be middle-income, at least to have middle-income values, a work ethic, a family ethic, a protect-our-women ethic.*

An abundance of real jobs in our communities could challenge the "jobs" provided by the underground criminal economy. It would be wonderful if we had more black entrepreneurs on our turf to offer jobs to youth and give them direct role models for achievement and success. There are programs for high school students to teach them the basics of how to start their own businesses and develop their entrepreneurial skills. Such programs should be expanded to help our youths turn their dreams and visions into realities that enrich our communities.

We have a long history of running our own businesses. After segregation, many of these businesses began to fade, but others have risen up, suggesting that black entrepreneurs may experience a comeback. There are more talented black people out there with advanced degrees—including many in law and business—than ever before. Working together, they can become a boon to black communities as entrepreneurs.

TAKE CARE OF OUR OWN

What we forgot to do when the new freedoms came, the legislative freedom, was to take care of certain things. One thing for sure was our own neighborhood. We forgot to become entrepreneurs. We forgot to put up shops. We forgot to look out for education. We forgot to look out for each other. We forgot so much that we used to know and do.

So did we actually forget, or were we just not ready at the time? When white people left the cities and moved into the suburbs, we stayed in the cities. They took their jobs with them, but we did not seize the entrepreneurial opportunities that were left behind. What blocked us from entrepreneurship? You can talk about "institutional racism" all you want, but black-owned businesses have faded even as institutional racism has lessened. Have we lost sight of our own intelligence and skills? So as far as we can see, there are few businesses left in our communities that we run, except maybe barber and beauty shops, funeral parlors, maybe a few restaurants. No one is telling us that black people can't have our own businesses. We are just telling ourselves.

We can't sit around cursing because other ethnic groups have established businesses in black neighborhoods. For new immigrants especially, opening a business is an extended family affair; they get group support both in labor and finance. We shouldn't complain about their success if we aren't willing to step up to the plate. It can be difficult for African Americans to get the support they need from local banks, but if we support one another, we can do it.

National corporate chains and banks have been moving into black communities, particularly when gentrification is underway. These changes bring jobs, but they often drive up the cost of housing, driving poor people further from the jobs being created. Black entrepreneurs, who have black community development on their agendas, can help solve problems before they take root.

SISTERS, SEIZE THE DAY!

Our impression is that both black men and women with law and business degrees are working in predominantly white businesses and corporations and have not yet learned to pool their talents for the mutual benefit of businesspeople and the black poor. Such black professionals can play key roles in the economic advancement of black communities just as many black doctors and dentists are doing in the health-care field.

Black women, you have a real opportunity to get more involved in the historically male-dominated world of entrepreneurship. You now represent two-thirds of our college and professional school graduates. Given the lack of educated males, many of you have had to defer starting families. Many of you have instead turned your creative instincts into building your credit and starting businesses, and this is a way of nurturing your community.

In the way of example, there is one woman we know who does marbleizing. She does walls and hallways and the like and does quite well at it, and she is not a college graduate. There are many comparable opportunities within the community. We are not trying to restrict anyone, but rather to alert folks to the possibilities.

Young women graduates would do well to get involved as entrepreneurs. This takes some mentoring, and we would strongly encourage successful entrepreneurs of whatever color to share their information on how to start up and maintain a prosperous business. If we made this information easily available, some of our young graduates might feel more comfortable taking advantage of it.

LIFE LESSONS

Born Catherine Elizabeth Woods in Omaha in 1947, Cathy Hughes went to work after college at KOWH, a black radio station in Omaha. Her good work there secured Hughes a job as a lecturer at the School of Communications at Howard University in Washington. While in

---

DC, she took a job at WHUR-FM and by 1975 was named the station's general manager. A persevering entrepreneur, she and her husband, Dewey Hughes, were turned down by thirty-two banks before finding one willing to lend them the money to buy WOL, a small Washington station, rechristened Radio One.

Over the objection of the bank, Hughes changed the format of the station from music to talk. It was no overnight success. After a divorce, she bought out her husband's share, and hard times forced her and her son, Alfred, to give up their home and move into the station. Based on the strength of her talk show, however, the audience grew and the station gained momentum.

Not content with one station, Hughes took Radio One nationwide and now owns seventy radio stations in nine major markets. Hers is the largest black-owned radio chain in the nation. And Alfred, who once lived at the station, now serves as CEO and president of Radio One, while his mom holds forth as chairperson. In January 2004, Radio One launched TV One, a national cable and satellite television network. "It is not enough for you to do your very best," said Hughes. "You must do what is required by the situation."

As an example, say that a few young women decided they wanted to make a healthier ice cream. How do they start? Perhaps a representative of Ben & Jerry's would lend a hand and explain the ins and outs of raising money, recruiting staff, marketing the business, and managing it. It can happen. It just takes the will.

Invest in Ourselves

In 2006, Dr. Muhammad Yunus of Bangladesh was awarded the Nobel Peace Prize for a concept entirely relevant to would-be black entrepreneurs, particularly women. He called it "microcredit." A PhD in economics, Yunus discovered in his research that very small loans with a reasonable rate of return could make a huge difference to a small, poor, start-up entrepreneur. He also discovered that "solidarity groups," small informal groups whose members apply together and act as co-guarantors of repayment, helped the business prosper and assured that the loans got repaid. He also quickly realized that women were a better investment than men. Although traditional bankers thought he was crazy, the bank he started has gone on to give six billion dollars in loans to seven million customers with a repayment rate above 98 percent. Yunus was the first person to win a Nobel Peace Prize for a profit-making venture, and he richly deserved it.

One area where a little microcredit would come in handy is food. For every one prosperous black-run restaurant there are a hundred Mexican and Chinese restaurants, and it is not because their food is better. Our belief is that we as a people can begin to enter areas that we have never really thought of, perhaps a chain featuring Southern cooking, run by African-American people doing the cooking. And we're talking high-end, fresh food, with real plates, knives, and forks that do not look like they came from the army navy store, real napkins, real tablecloths, and fantastic service. The opportunity is there. We just have to seize it.

Artists often lead the way in the gentrification of neighborhoods, and art presents another potential entrepreneurial opportunity—selling the works of painters, sculptors, furniture makers, photographers, clothing designers, and the like. Many of the artists do not want to think about making money, but still they want what they are producing to be seen or worn. If black neighborhoods are going to be gentrified, we might as well be doing the gentrifying.

One area that we dominate as a people is entertainment, but too often we find ourselves working for someone else. We don't have to. Young entrepreneurs could maybe buy or lease a movie theater near an African-American college or in an area with a strong support system, set up the popcorn machines, go to different film festivals, pay attention to

African-American filmmakers, pull out what are the best films, take out ads, and sell some tickets. This is all possible.

On the entrepreneurial front, black people have been showing improvement. In 2002, the number of black-owned businesses stood at 1.2 million. This represented a rise of 45 percent since 1997. Earl Graves Sr., Oprah Winfrey, Magic Johnson, Cathy Hughes, Edward Lewis, Bruce Llewellyn, Spike Lee, the late John H. Johnson and Eunice W. Johnson, and other black businessmen and businesswomen have provided a great deal of leadership for black business success. Significant employers of local black people have been black-owned businesses, such as beauty parlors, barbershops, and funeral homes. These efforts in helping African Americans overcome poverty must continue.

VICTIMS TO VICTORS

As we have explained, there are a thousand things you could be doing to help yourself and your community. You know what they are, and many of them are interrelated.

The most important thing that is within the reach of just about everyone is to make sure that every black child has two active parents in his or her lives. If something happens to the boy's natural father, it is time for the stepfather or the grandfather or the uncle or the godfather to fill the void. Likewise with the mother. A two-parent home is less likely to be poor, and the children it produces are much less likely to end up in prison. If, a generation from now, every black child grew up in a functional two-parent home, the problems of crime and poverty in black communities would greatly diminish.

Black women seem to understand this better than our men. Few of them, even those living in poverty, fit the stereotype society tends to impose. Most are trying to do the right thing for their families and children. Most care about their children getting an education and staying out of jail. Such parents and caregivers are involved with schools, churches, health clinics, and community settlement houses. Probably many more would be involved if they felt it was safe to go out without becoming a victim of crime or senseless violence. They are the key to reaching our men.

The young men need to learn that it is highly unlikely that they will grow up to star in the NBA or see their hip-hop CD go platinum. Although within reach, it will be a challenge for them, today at least, to graduate from college and start a successful business. But most youth can overcome the obstacles to their finishing high school and getting a legitimate job. And there is no reason in the world they cannot become good partners and fathers, especially since the women want them to be.

This is the base we build on. Children who are loved will have the confidence to succeed in school, to succeed on the job, to succeed in life.

Education plus jobs plus increased minimum wage plus entrepreneurship plus affordable housing plus decreased craving for material goods plus avoidance of credit card debt could equal the end of poverty—maybe. Poverty is deeply rooted in American society and our economic system. Black people have more than their share of poverty, which stunts their ambition and saddles them with a host of social burdens. But by doing the things we *can* do, we can make the future much brighter for poor black youth, much brighter for everyone.

No more excuses, no more delays.

Come on, people!

SPECIAL THANKS

We want to salute—as Dr. Johnnetta B. Cole would call her—"Sister Doctor" Camille Olivia Hanks Cosby for her unwavering integrity and steadfast support of the team.

She spent many hours providing her wisdom, her insights, and extensive editorial feedback for this book.

We thank you.

Bill Cosby
Alvin F. Poussaint, MD

ACKNOWLEDGMENTS

First and foremost we would like to thank those who have spoken at the call-outs across the country over the past three years. The passionate and powerful voices of those individuals bearing witness to their life journeys have deeply moved us. It is their voices telling of their hardships and triumphs that gave birth to this book. We were inspired and humbled by the stories we heard and the trials that were overcome. We thank you.

There were many people involved in making the call-outs happen. Our thanks to: Eugene Kane, *Milwaukee Journal Sentinel* (Central High School to Dobbins High School); and Dr. Rogers Onick, in Milwaukee, Wisconsin; Dr. Earl S. Richardson and Dr. Stanley Battle, in Baltimore, Maryland; Cynthia Tucker, *Atlanta Journal Constitution*; Ron Johnson, in Springfield, Massachusetts; Rochelle Riley, *Detroit Free Press*; Lauren A. Wally, in Pittsburgh, Pennsylvania; James Ragland, *Dallas Morning News*; James Campbell, *Houston Chronicle*; Ronald Ross, in Roosevelt, New York; Sylvester Brown, *St. Louis Post Dispatch*; Sam Fulwood, *Cleveland Plain Dealer*; Rochelle Riley and Luther Keith, in Detroit, Michigan; Howard Bingham, in Compton, California; Eddie Tanner, Barbara Moore, and Beth Bennett, in Panama City, Florida; Dwight Tillery, in Cincinnati, Ohio; Troy and Curressia Brown, in Greenwood, Mississippi; Lee Ivory, *USA Today*; Sondra Lawson and DeWayne Wickham, *USA Today*, in Washington DC; Tracy Hall; Lewis Diuguid, *Kansas City Star*; Eric

Wesson, in Kansas City, Missouri; David Muhammad, in Newark, New Jersey and Angela Hall, in Birmingham, Alabama.

The editors at Thomas Nelson Publishing worked exceedingly hard to craft one product out of multiple sources. We are also grateful to those whose behind-the-scenes labor helped us with the details required to bring this book to its final form: Helen Johnson, Jamey Phillips, Karen R. Berry, Esq., and Karen Lim. We appreciate all your hard work.

Barbara Sweeny, of Judge Baker Children's Center in Boston, gave generously in putting this project ahead of all else to make sure the book came to fruition. She provided critical editorial assistance and worked consistently to meet deadlines and support the authors' vision. She served as a critical link with our publishers and other members of our staff. She has our deepest gratitude.

And last but not least, we want to thank Tina Young Poussaint, MD, for her patience and support.

Bill Cosby

Alvin F. Poussaint, MD

FOR MORE INFORMATION

WHAT'S GOING ON WITH BLACK MEN?

BOOKS

Geoffrey Canada. *Reaching Up for Manhood: Transforming the Lives of Boys in America.* Boston: Beacon Press, 1998.

Anderson J. Franklin. *From Brotherhood to Manhood: How Black Men Rescue Their Relationships and Dreams from the Invisibility Syndrome.* Hoboken, NJ: Wiley, 2004.

John Head. *Standing in the Shadows: Understanding and Overcoming Depression in Black Men.* New York: Broadway Books, 2004.

Ronald B. Mincy (Editor). *Black Males Left Behind.* Washington DC: Urban Institute Press, 2006.

Andre C. Willis (Editor). *Faith of Our Fathers: African-American Men Reflect on Fatherhood.* New York: Dutton, 1996.

INTERNET

Dellums Commission. *A Way Out: Creating Partners for Our Nation's Prosperity by Expanding Life Paths of Young Men of Color.* Washington DC: Joint Center for Political and Economic Studies, 2006. www.jointcenter.org/publications1/publication-PDFs/Dellums%20PDFs/FinalReport.pdf.

IT TAKES A COMMUNITY

BOOKS

Gordon Willard Allport. *Nature of Prejudice.* New York: Perseus Books Group, 1979.

James Baldwin. *Collected Essays: Notes of a Native Son, Nobody Knows My Name, The Fire Next Time, No Name in the Street, The Devil Finds Work, Other Essays.* New York: Library of America, 1998.

Lisa Blitz and Mary Pender Greene (Editors). *Racism and Racial Identity: Reflections on Urban Practice in Mental Health and Social Services.* New York: Haworth Press, 2006.

Clayborne Carson and Kris Shepard (Editors). *A Call to Conscience: The Landmark Speeches of Dr. Martin Luther King, Jr.* New York: Warner Books, 2001.

Johnnetta B. Cole. *Conversations: Straight Talk with America's Sister President.* New York: Doubleday, 1993.

W.E.B. Du Bois. *The Souls of Black Folk.* New York: Oxford University Press, 2007.

John Hope Franklin and Alfred A. Moss Jr. *From Slavery to Freedom: A History of African-Americans,* eighth edition. New York: Alfred A. Knopf, 2005.

Dorothy Height. *Open Wide the Freedom Gates: A Memoir.* New York: Public Affairs, 2005.

Woody Klein (Editor). *Toward Humanity and Justice: The Writings of Kenneth B. Clark Scholar of the 1954* Brown v. Board of Education *Decision.* Westport, CT: Praeger, 2004.

Malcolm X. *The Autobiography of Malcolm X* (with the assistance of Alex Haley). New York: Ballantine Books, 1990.

Gunnar Myrdal. *An American Dilemma: The Negro Problem and Modern Democracy* (with a new introduction by Sissela Bok). New Brunswick, NJ: Transaction Publishers, 1996.

Kenneth O'Reilly. *Nixon's Piano: Presidents and Racial Politics from Washington to Clinton.* New York: Free Press, 1995.

Cornell West. *Race Matters.* Boston: Beacon Press, 1993.

Juan Williams. *Enough: The Phony Leaders, Dead-End Movements, and Culture of Failure That Are Undermining Black America—and What We Can Do About It.* New York: Crown Publishers, 2006.

WE ALL START OUT AS CHILDREN

BOOKS

Anne C. Beal, Allison Abner, and Linda Villarosa. *The Black Parenting Book: Caring for Our Children in the First Five Years.* New York: Broadway Books, 1998.

James P. Comer and Alvin F. Poussaint. *Raising Black Children: Two Leading Psychiatrists Confront the Educational, Social and Emotional Problems Facing Black Children.* New York: Penguin Books, 1992.

Joyce Ladner, with Teresa Foy DiGeronimo. *Launching Our Black Children for Success: A Guide for Parents of Kids from Three to Eighteen.* San Francisco, CA: Jossey-Bass, 2003.

David B. Pruitt (Editor). *American Academy of Child & Adolescent Psychiatry Handbook: Your Child: A Parent's Guide to the Changes and Challenges of Childhood.* New York: HarperCollins, 1998.

David B. Pruitt (Editor). *American Academy of Child & Adolescent Psychiatry Handbook: Your Adolescent: Emotional, Behavioral, and Cognitive Development from Early Adolescence Through the Teen Years.* New York: HarperCollins, 2000.

Murray A. Straus. *Beating the Devil Out of Them: Corporal Punishment in American Children.* New York: Transaction Publishers, 2001.

INTERNET
Center for Effective Discipline:
http://www.stophitting.com/.
Center for the Improvement of Child Caring: Effective Black Parenting:
http://www.ciccparenting.org/cicc_sbp_11.asp.

TEACH YOUR CHILDREN WELL

BOOKS
Dwight Allen and William H. Cosby Jr. *American Schools: The 100 Billion Dollar Challenge.* New York: iPublish.com, 2000.

Sheryl J. Denbo and Lynson Moore Beaulieu. *Improving Schools for African American Students: A Reader for Educational Leaders.* Springfield, IL: Charles C. Thomas, 2002.

Freeman A. Hrabowski III, Kenneth I. Maton, and Geoffrey L. Greif. *Beating the Odds: Raising Academically Successful African American Males.* New York: Oxford University Press, 1998.

Robert P. Moses and Charles Cobb. *Radical Equations: Math Literacy and Civil Rights.* Boston: Beacon Press, 2001.

Charles J. Ogletree. *All Deliberate Speed: Reflections on the First Half-Century of Brown v. Board of Education.* New York: WW Norton, 2004.

Gary Orfield (Editor). *Dropouts in America: Confronting the Graduation Rate Crisis.* Cambridge: Harvard Education Press, 2006.

Theresa Perry, Claude Steele, and Asa Hilliard III. *Young, Gifted and Black: Promoting High Achievement among African-American Students.* Boston: Beacon Press, 2003.

INTERNET

Pedro Antonio Noguera. *The Trouble with Black Boys: The Role and Influence of Environmental and Cultural Factors on the Academic Performance of African American Males.* Cambridge, MA. *In Motion* magazine, May 13, 2002. www.inmotionmagazine.com/er/ pntroub1.html.

Additional articles by Dr. Noguera:
http://www.inmotionmagazine.com/noguera.html.

THE MEDIA YOU DESERVE

BOOKS

Donald Bogle. *Prime Time Blues: African Americans on Network Television.* New York: Farrar, Straus and Giroux, 2001.

Sissela Bok. *Mayhem: Violence as Public Entertainment.* New York: Basic Books, 1999.

Jannette Dates and William Barlow. *Split Image: African Americans in the Mass Media.* Washington DC: Howard University Press, 1993.

Bakari Kitwana. *The Hip Hop Generation: Young Blacks and the Crisis in African American Culture.* New York: BasicCivitas Books, 2002.

Susan Linn. *Consuming Kids: The Hostile Takeover of Childhood.* New York: The New Press, 2004.

S. Craig Watkins. *Hip Hop Matters: Politics, Pop Culture, and the Struggle for the Soul of a Movement.* Boston: Beacon Press, 2005.

INTERNET

Industry Ears: Industry Ears is a new generation nonpartisan think tank aimed at addressing and finding solutions to disparities in media that negatively impact individuals and communities, http://www.industryears.com/.

DVD

Color Adjustment. Producer/Director: Marlon Riggs. Producer: Vivian Kleinman. Narrator: Ruby Dee. California Newsreel. 1991. Follows 40 years of race relations through the lens of prime time entertainment.

Ethnic Notions. Producer/Director: Marlon Riggs. Narrator: Esther Rolle. California Newsreel. 1987. Documentary of the history of American stereotypes and the evolution of racial consciousness in America.

HEALTHY HEARTS AND MINDS

BOOKS

Carl C. Bell. *The Sanity of Survival: Reflections on Community Mental Health and Wellness.* Chicago: Third World Press, 2004.

Diane Brown and Verna Keith (Editors). *In and Out of Our Right Minds: The Mental Health of African American Women.* New York: Columbia University Press, 2003.

W. Michael Byrd and Linda A. Clayton. *An American Health Dilemma: A Medical History of African Americans and the Problems of Race: Beginnings to 1900.* New York: Routledge, 2000; Volume 2: *An American Health Dilemma: Race, Medicine, and Health Care in the United States 1900-2000.* New York: Routledge, 2002.

Mayo Clinic Book of Alternative Medicine: The New Approach to Using the Best of Natural Therapies and Conventional Medicine. New York: Time Inc., 2007.

Alvin F. Poussaint and Amy Alexander. *Lay My Burden Down: Suicide and the Mental Health Crisis among African-Americans.* Boston: Beacon Press, 2000.

David Satcher and Rubens J. Pamies (Editors). *Multicultural Medicine and Health Disparities.* New York, McGraw-Hill: 2006.

Harriet A. Washington. *Medical Apartheid: The Dark History of Medical Experimentation on Black Americans from Colonial Times to the Present.* New York: Doubleday, 2006.

INTERNET

American Academy of Child & Adolescent Psychiatry: www.aacap.org. *Facts for Families.* They provide information on a wide range of mental health topics.

American Academy of Pediatrics: http://www.aap.org/.

American Academy of Pediatric Dentists: http://www.aapd.org/.

American Dental Association: http://www.ada.org/.

American Holistic Health Association: http://www.ahha.org/.

National Center for Complementary and Alternative Medicine: http://nccam.nih.gov/.

National Medical Association: http://www.nmanet.org/.

DVD

Big Bucks Big Pharma: Marketing Disease and Pushing Drugs. Narrated by Amy Goodman. The Media Education Foundation. 2006.

Pack of Lies: The Advertising of Tobacco. Narrated by Jean Kilbourne and Rick Pollay. The Media Education Foundation. 2002.

Spin the Bottle: Sex, Lies & Alcohol. Featuring Jackson Katz and Jean Kilbourne. The Media Education Foundation. 2004.

THE HIGH PRICE OF VIOLENCE

BOOKS

Geoffrey Canada. *Fist Stick Knife Gun: A Personal History of Violence in America.* Boston: Beacon Press, 1996.

James Garbarino. *See Jane Hit: Why Girls Are Growing More Violent and What We Can Do About It.* New York: Penguin Press, 2006.

Debra Niehoff. *The Biology of Violence: How Understanding the Brain, Behavior, and Environment Can Break the Vicious Circle of Aggression.* New York: The Free Press, 2002.

Deborah Prothrow-Stith and Howard R. Spivak. *Murder Is No Accident: Understanding and Preventing Youth Violence in America.* San Francisco: Jossey-Bass, 2004.

Amos N. Wilson. *Black-on-Black Violence: The Psychodynamics of Black Self-Annihilation in Service of White Domination.* New York: African World Info/Systems, 1991.

INTERNET

U.S. Department of Justice, Office of Justice Programs: Bureau of Justice—Homicide trends: http://www.ojp.usdoj.gov/bjs/homicide/tables/totalstab.htm.

FROM POVERTY TO PROSPERITY

BOOKS

Wendy Beech. *Black Enterprise Guide to Starting Your Own Business.* New York: John Wiley & Sons, Inc., 1999.

Benjamin P. Bowser. *The Black Middle Class: Social Mobility—and Vulnerability.* Boulder: Lynne Rienner Publishers, 2007.

Cheryl D. Broussard. *Sister CEO: The Black Woman's Guide to Starting Your Own Business*. New York: Penguin Books, 1997.

Mary Hunt. *The Complete Cheapskate: How to Get Out of Debt, Stay Out, and Break Free from Money Worries Forever!* New York: St. Martin's Griffin, 2003.

Michelle Singletary. *Spend Well, Live Rich: How to Get What You Want with the Money You Have*. New York: Ballantine Books, 2004.

Deborah Taylor-Hough. *Frugal Living for Dummies*. New York: Wiley Publishing, 2003.

William Julius Wilson and Richard P. Taub. *There Goes the Neighborhood: Racial, Ethnic, and Class Tensions in Four Chicago Neighborhoods and Their Meaning for America*. New York: Knopf, 2006.

INTERNET

National Federation of Independent Business Young Entrepreneur Foundation Entrepreneur-in-the-Classroom program: http://www.nfib.com/page/YoungEntrepreneurFoundation.

INDEX

Healthy Eating Initiative — on plane from Palm Beach to Newark NJ. 2/29/2008

locating grocery stores in low-income neighborhoods
- competitive prices
- wholesome foods, fresh fruits, lean meats, etc

subsidized chains

Sodexo — Susan + Tim Smith

+ cooking classes + food purchasing classes.
  buying in bulk advantages
  food storage + prep

+ dental classes + teach oral hygiene

+ health monitoring for kids + parents
    prenatal care.

+ JnJ somehow — Lee Hahn.

+ RWJF obesity initiative
    + Melanie Adams

+ small conference on this

- Sodexo is in the health business, not
  the food business.

+ Three doctors. dental + physical.
    - talk to Ramesh Hunt @ Princeton Medical Center.
    - Tony Hawes.

- get retired teachers involved w/ a basic food list + literacy classes for adults.
  (See buying BJ Collins

Support from Vanguard — Gov's Delko